ALSO BY AMITAV GHOSH

The Circle of Reason
The Shadow Lines

IN AN ANTIQUE LAND

IN AN
ANTIQUE
LAND

AMITAV GHOSH

ALFRED A. KNOPF
NEW YORK
1993

THIS IS A BORZOI BOOK
PUBLISHED BY ALFRED A. KNOPF, INC.

Translation © 1992 by Amitav Ghosh

Library of Congress Cataloging-in-Publication Data
Ghosh, Amitav.
In an antique land / by Amitav Ghosh.
p. cm.
ISBN 0-394-58368-X
1. Ghosh, Amitav—Journeys—Egypt. 2. Laṭâifa (Egypt)—
Description and travel. 3. Nashâway (Egypt)—Description
and travel. 4. Ben Yijû, Abraham 12th cent. 5. Merchants,
Jewish—Egypt—Biography. 6. Bomma, 12th cent.
7. Slaves—Egypt—Biography. I. Title.
DT56.2.G48 1993
962'.02'0922—dc20
[B]   92-54276
CIP

Manufactured in the United States of America

FIRST AMERICAN EDITION

For Debbie

CONTENTS

PROLOGUE

PROLOGUE

THE SLAVE OF MS H.6 first stepped upon the stage of modern history in 1942. His was a brief debut, in the obscurest of theatres, and he was scarcely out of the wings before he was gone again—more a prompter's whisper than a recognizable face in the cast.

The slave's first appearance occurred in a short article by the scholar E. Strauss, in the 1942 issue of a Hebrew journal, *Zion*, published in Jerusalem. The article bore the title 'New Sources for the History of Middle Eastern Jews' and it contained transcriptions of several medieval documents. Among them was a letter written by a merchant living in Aden—that port which sits, like a fly on a funnel, on the precise point where the narrow spout of the Red Sea opens into the Indian Ocean. The letter, which now bears the catalogue number MS H.6, of the National and University Library in Jerusalem, was written by a merchant called Khalaf ibn Isḥaq, and it was intended for a friend of his, who bore the name Abraham Ben Yijû. The address, written on the back of the letter, shows that Ben Yiju was then living in Mangalore—a port on the south-western coast of India. In Strauss's estimation, the letter was written in the summer of 1148AD.

In the summer of its writing, Palestine was a thoroughfare for European armies. A German army had arrived in April, led by the ageing King Conrad III of Hohenstaufen, known as Almân to the Arabs. Accompanying the king was his nephew, the young and charismatic Frederick of Swabia. The Germans struck fear into the local population. 'That year the German Franks arrived,' wrote an Arab historian, 'a particularly fearsome kind of Frank.' Soon afterwards, King Louis VII of France visited Jerusalem with his army and a retinue of nobles. Travelling with him was his wife, the captivating Eleanor of Aquitaine, the greatest heiress in Europe, and destined to be successively Queen of France and England.

It was a busy season in Palestine. On 24 June a great concourse of the crowned heads of Europe gathered near Acre, in Galilee. They were received by King Baldwin and Queen Melisende of Jerusalem, with their leading barons and prelates, as well as the Grand Masters of the Orders of the Temple and the Hospital. King Conrad was accompanied by his kinsmen, Henry Jasimirgott of Austria, Otto of Freisingen, Frederick of Swabia, Duke Welf of Bavaria, and by the margraves of Verona and Montferrat. Among the nobles accompanying the King and Queen of France were Robert of Dreux, Henry of Champagne, and Thierry, Count of Flanders.

Between festivities, the leaders of the crusading armies held meetings to deliberate on their strategy for the immediate future. 'There was a divergence of views amongst them,' their enemies noted, 'but at length they came to an agreed decision to attack the city of Damascus...' For the Muslim rulers of Jordan and Syria, who had only just begun to recover from the first hundred years of the Crusades, this was a stroke of unexpected good fortune because Damascus was at that time the only Muslim state in the region that had friendly relations with the Crusader kingdoms.

On 24 July 1148AD the greatest Crusader army ever assembled camped in the orchards around Damascus. Its leaders had some successes over the next couple of days, but the Damascenes fought back with fierce determination and soon enough the Crusaders were forced to pack up camp. But Turcoman horsemen hung upon their flanks as they withdrew, raining down arrows, and the retreat rapidly turned into a rout. After this battle 'the German Franks returned' wrote the Arab historian who had so dreaded their arrival, 'to their country which lies over yonder and God rid the faithful of this calamity.'

It was not until 1942, the very summer when Khalaf's letter slipped quietly into twentieth-century print, that the Middle East again saw so great and varied a gathering of foreigners. Nowhere were there more than in the area around Alexandria; the Afrika Corps and the Italian Sixth Army, under the command of Erwin Rommel, were encamped a bare forty miles from the city, waiting for their orders for the final push into Egypt, and in the city itself the soldiers of the British Eighth Army were still arriving—from every corner of the world: India, Australia, South Africa, Britain and America. That summer, while the fates of the two armies hung in the balance, Alexandria was witness to the last, most spectacular, burst of cosmopolitan gaiety for which the city was once famous.

WITHIN THIS TORNADO of grand designs and historical destinies, Khalaf ibn Ishaq's letter seems to open a trapdoor into a vast network of foxholes where real life continues uninterrupted. Khalaf was probably well aware of the events taking place farther north: the city he lived in, Aden, served as one of the principal conduits in the flow of trade between the Mediterranean and the Indian Ocean, and Khalaf and his fellow merchants had a wide network of contacts all over North Africa, the Middle East and southern Europe. They made it their business to keep themselves well-informed: from season to season they followed the fluctuations of the prices of iron, pepper and cardamom in the markets of Cairo. They were always quick to relay news to their friends, wherever they happened to be, and they are sure to have kept themselves well abreast of the happenings in Syria and Palestine.

But now, in the summer of 1148, writing to Abraham Ben Yiju in Mangalore, Khalaf spends no time on the events up north. He begins by giving his friend news of his brother Mubashshir (who has set off unexpectedly for Syria), letting him know that he is well. Then he switches to business: he acknowledges certain goods he has received from Ben Yiju—a shipment of areca nuts, two locks manufactured in India and two bowls from a brass factory in which Ben Yiju has an interest. He informs Ben Yiju that he is sending him some presents with the letter—'things which have no price and no value.' The list seems to hint at a sweet tooth in Ben Yiju: 'two jars of sugar, a jar of almonds and two jars of raisins, altogether five jars.'

It is only at the very end of the letter that the slave makes his entry: Khalaf ibn Ishaq makes a point of singling him out and sending him 'plentiful greetings.'

That is all: no more than a name and a greeting. But the reference comes to us from a moment in time when the only people for whom we can even begin to imagine properly human, individual, existences are the literate and the consequential, the wazirs and the sultans, the chroniclers and the priests—the people who had the power to inscribe themselves physically upon time. But the slave of Khalaf's letter was not of that company: in his instance it was a mere accident that those barely discernible traces that ordinary people leave upon the world happen to have been preserved. It is nothing less than a miracle that anything is known about him at all.

THIRTY-ONE YEARS were to pass before the modern world again caught a glimpse of the slave of MS H.6: the so-called Yom Kippur War was just over and the price of oil had risen 370 per cent in the course of a single year.

The Slave's second appearance, like his first, occurs in a letter by Khalaf ibn Ishaq, written in Aden—one that happened to be included in a collection entitled *Letters of Medieval Jewish Traders*, translated and edited by Professor S. D. Goitein, of Princeton University. Like the other letter, this one too is addressed to Abraham Ben Yiju, in Mangalore, but in the thirty-one years that have passed between the publication of the one and the other, the Slave has slipped backwards in time, like an awkward package on a conveyor belt. He is nine years younger—the letter in which his name now appears was written by Khalaf ibn Ishaq in 1139.

This is another eventful year in the Middle East: the atabeg of Damascus has been assassinated and the Levant is riven by wars between Muslim principalities. But as ever Khalaf, in Aden, is unconcerned by politics; now, even more than in the other

17

letter, business weighs heavily on his mind. A consignment of Indian pepper in which he and Ben Yiju had invested jointly has been lost in a shipwreck off the narrow straits that lead into the Red Sea. The currents there are notoriously treacherous; they have earned the Straits a dismal name, Bab al-Mandab, 'the Gateway of Lamentation'. Divers have salvaged a few pieces of iron, little else. In the meanwhile a shipment of cardamom sent by Ben Yiju has been received in Aden, and a cargo of silk dispatched in return. There are also accounts for a long list of household goods that Ben Yiju has asked for, complete with an apology for the misadventures of a frying-pan—'You asked me to buy a frying-pan of stone in a case. Later on, its case broke, whereupon I bought you an iron pan for a niṣâfî, which is, after all, better than a stone pan.'

Yet, despite all the merchandise it speaks of, the letter's spirit is anything but mercenary: it is lit with a warmth that Goitein's translation renders still alive and glowing, in cold English print. 'I was glad,' writes Khalaf ibn Ishaq 'when I looked at your letter, even before I had taken notice of its contents. Then I read it, full of happiness and, while studying it, became joyous and cheerful…You mentioned, my master, that you were longing for me. Believe me that I feel twice as strongly and even more than what you have described…'

Again the Slave's entry occurs towards the end of the main body of the text; again Khalaf sends him 'plentiful greetings' mentioning him by name. The Slave's role is no less brief upon his second appearance than it was in his first. But he has grown in stature now: he has earned himself a footnote.

The footnote is very brief. It merely explains him as Ben Yiju's Indian 'slave and business agent, a respected member of his household.'

The letter is prefaced with a few sentences about Ben Yiju. They describe him as a Jewish merchant, originally of Tunisia, who had gone to India by way of Egypt, as a trader, and had spent seventeen years there. A man of many accomplishments, a distinguished calligrapher, scholar and poet, Ben Yiju had returned to Egypt having amassed great wealth in India. The last years of his life were spent in Egypt, and his papers found their way into his synagogue in Cairo: they were eventually discovered in a chamber known as the Geniza.

I CAME UPON Professor Goitein's book of translations in a library in Oxford in the winter of 1978. I was a student, twenty-two years old, and I had recently won a scholarship awarded by a foundation established by a family of expatriate Indians. It was only a few months since I had left India and so I was perhaps a little more befuddled by my situation than students usually are. At that moment the only thing I knew about my future was that I was expected to do research leading towards a doctorate in social anthropology. I had never heard of the Cairo Geniza before that day, but within a few months I was in Tunisia, learning Arabic. At about the same time the next year, 1980, I was in Egypt, installed in a village called Laṭaîfa, a couple of hours journey to the south-east of Alexandria.

I knew nothing then about the Slave of MS H.6 except that he had given me a right to be there, a sense of entitlement.

LAṬAÎFA

1

I FIRST BEGAN to dream of Cairo in the evenings, as I sat in my room, listening, while Abu-'Ali berated his wife or shouted at some unfortunate customer who had happened to incur his displeasure while making purchases at his shop. I would try to shut out the noise by concentrating on my book or my diaries or by turning up the volume of my transistor radio, but Abu-'Ali's voice always prevailed, despite the thick mud walls of his house and the squawking of the ducks and geese who lived around my room.

Nobody in Lataifa liked Abu-'Ali; neither his relatives, nor his neighbours nor anyone else in the hamlet—not even, possibly, his own wife and children. Some actively hated him; others merely tried to keep out of his way. It was hard to do otherwise; he was profoundly unlovable.

Still, dislike him as they might, Abu-'Ali's neighbours and kinsmen also held him in fear. The children of the hamlet were always careful to be discreet when they mimicked him: they would look up and down the lanes to make sure that neither he nor his burly eldest son, 'Ali, were in sight, and then, screwing up their faces in imitation of his scowl, making imaginary sunglasses out of their fingers and thumbs, they would arch their backs and stagger down the lane, labouring under the weight of gigantic bellies.

Everybody in the area knew of Abu-'Ali's temper and most people did their best to avoid him, so far as they could. As for me, I had no choice in the matter: by the time I had learnt of Abu-'Ali's reputation, I was already his lodger, and he, on his own initiative, had assumed the role of surrogate father as well as landlord.

I was not the first person in the hamlet to find himself thrust into an unwelcome proximity with Abu-'Ali. It so happened that his house sat astride the one major road in the area, a narrow, rutted dirt track just about wide enough to allow two lightweight vehicles to squeeze past each other without toppling into the canal that ran beside it. The road served a large network of villages around Lataifa and a ragged procession of pick-up trucks roared up and down it all day long, carrying people back and forth from Damanhour, the capital of the Governorate and the largest city in the region.

Abu-'Ali's house was so placed that it commanded a good view of the road and, being the man he was, Abu-'Ali was diligent in exploiting the strategic potential of its location. He spent much of his time on a small veranda at the front of his house, lying on a divan and keeping a careful eye on the traffic. At the busier times of the day, he would lie on his side, with one arm resting voluptuously on the gigantic swell of his hip, watching the passing trucks through a pair of silver-tipped sunglasses; in the afternoons, once he had eaten his lunch, he would roll on his back and doze, his eyes half-shut, like an engorged python stealing a rest after its monthly meal.

One of the elders of the hamlet, Shaikh Musa, told me once,

when I was having dinner at his house, that Abu-'Ali had always been obese, even as a boy. He had never been able to work in the fields because he had hurt his leg as a child, and had soon grown much heavier than others of his age. People had felt sorry for him to begin with, but later the injury had proved such an advantage that everyone had begun to wonder about its authenticity: it had given him an excuse for not working on the land and as a result his father had allowed him to go through school. Nothing was heard of his injury thereafter. Later, he'd even gone on to college in Damanhour, which was unusual at the time for a fellah boy, the son of an unlettered peasant. Sure enough, he had seen to it that his time in college was well spent: he had cultivated contacts with students from influential families, and with bureaucrats and officials in Damanhour. It hadn't surprised anyone when he succeeded in getting a permit to set up a government-subsidized shop for retailing essential commodities at controlled prices.

That permit was to become Abu-'Ali's passport to prosperity: his was the only shop of its kind in the area (he had made sure of that) and everybody had to go to him if they wanted to buy sugar, tea, oil and suchlike at government-subsidized prices. Often his customers were more supplicants than patrons, for there was nothing to prevent him from choosing whom to sell to: people who got on the wrong side of him frequently discovered that he was out of tea or kerosene or whatever it was they wanted. It was all the same to Abu-'Ali: he had no shortage of customers—they had to come to him or go all the way to the next village, Nashâwy, a mile and a half down the road.

It was thus that Abu-'Ali had grown so large, Shaikh Musa said (he was generally extremely reluctant to discuss Abu-'Ali but on this occasion he permitted himself a laugh): for years he had eaten meat like other people ate beans, and eventually he had swollen up like one of the force-fed geese his wife reared on their roof.

'Women use their forefingers to push corn down the throats of their geese,' added Shaikh Musa's son Ahmed, an earnest young man, who was a great deal more heedful of my duties as a gatherer of information than I. 'Corn, as you ought to know, is harvested just before winter, towards the start of the Coptic year which begins in the month of Tût...'

It had long been a point of pride with Abu-'Ali that he possessed more—more gadgets, especially—than anyone else in Lataifa. It was therefore a matter of bitter chagrin to him that he had not been the first person in the village to buy a television set. One of his own half-brothers, a schoolteacher, had beaten him to it.

He was often reminded of this by a cousin's son, Jabir, a boy in his late teens, with bright, malicious eyes and a tongue that bristled with barbs. Sometimes, when we were sitting in Abu-'Ali's guest-room in the evenings, Jabir would turn to me and ask questions like 'What's the name of the captain of the Algerian soccer team?' or 'Who is the Raïs of India? Isn't it Indira Gandhi?' The questions were entirely rhetorical; he would answer them himself, and then, sighing with pleasure he would glance at his uncle and exclaim: 'Oh there's so much to be learnt from television. It's lucky for us there's one next door.'

It always worked.

'I don't understand this television business,' Abu-'Ali would roar. 'What's the point of buying a television set now, when our village doesn't even have electricity?'

Smiling serenely, Jabir would point out that a television set could be run perfectly well on car batteries.

'Car batteries!' Abu-'Ali's voice would be breathy with contempt. 'That's like burning up money. I'm telling you, and you pay attention, let the electricity come to Lataifa as the government's promised, and you'll be able to watch the biggest and best TV set you've ever seen, right here, in this room, God willing. It'll be better than the best television set in Nashawy, insha'allah, and it'll be in colour too.'

A sly smile would appear on Jabir's blunt-featured face, with its adolescent's crop of stubble and unquiet skin. 'There'll be other colour TVs here soon,' he would say, leaning back contentedly against the bolsters on the couch. 'My uncle Mustafa is going to get one for our house any one of these days, insha'allah.'

All Abu-'Ali could do in retaliation was glare at him; he knew he was no match for Jabir's tongue. He would have loved to ban Jabir from his house, but it so happened that Jabir's father was a cousin in the paternal line, and thus a member of the extended family, or lineage, of which Abu-'Ali was nominally the head: he couldn't have thrown Jabir out of his house without offending a whole platoon of relatives. Besides, it so happened that Jabir was also best friends with one of Abu-'Ali's sons, a schoolboy of his own age, about sixteen or so. The two of them were always together, with their arms around each others' shoulders, giggling, or talking in furtive, experimental whispers. There was little Abu-'Ali could do to rid his house of him; constrained as he was by the obligations of kinship, he had to choke daily on the gall of hearing about the soccer matches that his son and Jabir watched on the TV set in the house next door.

'What's in this soccer stuff, I want to know?' Abu-'Ali would explode from time to time. 'Isn't there work to do? Allah! Is the world going to live on soccer? What's going to become of...'

27

But laggardly though he may have been in the matter of television, Abu-ʿAli was undeniably the first person in the hamlet to acquire a form of motorized transport—a light Japanese moped, fragile in appearance, but extraordinarily sturdy in build. The moped was normally used by one of his older sons, who drove it to his college in Damanhour every day. He was very jealous of his custodianship of the vehicle and would never allow his brothers or cousins to use it—but his father, of course, was another matter altogether.

Every now and again, Abu-ʿAli would roll off his divan, send his wife in to fetch his best dark glasses, and shout for the moped to be wheeled out into the courtyard. He would hitch up the hem of his jallabeyya and then, lifting up his leg, he would mount the vehicle with a little sidelong hop, while his son held it steady. To me, watching from the roof, it seemed hardly credible that so delicate a machine would succeed in carrying a man of Abu-ʿAli's weight over that bumpy dirt track. But to my astonishment it invariably did: he would go shooting off down the road, his jallabeyya ballooning out around him, while the moped, in profile, diminished into a thin, sharp line—it was like watching a gargantuan lollipop being carried away by its stick.

It was no accident that Abu-ʿAli had acquired so many possessions: everyone agreed that he had a remarkable talent for squeezing the last piastre from everything that came his way. People often said that it was useless to bargain with Abu-ʿAli: in the end he would get exactly what he wanted.

I was soon to discover the truth of this for myself.

One afternoon, about a month or so after I had arrived in Lataifa, Abu-ʿAli came up to my room to pay me a visit. This was an unusual event because it called for the climbing of a narrow flight of stairs. I lived on the roof of his house, in an old chicken-coop, which his wife had once used for her poultry. Her stock of ducks, chickens, pigeons and geese had been moved to a pen, at the far end of the roof, and the coop had been turned into a makeshift room for my benefit, with a bed, a desk and a chair.

I had discovered since moving in that an afternoon visit from Abu-'Ali was generally good cause for apprehension. At that time of the day he was normally to be found lying inert upon his divan, resting after his midday meal; it was unusual for him to so much as turn on his side, much less attempt an assault on the stairs that led to the roof. He had only visited me twice before in the afternoon, and on both occasions it was because he had wanted a discussion in private, while his children were away at work or in school. On one of those occasions he had tried to lay claim to my transistor radio, my best-loved possession, and on the other he had indicated, after a prolonged and roundabout conversation, that the rent I was paying was not satisfactory and that either I or the 'doktór' who had brought me to his house would have to do something about it.

I had been brought to Abu-'Ali's house by Doctor Aly Issa, Professor in the University of Alexandria, and one of the most eminent anthropologists in the Middle East. An acquaintance of Doctor Issa's had led us to Abu-'Ali, who had declaimed: 'I swear to you, ya doktór, the Indian shall stay here and we will look after him as we do our own sons, for your sake, ya doktór, because we respect you so much.'

Being the kindest and most generous of men, Doctor Issa had all too easily allowed himself to take Abu-'Ali at his word. It had been agreed upon very quickly—all except how much I was to pay. The Professor had brushed aside my anxiety on that score:

'That will be easily settled, I will write him a letter—don't worry about it.'

And so he had, but Abu-'Ali had seen little merit in Doctor Issa's letter. Now, having settled himself on my bed, he took the dog-eared letter out of the pocket of his jallabeyya once again, and read it through, clicking his tongue and frowning.

'Tell me,' he said at last, 'where did you stay while you were in Alexandria?'

'A small hotel,' I answered.

'And how much did it cost?'

'Two pounds a night.'

He gave a little nod of satisfaction and put the letter away. 'Hotels are expensive,' he said, 'you're lucky to be staying here with us. We will cook for you, wash your clothes for you, provide you with anything you need. You must ask for whatever you want whenever you want it. To us you are just like our sons—why we will even give you our own money if you like.'

He reached into his pocket for his wallet and held it out to me, smiling, his eyes vanishing into the folds of his immense, fleshy face. 'You can take this,' he said. 'You can have our money.'

I stared at the wallet, mesmerized, wondering whether custom demanded that I touch it or make some other symbolic gesture of acceptance or obeisance, like falling at his feet. I saw myself shrinking, dwindling away into one of those tiny, terrified foreigners whom Pharaohs hold up by their hair in New Kingdom bas-reliefs.

But the wallet vanished back into his pocket in a flash, before I had time to respond. 'You see,' he said, 'that is how much we love you.'

'I was just thinking,' I stammered, at last, 'maybe I could buy my own food.'

'How can you do that?' he responded indignantly. 'The shops are far away, and you know it would cost you at least a pound a day if you were to buy your food in town. No, no, you must eat with us.'

'No, I meant, I could give you the money...' My Arabic had begun to falter now under the strain of bargaining, and I was slowly sinking into a tongue-tied silence.

'No, no, it's not a question of money. You are our honoured guest. You can see that I don't care for money. I have a big shop downstairs, and I sell many things there. Next year I will add a second floor to my house, insha'allah. You know I have sent my sons to school and college; you can see that I don't care for money at all.'

'Please tell me,' I said, 'how much do you think I should pay?'

He sighed thoughtfully, rubbing his moustache.

'No,' he said, 'you must tell us how much you would like to give us.'

And so it went on for a good hour or so, before he would allow himself to be cajoled into naming a sum.

That evening, at sunset, I was standing on the roof, looking out over the tranquil, twilit cottonfields, when Abu-'Ali's voice exploded out of the porch below, roaring abuse at his wife. I went back into my room and in an effort to shut out the noise, I began to turn the dial on my radio, scanning the waves for the sound of a familiar language, listening for words that would make me feel a little less alone. As the night wore on, the thought of hearing Abu-'Ali's voice for months on end, perhaps years, began to seem utterly intolerable.

It was on nights like that that my dreams of Cairo were most vivid.

2

CAIRO IS EGYPT'S own metaphor for itself.

Everywhere in the country except the city itself, Cairo *is* Egypt. They are both spoken of by the same name, Maṣr, a name that is appropriate as well as ancient, a derivative of a root that means 'to settle' or 'to civilize'. The word has a long history in Arabic; it occurs in the Qur'ân but was in use even before the advent of Islam. It is the name by which the country has been known, in its own language, for at least a millennium, and most of the cultures and civilizations with which it has old connections have accepted its own self-definition. The languages of India, for example, know Masr by variations of its Arabic name: 'Mishor' in Bengali, 'Misar' in Hindi and Urdu. Only Europe has always insisted on knowing the country not on its own terms, but as a dark mirror for itself. 'Egyptian darkness,' says the Oxford English Dictionary, quoting the Bible, 'intense darkness (see Exodus x.22).' Or 'Egyptian days: the two days in each month which were believed to be unlucky'; and: 'Egyptian bondage: bondage like that of the Israelites in Egypt.'

Like English, every major European language derives its name for Egypt from the Greek Ægyptos, a term that is related to the word 'Copt', the name generally used for Egypt's indigenous Christians. Thus German has its Ägypten, Dutch Egypte, Polish and Estonian Egipt: old resonant words, with connotations and

32

histories far in excess of those that usually attach to the names of countries. A seventeenth-century English law, for example, states: 'If any transport into England or Wales, any lewd people calling themselves Egyptians, they forfeit 40 £'—a reminder that words like 'gypsy' and 'gitano' derived from 'Egyptian'.

Europe's apparently innocent 'Egypt' is therefore as much a metaphor as 'Masr', but a less benign one, almost as much a weapon as a word. Egypt's own metaphor for itself, on the other hand, renders the city indistinguishable from the country; a usage that brims with pleasing and unexpected symmetries.

Like Egypt, Cairo dwindles into a thin ribbon of settlements at its southern extremity; towards the north it gradually broadens, like the country itself, into a wide, densely populated funnel. To the south lies Upper Egypt, the Ṣaʿîd, a long thin carpet of green that flanks the Nile on both sides; to the north is the triangle created by the river, as perfect as any in Nature, the Delta. Egypt's metaphor, Egypt itself, sits in between like a hinge, straddling the imaginary line that since the beginning of human history has divided the country into two parts, each distinct and at the same time perfectly complementary.

To most Egyptians outside Cairo, their metaphor stands for the entire city: the whole of it is known as Masr—the city's formal name al-Qâhira is infrequently used. But Cairo, like Delhi or Rome, is actually not so much a single city as an archipelago of townships, founded on neighbouring sites, by various different dynasties and rulers.

When the people of Cairo speak of Masr, they often have a particular district of the city in mind. It lies towards the south, and it goes by several names. Sometimes it is spoken of as Old Cairo, Maṣr al-Qadîma or Maṣr al-ʿAtîqa, sometimes as Mari Gargis, but most often as Fusṭâṭ Maṣr, or simply Fusṭâṭ. On a map, the quarter seems very small, far too small to be so rich in names. But in fact, small as it is, the area is not a single island within Cairo, but rather a second archipelago within the first.

It was a small enclave within this formation that eventually became home to Abraham Ben Yiju, the master of the Slave of MS H.6: a Roman fortress called Babylon. The fort was built by the emperor Trajan in 130AD, on the site of an even earlier structure, and the Romans are said to have called it Babylon of Egypt, to distinguish it from the Mesopotamian Babylon. The name may have come from the Arabic Bâb il-On, 'The Gate of On', after the ancient sanctuary of the Sun God at Heliopolis, but there are many contending theories and no one knows for sure. The fort has had other names, most notably Qaṣr al-Shamaʿ, Fortress of the Lamp, but it is Babylon that has served it longest.

The entrance to Babylon was once guarded by two massive, heavily buttressed towers: one of them is now a ruined stump, and the other was incorporated several centuries ago into the structure of a Greek Orthodox church. Today the towers, and the gateway that lies between them, are separated from the Nile by several hundred metres. But at the time when the fortress was built the river flowed directly beside it: the reason why the towers were so solidly constructed is that they served as Babylon's principal embankment against the annual Nile flood. In the early years of Babylon's history, the towers were flanked by a port. As the centuries advanced and the conurbation around the fortress grew in size and importance, the river retreated westwards and the docks and warehouses gradually expanded along the newly emerged lands on the bank. In Ben Yiju's time the port was one of the busiest in the Middle East; it was said to handle more traffic than Baghdad and Basra combined.

Today there is a steel gate between Babylon's twin towers, and millions of visitors pour through it every year. But the fort's second great gateway, in its southern wall, is no longer in use: its floor is deep in water now, swamped by Cairo's rapidly rising water-table. A thick film of green slime shimmers within its soaring, vaulted interior, encircling old tyres and discarded plastic bottles. Incredible as it may seem, this putrefying pit marks the site of what was perhaps the single most important event in the history of Cairo, indeed of Egypt: it was through this gateway that the Arab general 'Amr ibn al-'Âs is thought to have effected his entry into Babylon in 641AD—the decisive event in the futûḥ, the Muslim victory over the Christian powers in Masr.

For Babylon, ironically, the moment of capitulation marked its greatest triumph for it was then that this tiny fortress fixed the location of the country's centre of gravity, once and for all. It was Alexandria that was Egypt's most important city at the time of the Arab invasion; founded by Alexander the Great in 332BC it had served as the country's capital for almost a thousand years. Babylon, on the other hand, was a mere provincial garrison, a small military outpost. By rights therefore, it was Alexandria's prerogative to serve as the funnel for the assimilation of the newcomers.

But the conquering Muslim general, 'Amr ibn al-'As, broke with the usual practice of invaders by electing to base his army not in the country's capital, but in an entirely new city. The location he chose was the obvious one—the site the Arab army had used for its camp while laying siege to Babylon. The fortress was thus the promontory that served to anchor the Cairo archipelago: ever afterwards Egypt's capital, Masr, Egypt's metaphor for itself, has lain within a few miles of Babylon.

The legend goes that on the morning when 'Amr was to lead his army against Alexandria he woke to find a dove nesting on top of his tent. Loath to invite misfortune by disturbing the bird, he left the tent behind and upon returning to Babylon after his successful assault on Alexandria, laid out his new city around the nest-topped tent. The legend is universally believed in Cairo, and everyone who repeats it adds that the name of 'Amr's city, al-Fusṭâṭ, was derived from the Arabic for tent. But in fact the story came into circulation long after the event and is almost certainly apocryphal. It is possible that the name does not come from an Arabic source at all, being related instead to the Latin-Greek word 'fossaton', which is also the parent of an archaic and unglamorous English word, 'fosse', or ditch.

Fustat served as Egypt's capital for more than three centuries, but then a new invasion and a new set of conquerors moved the centre of power a couple of miles northwards. The new rulers were the Fatimids, a dynasty which had its beginnings in North Africa, in an esoteric Shî'a sect whose members were known as Ismâ'îlîs. In 969AD one of their generals, a former Greek slave called Jawhar al-Rûmî, marched against Egypt with a hundred thousand men. Their army routed the Egyptians in a battle near Fustat and the inhabitants of the city soon sued for peace. Like 'Amr ibn al-'As before him, Jawhar the Greek marked out the boundaries of a new township right beside the conquered city. Soothsayers are said to have named the town al-Qâhira, the Martial, or the Victorious, because the planet Mars, al-Qâhir, was in the ascendant at the time of the foundation ceremony. It was this name that was to pass into European languages as Cairo, Le Caire and the like.

In its original conception al-Qahira was a planned capital, an early forebear of New Delhi, Canberra, Brasilia and other such haunts of officialdom. The Caliph had his residence there and it contained many notable buildings, but everything in it was the personal property of the rulers and its shops and bazaars existed only to serve him and his entourage. In time the character of al-Qahira was to change entirely and it was to become a frantic, crowded district, the bustling nucleus of the conurbation of Cairo. But all that came later: in the early years of the twelfth century when Ben Yiju first came to Masr it was probably still a relatively solemn, bureaucratic kind of place. At the time, the Fatimids, who had long since embarked on a course of catastrophic decline, were clinging to the last tatters of their power, and their capital was still largely a ceremonial and administrative township. It was Fustat then that probably had something of the busy, market-place character of al-Qahira today.

Thriving hub though it was, medieval Fustat probably presented an unremarkable kind of appearance. Archæological excavations have shown that its dwellings were, for the most part, made of the material that is still most in evidence in rural Egypt today, dried mud and straw—a substance that sounds somehow more glamorous when spoken of by the term 'adobe', a term appropriately applied here, since the word probably derives from the Arabic al-ṭûb, 'the brick'. Possibly Fustat even had something of the distinctive look of an Egyptian village: that tousled, mop-haired appearance that is characteristic of fellah houses, with great ricks of straw and firewood piled high on their roofs.

But in fact there was nothing remotely rustic about medieval Fustat, whatever its appearance. With the political ascendancy of the Fatimid Empire, it had come to play a pivotal role in the global economy as the entrepôt that linked the Mediterranean and the Indian Ocean: the merchandise that flowed through its bazaars came from as far afield as East Africa, southern Europe, the western Sahara, India, China and Indonesia. By Ben Yiju's time Fustat had long since become the largest island in the emerging archipelago of Masr: the juncture of some of the most important trade routes in the known world and the nucleus of one of the richest and most cosmopolitan cities on earth.

But although it may have been Fustat's markets that first attracted Ben Yiju to Masr it was Babylon that was to become his spiritual home there. The fortress had remained relatively unchanged over several centuries and was still largely populated by Christians of various denominations, with Copts in the majority. But there were also at least three Jewish groups in Babylon, each with a synagogue of its own—they were the 'Iraqis', the 'Palestinians' and the Karaites. The 'Palestinian' congregation followed the rites of the school of Jerusalem, and despite its name, it included the indigenous Jews of Egypt. It was the Palestinian synagogue that Ben Yiju was to join.

By the time Ben Yiju came to Masr, Babylon had long since been eclipsed by the thriving township of Fustat. But in the end it was the hardy little fortress that proved to have the greater staying power. Today, the entrance to what remains of Fustat lies a short distance from Babylon's towers, but very few tourists pass through it. Fustat can be smelt before it is seen—it is a gigantic open refuse-pit, an immense rubbish-dump.

The site is guarded by a large steel gate which looks as though it belongs in a prison. But it swings open easily enough, with a push, and a dusty path curls away from it, between the mounds of refuse, towards a stretch of reed-filled marshland in the distance. In places, where the decomposing matter has caught fire spontaneously under the fierce glare of the Cairo sun, thin tendrils of smoke spiral torpidly towards the sky. Children play in puddles of grey ooze and a few figures in torn, flapping jallabeyyas move slowly through the refuse, dragging piles of cardboard and plastic behind them. Incredible as it may seem, excavations in this suppurating wasteland have yielded huge quantities of Chinese pottery and other riches: it was here that some of the earliest and most valuable fragments of Indian textiles have been found.

The last skeletal remains of the city whose markets once traded in the best the world could offer lie a little further along the path: the outlines of a few foundations and some brick walls and arches, pushing through pools of oily slime, clawing at the earth. In the distance shanties grow in tiers upon the ruins, and they in turn fade gently, imperceptibly, into the scraggy geometry of Cairo's skyline—into a tableau of decay and regeneration, a metaphor for Masr.

3

I OFTEN THOUGHT of telling Shaikh Musa that I wanted to move out of Abu-'Ali's house; for a while I even considered asking him to help me make some other arrangement. I had always felt secure in his friendship, from the moment of our first meeting: there was a gentleness and a good humour about him that inspired trust, something about the way he rocked his short, portly frame from side to side as we talked, the way he shook my hand every time we met, his round, weathered face crinkling into a smile, and cried: 'Where have you been all this while? Why haven't you come to see me?'

There were times when I had the distinct impression that Shaikh Musa was trying to warn me about Abu-'Ali. The two of them were of the same age after all, in their mid-fifties; they had grown up together, and Shaikh Musa probably knew him as well as anyone in the hamlet. Once, while dining with Shaikh Musa and his family, I had the feeling that he was cautioning me, in an oblique and roundabout way, telling me to be careful with Abu-'Ali. It was only because of a series of unfortunate interruptions that I didn't beg him right then to find me some other house to live in.

We were sitting in his bedroom that evening. Shaikh Musa, his son Ahmed, his two grandsons and I were eating out of one tray, while the women of the household were sharing another, at the other end of the room. It was something of a special occasion for I had just crossed an invisible barrier. Whenever I had eaten at Shaikh Musa's house before, it had been in the 'mandara', the guest-room on the outside of the house, facing the lane; every house had one, for this was the room where male guests were usually received. But on this occasion, after saying his evening prayers, Shaikh Musa had risen to his feet and led me out of the guest-room, into the lamplit interior of the house.

We had gone directly to his bedroom, pushing past a nuzzling sheep tethered by the door. Shaikh Musa chased a brood of chickens off an old sheepskin, sending them scuttling under his bed, and we seated ourselves on the floor and played with Ahmed's two young sons while waiting for the rest of the family. After Ahmed returned from the mosque, two women came into the room carrying a pair of trays loaded with food. The trays were set out on the floor, and the women gathered around one, while we seated ourselves at the other; each tray was as big as a cartwheel, and there was plenty of room for all of us.

There were three women in the room now, all of them young, one in the first bloom of her adolescence with a gentle, innocent face and a rosy complexion—a family inheritance shared by many of the inhabitants of Lataifa. From the strong resemblance she bore to Ahmed, I knew at once that she was his sister. The other two women were a good deal older, perhaps in their mid-twenties. One was a pale, pretty, self-possessed young woman, dressed in a long, printed skirt. The other was dark and thick-set, and she was wearing a black fusṭân, a heavy, shapeless robe that was the customary garb of a fellah woman.

I had encountered all of them before, occasionally at the doorway to Shaikh Musa's house and sometimes in the guest-room when they came in to hand out tea. There were times when I had the impression that I had passed them in the lanes of the hamlet, but I was never quite sure. The fault for this lay entirely with me, for neither they nor anyone else in Lataifa wore veils (nor indeed did anyone in the region), but at that time, early in my stay, I was so cowed by everything I had read about Arab traditions of shame and modesty that I barely glanced at them, for fear of giving offence. Later it was I who was shame-stricken, thinking of the astonishment and laughter I must have provoked, walking past them, eyes lowered, never uttering so much as a word of greeting. Shaking hands with them now, as we sat down to dinner, I tried to work out the connections between them and the rest of the family. The pretty woman in the printed dress was Ahmed's wife, I decided: her clothes and her bearing spoke of a college, or at least a high-school, education. Since Ahmed had been through school and college too, I had every reason to assume that they were a couple. As for the other woman, the dark one in the black dress, it took me no more than a moment's thought to reach a conclusion about her: she was the wife of Shaikh Musa's other son, I decided, Ahmed's younger brother, Hasan.

I had never met Hasan, for he was away, serving his draft in the army, but I had heard a great deal about him. Shaikh Musa spoke of him often, and with something more than the usual warmth of a father remembering a son long absent. He had shown me a picture of him once: he was a strikingly good-looking young man, with a broad, strong face and clear-cut features; in fact, he bore a marked resemblance to a picture of Shaikh Musa that hung on the wall of his guest-room, a photograph taken in his youth, in army uniform.

Unlike Ahmed, who had been through school and college, Hasan had not had an education. He had been taken out of school at a fairly early age; Shaikh Musa had brought him up as a fellah, so that at least one of his sons would profit from the land their ancestors had left them. It was that shared background perhaps that lent Shaikh Musa's voice a special note of affection when he spoke of Hasan: Ahmed was the most dutiful of sons and he helped Shaikh Musa on the land as often as he could, but there was an unbridgeable gap between them now because of his education. Ahmed worked as a clerk, in a factory near Damanhour, and he was thus counted as a mowazzaf, an educated, salaried man, and like all such people in the village, his clothes, his speech, his amusements and concerns, were markedly different from those of the fellaheen. Hasan, on the other hand, fell on his father's side of that divide, and it was easy to see that their shared view of the world formed a special bond between them.

I was soon sure that the woman in the black dress was Hasan's wife. I overheard Shaikh Musa saying a few words to her and, detecting a note of familiarity in his voice, I attributed it to his special closeness to his younger son. But now I began to wonder where his own wife was and why she had not joined us at our meal.

The meal that was set out on the tray in front of us was a very good one: arranged around a large pile of rice were dishes of fried potatoes, cheese preserved in brine, salads of chopped tomatoes and fresh dill, plates of cooked vegetables, large discs of corn-meal bread, and bowls of young Nile perch, baked with tomatoes and garlic. Everything was fresh and full of flavour, touched with that unnameable quality which makes anything grown in the soil of Egypt taste richer, more distinctively of itself, than it does anywhere else.

It was when I complimented him on the food that Shaikh Musa suddenly raised his head, as though a thought had just struck him.

'Things are cheap in the countryside,' he said, 'much cheaper than they are in the city. In the city people have to buy everything in the market, for cash, but here it isn't like that; we get everything from the fields. You should not expect to pay as much here as you would in the city. This is just a little hamlet —not even a big village like Nashawy.'

I was taken aback for a moment, and then I realized that he was referring obliquely to Abu-'Ali: he had asked me once how much I paid him and had sunk into an amazed silence when I quoted the sum. But before I could say anything, Shaikh Musa changed the subject: resorting to one of his favourite ploys he began to talk about agriculture.

'And these,' he said, pointing at the cucumbers on the tray, 'are called khiyâr. The best are those that are sown early, in spring, in the month of Amshîr by the Coptic calendar.'

Not one to be left behind in a conversation of that kind,

43

Ahmed immediately added: 'Amshir follows the month of Ṭūba, when the earth awakes, as we say, and after it comes Barmahât…'

Later, after dinner, when Shaikh Musa and I were alone in the room for a while, he began to wax expansive, talking about his boyhood in Lataifa and about Abu-'Ali as a child. But once the family returned he cut himself short, and there was no opportunity to discuss the matter again for shortly afterwards he got up and left the room.

No sooner had Shaikh Musa left than Ahmed began to tell me how cotton was rotated with the fodder crop berseem. 'Write it down,' he said, handing me my notebook, 'or else you'll forget.'

I scribbled desultorily for a while, and then, searching desperately for something else to talk about, I happened to ask him if his mother was away from the hamlet.

A hush immediately descended upon the room. At length, Ahmed cleared his throat and said: 'My mother, God have mercy on her, died a year ago.'

There was a brief silence, and then he leaned over to me. 'Do you see Sakkina there?' he asked, gesturing at the woman in the black fustan. 'My father married her this year.'

For a moment I was speechless: in my mind Shaikh Musa was very old and very venerable, and I was oddly unsettled by the thought of his marrying a woman a fraction his age.

His wife noticed me staring and smiled shyly. Then, Ahmed's wife, the self-possessed young woman in the cotton dress, turned to me and said: 'She's heard about you from her family. You have met her uncle, haven't you? Ustaz Mustafa?'

Again I was taken completely by surprise. But now things began to fall into place.

4

JABIR, ABU-'ALI'S YOUNG relative, had woken me one morning, soon after I arrived in Lataifa. 'Get up, ya mister,' he said, shaking me. 'Get up and meet my uncle.'

I sat up bleary-eyed and found myself looking at a short, plump man who bore a strong family resemblance to Jabir; he had the same rosy complexion, blunt features and bright, black eyes. He also had a little clipped moustache, and the moment I saw it I knew it was the kind of moustache that Jabir was sure to aspire to once his feathery adolescent whiskers had matured.

At that time, I was still innocent of some of the finer distinctions between salaried people and fellaheen but I could tell at once, from his starchy blue jallabeyya and white net skull-cap, that Jabir's uncle did not make his living from ploughing the land. Jabir's introduction made things clearer, for he added the word Ustaz, 'Teacher', to his uncle's name—a title usually given to men who had been educated in modern, rather than traditional, forms of learning.

'This is Ustaz Mustafa,' said Jabir. 'My uncle. He studied law at the University of Alexandria.'

Ustaz Mustafa smiled and, nodding vigorously, he addressed me in classical, literary Arabic. 'We are honoured,' he said, 'to have Your Presence amongst us.'

I was dismayed to be spoken to in this way, for in concentrating on learning the dialect of the village I had allowed my studies of classical Arabic to fall into neglect. I stuttered, unsure of how to respond, but then, unexpectedly, Jabir came to my rescue. Clapping me on the back, he told his uncle: 'He is learning to talk just like us.'

Ustaz Mustafa's face lit up. 'Insha'allah,' he cried, 'God willing, he will soon be one of us.'

I noticed that he had a habit of flicking back the cuff of his jallabeyya every few minutes or so to steal a quick look at his watch. I was to discover later that this gesture was rooted in an anxiety that had long haunted his everyday existence: the fear that he might inadvertently miss one of the day's five required prayers. That was why he looked much busier than anyone else in Lataifa—he was always in a hurry to get to the mosque. 'I have read all about India,' said Ustaz Mustafa, smiling serenely. 'There is a lot of chilli in the food and when a man dies his wife is dragged away and burnt alive.'

'Not always,' I protested, 'my grandmother for example...'

Jabir was drinking this in, wide-eyed.

'And of course,' Ustaz Mustafa continued, 'you have Indira Gandhi, and her son Sanjay Gandhi, who used to sterilize the Muslims...'

'No, no, he sterilized everyone,' I said.

His eyes widened and I added hastily: 'No, not me of course, but...'

'Yes,' he said, nodding sagely. 'I know. I read all about India when I was in college in Alexandria.'

He had spent several years in Alexandria as a student, he said; he had specialized in civil and religious law and now practised in a court in Damanhour. He talked at length about his time at university, the room he had lived in and the books he had read, and in the meanwhile two of Abu-'Ali's sons came up to join us, carrying a tray of tea.

Soon, the conversation turned to village gossip and for a while, to my relief, I was forgotten. But Jabir was not going to allow me so easy an escape: he had noticed that Ustaz Mustafa's questions had unsettled me and he was impatient for more entertainment.

46

'Ask him more about his country,' he whispered to his uncle. 'Ask him about his religion.'

The reminder was superfluous for, as I later discovered, religion was a subject never very far from Ustaz Mustafa's mind. 'All right then,' he said to me, motioning to the boys to be quiet. 'Tell me, are you Muslim?'

'No,' I said, but he didn't really need an answer since everyone in the hamlet knew that already.

'So then what are you?'

'I was born a Hindu,' I said reluctantly, for if I had a religious identity at all it was largely by default.

There was a long silence during which I tried hard to think of an arresting opening line that would lead the conversation towards some bucolic, agricultural subject. But the moment passed, and in a troubled voice Ustaz Mustafa said: 'What is this "Hinduki" thing? I have heard of it before and I don't understand it. If it is not Christianity nor Judaism nor Islam what can it be? Who are its prophets?'

'It's not like that,' I said. 'There aren't any prophets...'

'So you are like the Magi?' he said, bright-eyed. 'You worship fire then?'

I shook my head vaguely, but before I could answer, he tapped my arm with his forefinger. 'No,' he said, smiling coquettishly. 'I know—it's cows you worship—isn't that so?'

There was a sharp, collective intake of breath as Jabir and the other boys recoiled, calling upon God, in whispers, to protect them from the Devil.

I cleared my throat; I knew a lot depended on my answers. 'It's not like that,' I said. 'In my country some people don't eat beef because...because cows give milk and plough the fields and so on, and so they're very useful.'

47

Ustaz Mustafa was not to be bought off by this spurious ecological argument. 'That can't be the reason,' he began, but then his eyes fell on his watch and a shadow of alarm descended on his face. He edged forward until he was balanced precariously on the rim of the bed.

'You still haven't told me about this "Hinduki" business,' he said. 'What is your God like?'

I tried to stutter out an answer of some kind, but fortunately for me Ustaz Mustafa wasn't really paying attention to me any more.

'Well thanks be to Allah,' he said quickly, eyeing his watch. 'Now that you are here among us you can understand and learn about Islam, and then you can make up your mind whether you want to stay within that religion of yours.'

He jumped to his feet and stretched out his hand. 'Come with me to the mosque right now,' he said. 'That is where we are going—for the noon prayers. You don't have to do anything. Just watch us pray, and soon you will understand what Islam is.'

I hesitated for a moment, and then I shook my head. 'No,' I said. 'I can't. I have many things to do.'

'Things to do?' cried Ustaz Mustafa. 'What is there to do here that you can't do later? Come with us—it's very important. Nothing could be more important.'

'No,' I said. 'I can't.'

'Why not?' he insisted quietly. 'Just come and watch—that's all I'm asking of you.'

And just then the voice of the muezzin floated over from a nearby mosque, singing the call to prayer, and before I could say another word Ustaz Mustafa and the boys had vanished from the room.

But I couldn't go back to work even after I was alone again. I began to wonder why I had not accepted Ustaz Mustafa's invitation to visit the mosque and watch him at his prayers; he had meant well, after all, had only wanted to introduce me to the most important element of his imaginative life. A part of me had wanted to go—not merely that part which told me that it was, in a sense, my duty, part of my job. But when the moment had come, I'd known that I wouldn't be able to do it: I had been too afraid, and for the life of me I could not understand why.

But soon enough, Ustaz Mustafa came back to talk to me again. This time he had a child in his arms. 'This is my son,' he said, tweaking the child's cheeks. He glowed with love as he looked at the boy.

'Say salâm to the mister,' he said, and the child, alarmed, hid his face in his father's shoulder.

Ustaz Mustafa laughed. 'I missed you the last few days,' he said to me. 'I was busy in the evenings—I had to go and meet someone in Nashawy, so I couldn't come to talk to you. But today I decided that I would come over as soon as I got back from work.'

I was better prepared for him this time, and I began to talk at length about the hamlet's history and his family's genealogy. But Ustaz Mustafa had little time for matters of that kind, and soon he began to steal anxious glances at his watch over his son's back.

Eventually he brushed my patter aside and began to ask questions, first about my family and then about Indian politics—what I thought of Indira Gandhi, was I for her or against her, and so on. Then, with a wry, derisory smile he began to ask me about 'The Man from Menoufiyya'—the current nickname for the President, the Raïs—phrasing his questions in elaborately allusive, elliptical forms, like riddles, as

In an Antique Land

though he were mocking the Raïs's habit of spreading surrogate ears everywhere. My answers left him a little disappointed however, for many of his riddles had stock responses with which I was not then familiar.

Suddenly the bantering note went out of his voice.

'Tell me something,' he said, 'tell me, are you a communist?'

He used a word, shiyu'eyya, which could mean anything from 'communist' to 'atheist' and 'adulterer' in the village dialect; my understanding of it was that it referred to people who rejected all moral and ethical laws.

'No,' I said.

'All right then,' he said, 'if you're not a communist, tell me this: who made the world, and who were the first man and woman if not Âdam and Hawâ?'

I was taken aback by the abruptness of this transition. Later I came to expect elisions of this kind in conversations with people like Ustaz Mustafa, for I soon discovered that salaried people like him, rural mowazzafeen, were almost without exception absorbed in a concern which, despite its plural appearance, was actually single and indivisible—religion and politics—so that the mention of the one always led to the other. But at the time I was nonplussed. I mumbled something innocuous about how, in my country, people thought the world had always existed.

My answer made him flinch. He hugged his sleeping son hard against his chest and said, 'They don't think of Our Lord at all, do they? They live only for the present and have no thought for the hereafter.'

I began to protest but Ustaz Mustafa was not interested in my answers any more. His eyes had fallen on his watch, and he rose hurriedly to his feet. 'Tomorrow,' he said, 'I will take you with me to the graveyard, and you can watch me reciting the Quran

50

over my father's grave. You will see then how much better Islam is than this "Hinduki" of yours.'

At the door he turned back for a moment. 'I am hoping,' he said, 'that you will convert and become a Muslim. You must not disappoint me.'

Then he was gone. A moment later I heard the distant voice of a muezzin, chanting the call to prayer.

He had meant what he said.

He came back the next evening, his Quran in his hands, and said: 'Come, let's go to the graveyard.'

'I can't,' I said quickly. 'I have to go out to the fields.'

He hesitated, and then, not without some reluctance, decided to accompany me. The truth was that walking in the fields was something of a trial for Ustaz Mustafa: it demanded ceaseless vigilance on his part to keep particles of impure matter, like goat's droppings and cow dung, from touching his jallabeyya, since he would otherwise be obliged to change his clothes before going to the mosque again. This meant that he had to walk with extreme care in those liberally manured fields, with his hem plucked high above his ankles, very much in the manner that women hitch up their saris during the monsoons in Calcutta.

Before we had gone very far we came upon some of his relatives, working in a vegetable patch. They invited us to sit with them and began to ask me questions about the soil and the crops in India. Ustaz Mustafa soon grew impatient with this and led me away.

'They are fellaheen,' he said apologetically. 'They don't have much interest in religion or anything important.'

'I am just like that myself,' I said quickly.

'Really?' said Ustaz Mustafa, aghast. We walked in silence for a while, and then he said: 'I am giving up hope that you will become a Muslim.' Then an idea occurred to him and he turned to face me. 'Tell me,' he said, 'would your father be upset if you were to change your religion?'

'Maybe,' I said.

He relapsed into thoughtful silence for a few minutes. 'Has your father read the holy books of Islam?' he asked, eagerly.

'I don't know,' I answered.

'He must read them,' said Ustaz Mustafa. 'If he did he would surely convert himself.'

'I don't know,' I said. 'He is accustomed to his own ways.'

He mulled the issue over in his mind, and when we turned back towards Lataifa he said: 'Well, it would not be right for you to upset your father. That is true.'

After that the heart went out of his efforts to convert me: he had a son himself and it went against his deepest instincts to urge a man to turn against his father. And so, as the rival moralities of religion and kinship gradually played themselves to a standstill within him, Ustaz Mustafa and I came to an understanding.

A connection was already beginning to form in my mind now, as I turned towards Shaikh Musa's wife. 'Is Ustaz Mustafa really your uncle?' I asked her, uncertain of whether she was using the word in a specific or general sense. 'Your father's real brother, your 'amm shagîg?'

She was too shy to address me directly, at least in Ahmed's presence, so he spoke for her. 'Ustaz Mustafa is her real uncle,' he said. 'Her father and he were carried in the same belly. They still live in the same house.'

'But then Jabir must be her cousin,' I said in astonishment. 'They must have grown up in the same house.'

'Yes,' said Ahmed, 'she is Jabir's bint 'amm, his father's brother's daughter.'

He could have added: 'If Jabir were older he could have married her himself.' Certainly Jabir's parents and relatives would probably have wished for nothing better, since a marriage between first cousins, the children of brothers, was traditionally regarded as an ideal sort of union—a strengthening of an already existing bond.

'So she is of Abu-'Ali's lineage then?' I asked Ahmed.

'Yes,' said Ahmed, 'Abu-'Ali is her father's first cousin. His half-sister is her grandmother as well as Jabir's. She still lives in their house: you've met her.'

And so I had, a portly matriarch dressed in black, with fine features and delicate papery skin: she bore not the remotest resemblance to Abu-'Ali. I remembered her because of the posture of command she had assumed, perfectly naturally, with one knee flat on the floor and the other drawn up to support her arm and clenched fist. A glance from her had been enough to keep even Jabir quiet.

'Yes,' said Ahmed, 'Abu-'Ali's father was her great-grandfather's brother. And of course, his father, Abu-'Ali's grandfather, was my great-great-grandfather's brother.'

By this time I had lost my way in this labyrinth of relationships. It was only much later, when Shaikh Musa helped me draw up a complete genealogy of hamlet of Lataifa (all of whose inhabitants belonged ultimately to a single family called Latíf) that I finally began to see why he was always so careful never to voice a word of criticism about Abu-'Ali: his wife, Sakkina, was Abu-'Ali's great-grand-niece. The lines of the genealogy led inexorably to the conclusion that Abu-'Ali had played a crucial part in arranging the marriage.

It became clear to me then that there were complexities in Shaikh Musa's relationship with Abu-'Ali that I did not understand, and probably never would; that it would be deeply embarrassing for him if I were to ask him to help me find some other house, or family, to live in.

I realized then that my deliverance from Abu-'Ali would not come as easily as the dreams that took me to Cairo.

5

FOR BEN YIJU the centre of Cairo would have lain in a modest building near the eastern walls of the fortress of Babylon: the Synagogue of Ben Ezra, also known as the 'Synagogue of the Palestinians'. The building was destined to last until a good seven hundred years after Ben Yiju's lifetime; it was still standing late into the nineteenth century. In 1884 it was described, by a British historian and archæologist, A. J. Butler, as a small and somewhat simplified version of a Coptic basilica. By then most of its woodwork was gone and in 'point of detail there is not much remaining…'

When Ben Yiju first saw it, the building probably had a faint whiff of novelty about it, having been completely rebuilt only a hundred years or so earlier, in about 1025. It is known to have had two entrances then: one for the men, the main gateway, and a 'secret door' leading to a wooden platform inside the building, the women's gallery. The main chamber of the synagogue had a gabled ceiling and glass windows, and it was decorated with woodwork of very fine quality: some of it has survived and can still be seen in the Louvre, and in museums in Cairo and Jerusalem.

As far as Ben Yiju was concerned, his membership of this synagogue was probably more a matter of birth than personal preference. His origins lay in a region that was known as Ifrîqiya in the Arabic-speaking world of the Middle Ages—an area centred around what is now Tunisia. The region had fared badly in the eleventh century and over a period of several decades, since well before Ben Yiju's lifetime, its merchants and traders had been moving eastwards, towards Egypt. Jews figured prominently among these migrants and those amongst them who moved to Masr generally chose to join the 'Palestinian' congregation in Babylon. Ben Yiju was thus following a well-marked trail.

For the Synagogue of Ben Ezra the influx of migrants from Ifriqiya was to prove providential: the newcomers proved to be the most industrious members of the community and they soon assumed its leadership, setting the pattern for the others in matters of language and culture, as well as trade and commerce. The North Africans appear to have had a particular affinity for the flourishing trade between the Mediterranean and the Indian Ocean and over a period of several centuries the Jewish traders of Fustat counted as an integral part of the richly diverse body of merchants who were involved in the conduct of business in Asian waters. Carried along by the movements of that cycle of trade many of them travelled regularly between three continents—men whose surnames often read like the chapter headings of an epic, linked them to sleepy oases and dusty Saharan market towns, places like El Faiyum and Tlemcen.

Thus it was no ordinary congregation that Ben Yiju joined in Masr: it consisted of a group of people whose travels and breadth of experience and education seem astonishing even today, on a planet thought to be newly-shrunken. Yet, unlike others of that time who have left their mark on history, the members of this community were not born to privilege and entitlement; they were neither aristocrats nor soldiers nor professional scholastics. The vast majority of them were traders, and while some of them were wealthy and successful, they were not, by any means, amongst the most powerful merchants of their time—most of them were small traders running small family businesses. Yet, despite their generally modest circumstances, a majority of the men were endowed with a respectable level of education, and some were among the most learned scholars of their time. Their doctors, for example, studied Hippocrates and Galen in Arabic translation, as well as the medical writings of Arab physicians and scholars, such as Ibn Rushd (Averroes) and al-Râzî. Indeed, one member of the Synagogue's congregation is reckoned to have been one of the finest minds of the Middle Ages: the great doctor, scholar and philosopher Mûsa ibn Maimûn, known as Maimonides. Like so many others in his community, he too had close familial links with the India Trade.

The greatest achievement of the Ben Ezra congregation, however, was the product of largely fortuitous circumstances. The Synagogue's members followed a custom, widespread at the time, of depositing their writings in a special chamber in the synagogue so that they could be disposed of with special rites later. This practice, which is still observed among certain Jewish groups today, was intended to prevent the accidental desecration of any written form of God's name. Since most writings in that epoch included at least one sacred invocation in the course of the text, the custom effectively ensured that written documents of every kind were deposited within the Synagogue. The chambers in which the documents were kept were known by the term

'Geniza', a word that is thought to have come into Hebrew from a Persian root, ganj, meaning 'storehouse'—a common element in place-names in India and Iran, particularly beloved of the British who sprinkled it liberally across their Indian settlements, in odd Anglicized forms like 'Ballygunge' and 'Daltongunj'.

Every synagogue in the Middle East once had a Geniza and in accordance with custom, their contents were regularly emptied and buried. The Geniza of the Synagogue of Ben Ezra was added when the synagogue was rebuilt in 1025AD, but for some reason—possibly reverence for the past, possibly mere oversight—it was never cleared out. For more than eight centuries papers continued to accumulate inside the Geniza. At the peak of the community's prosperity, during the first two and a half centuries after the rebuilding of the Synagogue in 1025, great quantities of manuscripts poured in. Then, towards the middle of the thirteenth century, the flow dried to a trickle, and only swelled again some three hundred years later, when the Spanish Inquisition sent yet another wave of Jewish immigrants flooding in to Egypt. Papers (and later, books) continued to accumulate intermittently in the Geniza until the nineteenth century, by which time Fustat had become a poor neglected backwater in Cairo's rapidly expanding archipelago. The document that is thought to be the last to be deposited in the Geniza bears the date 1875: it was a divorce settlement written in Bombay.

For centuries the Synagogue of the Palestinians lay forgotten within the half-abandoned precincts of the ancient fortress of Babylon. In about 1890, the eleventh-century building, the structure that Ben Yiju saw, was finally torn down and a new one was erected in its place: it still stands on the site today.

Until recently the site of the Synagogue of Ben Ezra lay at one end of a plateau of rubble; an expanse of shattered brick and stone, that looked as though it had been flattened by a gigantic hammer. The Synagogue itself, an undistinguished, rectangular building, seemed just barely to have survived: much of its masonry had crumbled, and the shutters had fallen away from many of its windows. Its most striking feature was a pair of wrought-iron gates; although much discoloured and corroded, they were still graceful, their sinuous forms exuberantly Art Deco: they looked as though someone had ordered them from Paris in a flush of enthusiasm after a summer holiday. Above the narrow gateway, held in place by a length of iron tubing and a few heavy stones, was a Star of David, a little askew and festooned with cobwebs.

Today the building is once again rejuvenated, its exterior scrubbed and well-tended. Prefabricated huts have sprouted in the rubble outside, where young engineers stand behind drawing-boards, their toes tapping gently to the beat of muted rock music: a team of Canadian experts and restorers has arrived, Mountie-like, to rescue the Synagogue from the assaults of Time.

A few men wait for tourists at the entrance to the Synagogue, standing behind desks spread with beads, necklaces, bronze scarabs and busts of Nefertiti. One of them has been there for years, a plump, smiling man, dressed in a shirt and trousers. His trinkets and souvenirs do not seem to change much from year to year—in fact he never seems to do much business at all—but he is always full of smiles, good-natured, and helpful. He explains that 'Amm Shahata, the caretaker, is inside, he can take visitors in and explain everything—he is Jewish, *yahûdi*, he knows all about the Synagogue.

In a while 'Amm Shahata appears, a sprightly old man, very thin and a little stooped. He too is dressed in a shirt and trousers, and his skull-cap is very much like any Egyptian Muslim's. The two men exchange some companionable banter; his Arabic is indistinguishable from theirs, the staccato speech of working-class Cairo. He tells you his name: 'Nathan in Hebrew and Shahata in Arabic.' Close up he looks unexpectedly old, his teeth are gone and veins stand out on his forehead.

'Amm Shahata soon lets it be known that he is a busy man: he has no time to waste; he ushers you briskly through the gateway and leads you into the main chamber of the Synagogue. Prisms of light shine through coloured windows; you are in a room with a very high ceiling, but otherwise of modest, schoolroom size. In the centre is a raised, octagonal altar, with benches arranged in rows on either side. The room has two levels. At the upper level is the women's gallery, which runs around three sides of the room. At the far end of the gallery, on the left, is a small hole, high up in the wall; it opens into an empty chamber adjoining the back wall. 'Amm Shahata points at the opening; that is the Geniza, he tells you, where a lot of papers were found, years and years ago.

You wish it were indeed the old Geniza, but it cannot be. It is no higher than a bare six feet or so while the Geniza of the old Synagogue is known to have been at least as tall as the rest of the building, some two and a half storeys high. The old Geniza was probably left standing for a while, after the rest of the structure was torn down, but it must have perished later.

Of course, you have no cause to be disappointed. The Synagogue's location has not altered, whatever the changes in its outer shell. The fact is that you are standing upon the very site which held the greatest single collection of medieval documents ever discovered.

It was here, in this forlorn corner of Masr, that the memories of Abraham Ben Yiju and his slave lay preserved for more than seven hundred years.

6

ONCE, ON A very hot afternoon, when the sweat was dribbling off my face on to my notebooks, I gave up trying to work, and sat in my room with the door open, hoping to trap a breath of fresh air. It was very still that day, with the moisture from the freshly-watered cotton fields and rice paddies hanging heavy in the air. At intervals, as though frightened by the stillness, the ducks and chickens with whom I shared the roof would burst into an uproar, erupt out of their coops and flap around the roof in a gale of frenzied squawks, undaunted by the flat, white heat of the afternoon.

As I sat watching, a pair of ducks began to race around and around the roof, one in pursuit of the other. They were of a species I had never seen before I came to Egypt: squat, ugly creatures, almost suicidally self-absorbed, with large red warts on their necks and mangy black and white bodies. The pursuer was the bigger of the two, and it soon caught up with the other and pinned it to the floor with its beak. Then, after it had hoisted itself on top, it raised one leg and suddenly its penis appeared, a bright, wet pink, about as long as a thumbnail. It flapped its tailfeathers for a moment, pressing against its mate, and then tumbled off, a look of bafflement on its face. I watched spellbound: I had had no conception that ducks had penises and vaginas.

I happened to look up then and I saw Jabir, standing silently in the stairway, watching me.

He began to laugh.

'You were watching like it was a film, ya Amitab,' he said, laughing. 'Haven't you seen ducks do that before?'

'No,' I said.

His laughter was infectious; I found myself laughing with him.

He came into the room and seated himself on the chair, taking care to keep his clean jallabeyya from touching the floor.

'So tell me then,' he said, throwing me a glance of interested inquiry. 'What do you know on the subject of…?'

He used a word I had not heard before. I must have looked puzzled, for he gave an incredulous gasp and said: 'You mean you've never heard of…?'

It was the same word again.

I shook my head and he sank back in the chair, knocking his head with his fist, nearly dislodging his white skull-cap.

'Ya Amitab,' he said in mock despair. 'What are you going to do in life if you don't know about that?'

'About what?' I said.

This only made him laugh. 'If you don't know you don't know,' he muttered mysteriously.

'Don't know about what?' I said, in exasperation.

'It's not important,' he said, grinning, elliptical. 'It's good to put a distance between your thoughts and things like that. But tell me this—of course you have circumcision where you come from, just like we do? Isn't that so, mush kida?'

I had long been dreading this line of questioning, knowing exactly where it would lead.

'Some people do,' I said. 'And some people don't.'

'You mean,' he said in rising disbelief, 'there are people in your country who are not circumcised?'

In Arabic the word 'circumcise' derives from a root that means 'to purify': to say of someone that they are 'uncircumcised' is more or less to call them impure.

'Yes,' I answered, 'yes, many people in my country are "impure".' I had no alternative; I was trapped by language.

'But not you...' He could not bring himself to finish the sentence.

'Yes,' I said. My face was hot with embarrassment and my throat had gone dry: 'Yes, me too.'

He gasped and his incredulous eyes skimmed over the front of my trousers. For a moment he stared in disbelieving curiosity, and then, with an effort, he said: 'And when you go to the barber to have your hair cut, do you not shave your armpits like we do?'

'No,' I said.

He leant forward, frowning intently. 'So tell me then,' he said, pointing a finger at my crotch. 'Don't you shave there either?'

'No,' I said.

'But then,' he cried, 'doesn't the hair grow longer and longer until...'

Inadvertently his eyes dropped and he stole a quick look at my ankles. I am convinced, to this day, that he fully expected to see the ends of two long, curly braids peeping out from the ends of my trousers.

That evening, towards sunset, I went for a walk in the fields. A fair distance from the hamlet I came upon Jabir and some other boys of his age, sitting beside a small canal. They had their textbooks with them and they were taking advantage of the comparative quiet of the fields to catch up with their schoolwork. I stopped dead when I saw Jabir; I was not sure whether we were still on speaking terms. But to my relief he waved cheerfully when he saw me coming, and then he and his friends jumped to their feet and fell in beside me.

'You should go on with your studies,' I said. 'There's still plenty of light.'

'We should be returning now,' Jabir said, 'it will soon be time for the evening prayers. Look—the moon is already up.'

I looked up and saw a full moon, brilliant against the fading purple of the evening sky. It was very quiet, except for the creak of distant water-wheels; in Lataifa, far away, the first lamps were beginning to shine.

Jabir had his arms around the shoulders of the other boys. 'Do you want to hear something?' he said. He was whispering but I could hear him clearly in the sunset hush.

'I was talking to him this afternoon,' he said, gesturing at me with his chin. 'And do you know, he doesn't know what sex is?'

I had checked in the dictionary as soon as he'd left: he was using the same word he'd used that afternoon.

'What's this you're saying, ya Jabir?' one of the boys exclaimed. 'He doesn't know what sex is?'

'What am I telling you?' Jabir retorted. 'He doesn't know. I asked him.'

'And he looks so grown up and all.'

'But he doesn't know a thing,' said Jabir. 'Not religion, not politics, not sex, just like a child.'

There was an awed silence. 'Do you think he doesn't know about "beating the ten" either?' one of the boys whispered. I was not familiar with this expression at the time, but the gesture of the fist that accompanied it gave me a fair idea of its meaning.

'No,' said Jabir, 'he's like a child, I told you. That's why he's always asking questions.'

'Shouldn't we tell him?' one of the boys said. 'How's he going to grow up if he doesn't beat the ten?'

'It's no use,' said Jabir. 'He won't understand; he doesn't know a thing. Look, I'll show you.'

He detached himself from the others and called out to me: 'Ya Amitab—stop, wait a minute.'

Taking hold of my elbow he led me to the edge of the canal. 'Look at that,' he said, pointing at the reflection of the full moon on the water. 'What is it? Do you know?'

'Of course I know,' I scoffed. 'It's Ahmed, Shaikh Musa's son, shining his torch on the water.'

There was a hushed silence and Jabir turned to cast the others a triumphant look while I walked on quickly.

'No, ya Amitab,' one of the boys said, running after me, his voice hoarse with concern. 'That's not so. It's not Ahmed shining his torch in the water—that's a reflection of the full moon.'

'No,' I said. 'You're absolutely wrong. Ahmed told me he would be going out for a walk today with his torch.'

'But if it's Ahmed how is it that we didn't see him?'

'We didn't see him because he was a long way off. His torch is very powerful. It works on four batteries. He's just bought new batteries—yesterday in Damanhour.'

And thus we argued, back and forth, and by the time we reached Lataifa I had nearly won the argument.

7

FOR A LONG time afterwards, I remained a child in Jabir's eyes.

One evening, shortly after the start of Ramadan (which stretched over July and August that year), Jabir took me to a mowlid, a fair in honour of a saint's birthday, in a village that lay across the fields. Several other boys from Lataifa went with us, among them Jabir's younger brother, Mohammad, and a nephew of Shaikh Musa's, a shy, quiet boy of fifteen, called Mabrouk.

As we walked across the fields towards the distant lights of the mowlid, Jabir and the other boys told me about the legend of Sidi 'Abbas of Nakhlatain, in whose honour the mowlid was being celebrated.

Sidi 'Abbas had lived in Nakhlatain long, long ago, long before anyone could remember, and he had been famous throughout the region for his godliness and piety: people had said of him that he was a 'good man', gifted with 'baraka', the power of conferring blessings. Such was his fame that a large crowd gathered in his village when he died, and so many people were witness to the miraculous events that graced his funeral. Trying to lift the Sidi's bier, the men of the village found, to their amazement, that they couldn't move it at all; dozens of them tried, only to find that they could not so much as budge it. It was only when the Sidi's son lent a hand that the body began to move, but even then, it was not he who moved the body: the Sidi had moved of his own volition.

The Sidi's body had led the wonderstruck people of the village into a mosque, and there the Sidi had communicated with them, telling them to build him a domed tomb, a maqâm: they were to celebrate his mowlid there every year. The people of the village had done as he had said, and in the following years the Sidi

65

demonstrated his power to them time and time again, through miracles and acts of grace. Once, for instance, some thieves who were escaping with a herd of stolen water-buffalo were frozen to the ground, buffaloes and all, when they drew abreast of the Sidi's tomb. Such was the Sidi's power that anything left touching his tomb was safe: farmers who were late going home in the evening would even leave such valuable things as their wooden ploughs leaning against its walls, knowing that they would not be touched. Once, someone left a plough with leather thongs there, propped up against the tomb. After a while a mouse came along and, since mice like to nibble at leather, it had bitten into the plough's thongs. But no sooner had its teeth touched the plough than it was frozen to the ground; that was how it was found next morning, with its teeth stuck in the thongs. Even animals were not exempt from the rules of sanctuary that surrounded the Sidi's tomb.

The tomb was visible from a long way off, across the fields: a simple, rectangular structure with a low dome and a large open space in front which served as a public space—a common threshing-floor, as well as the site of the village's weekly market. Now the tomb was festooned with dozens of small bulbs, its freshly whitewashed walls dotted with puddles of coloured light. The square in front was crowded with people, some thronging into the tomb, and others circulating amongst the fairground stalls that had been erected all around it.

A stall-owner called out to us as we walked into the square. 'Come on,' he said, 'let's see what you young fellows can do.'

There were several airguns balanced on his counter, pointing at a board with dangling balloons and candles. Smiling encouragement, he thrust a couple of guns into our hands. I was stooping to take aim when I heard Jabir's voice behind me:

'From India…'

I looked over my shoulder and quickly turned back again. A large crowd had gathered around me; much larger than the crowds in any of the other stalls. 'Doesn't know anything,' I heard Jabir say, 'Nothing at all…' I squeezed the trigger, trying to keep my sights steady on a large balloon.

'You missed,' said Jabir.

Ignoring my mumbled retort, he turned back to his audience. 'Didn't I tell you?' he whispered. 'Doesn't know a thing.'

I tried to fix the balloon in my sights again, while people clustered eagerly around Jabir. 'Doesn't pray, doesn't even know Our Lord…'

'What're you saying? Doesn't know Our Lord!'

I squeezed the trigger, and once again the pellet thudded into the board, wide of the balloon.

'Doesn't know the Lord! Oh the Saviour!'

I shuffled off quickly to the next stall where a boy was selling pink, fluffy candy. Jabir's voice followed me: 'Reads books and asks questions all day long; doesn't have any work to do…'

'Can we talk to him?' somebody asked.

'No,' Jabir said magisterially. 'He won't understand a word you say. Only we in Lataifa know how to talk to him.'

I began to push my way quickly through the crowd, towards the other end of the square: I was hoping to put a distance between myself and Jabir, but he was not to be shaken off and followed hard on my heels. But then, providentially, I earned a brief respite; he and his cousins spotted a row of swings on the edge of the square and went running off to join the queue.

By the time I worked my way through the crowd their turns had come and they were heaving themselves back and forth, their jallabeyyas ballooning out around them, each trying to outdo the other. The crowd began to cheer them on and one of the boys swung high enough to go all the way around the bar in a complete circle. Jabir attempted a couple of mighty heaves himself, to no effect, so he jumped off, shrugging dismissively. 'I wasn't trying,' he said, dusting his hands. 'I can do it when I try.'

Then he marched us off across the square again, towards the Sidi's tomb. 'We should see the zikr,' he said sternly to his cousins. 'That's the most important part of the mowlid.'

A group of about thirty men, of all ages, had gathered in front of the tomb. Standing in rows, with their feet apart, they were jerking their heads and their torsos from side to side while a man dressed in a white turban chanted into a microphone. They swung their bodies in time with the rhythm, only their heads and their upper bodies moving, their feet perfectly still.

'They are Sûfis,' Jabir said for my benefit. 'They are invoking God by chanting his name.'

Some of the men had shut their eyes, and the others looked rapt, mesmerized by the rhythm and the movement. As the singer increased the tempo, their heads began to move faster, keeping time, their eyes becoming increasingly glazed, unseeing.

Jabir and his cousins were soon bored by the zikr. 'Makes me dizzy,' one of them said, and we went off to look at the stalls again.

It was not long before Jabir had a new audience.

'Doesn't know Our Lord, doesn't know anything…if you ask him how water-wheels are made, he'll say: "They have babies".'

'Oh the black day!'

'No!'

'Go on, ask him.'

'Do water-wheels have babies, ya doktór?' one of the boys said.

'No,' I said. 'They lay eggs.'

'Did you hear that? He thinks water-wheels lay eggs.'

I began to yearn for the solitude of my room, and to my relief, I did not have to wait long before the boys decided to head back across the cotton fields.

Early next morning, Jabir burst in, his face flushed with excitement. 'Do you know what happened last night?' he said, shaking me out of bed. 'There was a murder—a man was murdered at the mowlid.'

'What happened?' I said confusedly.

It had happened near the swings, Jabir said, exactly where we had been last night. The murdered man had been sitting on a swing when someone had come along and asked him to get off. He was pushed when he refused, and had fallen off and died, hitting his head on a rock.

And now, Jabir said, drawing himself up to his full height, there would be a blood feud. That was the law of the Arabs: 'Me and my brother against my cousin; me and my cousin against the stranger.' This was a serious matter: if a man killed someone, then he and all his male kin on the paternal side could be killed in revenge by the dead man's family. They would have to go and hide with their maternal relatives until their uncles and the shaikhs of the land could talk to the dead man's family and persuade them to come to a council of reconciliation. Then, when the grief of the dead man's family had eased a little, an amnesty would be declared. The two lineages would meet in some safe central place, and in the presence of their elders they would negotiate a blood-money payment. That was thâr, the law of feud; damm, the law of blood; the ancient, immutable law of the Arabs.

'All that for pushing a man off a swing?' I asked, bleary-eyed.

Jabir paused to think. 'Well, maybe a little one,' he said wistfully. 'Just a small feud.'

'Who was the man who was killed?'

'His name was Fathy,' said Jabir, 'but people called him "the Sparrow". He was from the village down the road: Nashawy. Now there'll be a feud there.'

I was somehow very doubtful, but for all the attention Jabir paid me, I could have been a six-year-old child.

8

IT WAS MABROUK, Shaikh Musa's nephew, who was responsible for improving my standing in Jabir's eyes.

That year Mabrouk's father had done exceptionally well from his vegetable plot. He'd taken a risk the autumn before by planting a lot of carrots after the cotton harvest. Everyone had tried to dissuade him—his wife, his brothers (including Shaikh Musa) and most of his cousins and relatives. The carrots would have to be harvested all at the same time, they had said, and what if the prices in the market were low that week? He would end up selling a whole truckload of carrots at a loss; it was better to plant many different kinds of vegetables, less of a risk.

Mabrouk's father had not paid any attention. He was an obstinate sort of man, and their arguments had only served to settle his resolve. As it turned out, he had been lucky. The price of carrots happened to be exceptionally high at the time of his harvest, and he made an unexpectedly large profit.

A few weeks later, he put all his savings together, and he and two of his brothers hired a truck and went off to Damanhour. When the truck returned, several hours later, the three brothers —all men of ample girth—were sitting in front, squeezed in beside the driver. In the back was a mysterious object, about as big as a calf but of a different shape, wrapped in several sheets of tarpaulin. The truck went quietly around to Mabrouk's house, and the object was unloaded and carried in through a back entrance, still wrapped in its tarpaulin sheets.

I knew nothing of this until Mabrouk burst into my room that afternoon: I heard the sound of feet flying up the stairs, and then Mabrouk threw the door open and caught hold of my arm.

'Come with me, ya doktór,' he cried. 'You have to come with me right now, to our house. My father and my family want you.' He was in a state of such feverish excitement that he could not bring himself to wait until I closed my notebook; he virtually dragged me out of the room right then, never letting go of my elbow.

Abu-'Ali and his family were astonished to see Mabrouk racing through their house, for he had always had a reputation for being unusually shy. Jabir told me once that despite being the tallest and fastest amongst the boys of their age, Mabrouk wasn't allowed to play in the forward line of their soccer team: the sight of an open goal was sometimes enough to bring on one of his attacks of shyness.

But now, Mabrouk was transformed; as we hurried through the lanes he talked volubly about how his father and his uncles had hired a truck and gone to Damanhour. But when I asked what exactly they had bought, he shook his head and smiled enigmatically. 'Wait, wait,' he said, 'you will see.'

By the time we got there, a crowd had collected in Mabrouk's lane, and his house was in an uproar. His father had been waiting for me, and after a hurried exchange of greetings, he spirited me past the crowd in his guest-room and led me quickly to a walled courtyard at the back, next to the pen where the livestock was kept—the most secret, secluded part of the house, the zarîba. Their acquisition was standing in the middle of the courtyard, like a newborn calf, with an old shoe hanging around it to fend off the Evil Eye.

It was a brand-new diesel water-pump, the first of its kind to come to Lataifa. There were several such pumps in the surrounding villages: they were known generically as 'al-makana al-Hindi', the Indian machine, for they were all manufactured in India.

Mabrouk, his father, his mother and several cousins and uncles, were standing around me now, in a circle, looking from me to the machine, bright-eyed and expectant.

'Makana hindi!' I said to Mabrouk's father, with a show of enthusiasm. 'Congratulations—you've bought an "Indian machine"!'

Mabrouk's father's eyes went misty with pride as he gazed upon the machine. 'Yes,' he sighed. 'Yes, that's why we asked you to come. You must take a look at it and tell us what you think.'

'Me?' I said. I was aghast; I knew nothing at all about water-pumps; indeed, I could not recall ever having noticed one before coming to Lataifa.

'Yes!' Mabrouk's father clapped me on the back. 'It's from your country, isn't it? I told the dealer in Damanhour, I said, "Make sure you give me one that works well, we have an Indian living in our hamlet and he'll be able to tell whether we've got a good one or not."'

I hesitated, mumbling a few words of protest, but he nudged me eagerly forward. A quick look at the anxious, watchful faces around me told me that escape was impossible: I would have to pronounce an opinion, whether I liked it or not.

A hush fell upon the courtyard as I walked up to the machine; a dozen heads craned forward, watching my every move. I went up to the machine's spout, stooped beside it and peered knowledgeably into its inky interior, shutting one eye. Standing up again, I walked around the pump amidst a deathly silence, nodding to myself, occasionally tapping parts of it with my knuckles. Then, placing both hands on the diesel motor, I fell to my knees and shut my eyes. When I looked up again Mabrouk's father was standing above me, anxiously awaiting the outcome of my silent communion with this product of my native soil.

Reaching for his hand I gave it a vigorous shake. 'It's a very good makana Hindi,' I said, patting the pump's diesel tank. 'Excellent! 'Azeem! It's an excellent machine.'

At once a joyful hubbub broke out in the courtyard. Mabrouk's father pumped my hand and slapped me on the back. 'Tea,' he called out to his wife. 'Get the doktór al-Hindi some tea.'

Next day Jabir came to visit me in my room, late in the evening. He seemed somehow subdued, much quieter and less cocky than usual.

'I was talking to Mabrouk,' he said, 'I heard he took you to his house to see their new "Indian machine".'

I shrugged nonchalantly. 'Yes,' I said. 'He did.'

'And what was your opinion?' he asked.

'They've bought a good machine,' I said. 'A very good one.'

Jabir sank into silence, nodding thoughtfully. Later, when he rose to leave, he stopped at the door and declared: 'My father and my uncles are thinking of buying an Indian machine too, insha'allah.'

'Good,' I said.

'I hope you'll come with us,' he said.

'Where?'

'When we go to Damanhour to buy it,' he said, shyly. 'We would profit from your opinion.'

I stayed up a long time that night, marvelling at the respect the water-pump had earned me; I tried to imagine where I would have stood in Jabir's eyes if mine had been a country that exported machines that were even bigger, better and more impressive—cars and tractors perhaps, not to speak of ships and planes and tanks. I began to wonder how Lataifa would have looked if I had had the privilege of floating through it, protected by the delegated power of technology, of looking out untroubled through a sheet of clear glass.

9

SOON THE MONTH of Ramadan arrived and I began to think of taking a holiday. First I would go to Alexandria, I decided, to talk to Doctor Issa, and to see whether I could make arrangements for moving out of Abu-'Ali's house. After that I would go to Cairo: I had spent one night there when I first arrived, but I had seen nothing other than the airport, and the station. Now at last, the time had come to pay the city a proper visit.

As the days passed the thought of my trip became ever more exciting. We were then well into Ramadan, and I was one of the handful of people in the hamlet who were not fasting. I had wanted to join in the fast, but everyone insisted, 'No, you can't fast, you're not Muslim—only Muslims fast at Ramadan.' And so, being reminded of my exclusion every day by the drawn, thirsty faces around me, the thought of Cairo and Alexandria, and the proximity of others among the excluded, grew ever more attractive.

From the very first day of the lunar month the normal routines of the village had undergone a complete change: it was as though a segment of time had been picked from the calendar and turned inside out. Early in the morning, a good while before sunrise, a few young men would go from house to house waking everyone for the suḥûr, the early morning meal. After that, as the day progressed, a charged lassitude would descend upon Lataifa. To ease the rigours of the fast people would try to finish all their most pressing bits of work early in the morning, while the sun was still low in the sky; it was impossible to do anything strenuous on an empty stomach and parched throat once the full heat of the day had set in. By noon the lanes of the hamlet would be still, deserted. The women would be in their kitchens and oven-rooms, getting their meals ready for the breaking of the fast at sunset. The men would sit in the shade of trees, or in their doorways, fanning themselves. Their mouths and lips would sometimes acquire thin white crusts, and often, as the hours wore on, their tempers would grow brittle.

I often wondered whether there were any people in the village who were occasionally delinquent in their observance of the fast. It was true that the most vulnerable people—pregnant women, young children, the sick, the elderly, and so on—were exempted by religious law, but even for those of sound body the fast must have been very hard: those were long, fiercely hot summer days, and it must have been difficult indeed to last through them without food, water or tobacco. Yet I never once saw a single person in Lataifa breaking the fast, in any way: there were occasional rumours that certain people in such and such village had been seen eating or drinking, but even those were very rare.

In every house as the sun sank slowly towards the horizon, the women would lay out their trays and serve the food they had cooked during the day. Their families would gather around, ravenous now, with cool, tall glasses of water resting in front of them. They would sit watching the lengthening shadows, tense and still, listening to their radios, waiting for the shaikhs of the mosque of al-Azhar in Cairo to announce the legal moment of sunset. It was not enough to see the sun going down with one's eyes; the breaking of the fast was the beginning of a meal of communion that embraced millions of people and the moment had to be celebrated publicly and in unison.

When the meal was finished and the trays had been cleared away, the men would wash and change and make their way to the mosque, talking, laughing, replete with a sense of well-being which the day's denials had made multiply sweet. I would go up to my room alone and listen to the call of the muezzin and try to think of how it must feel to know that on that very day, as the sun travelled around the earth, millions and millions of people in every corner of the globe had turned to face the same point, and said exactly the same words of prayer, with exactly the same prostrations as oneself. A phenomenon on that scale was beyond my imagining, but the exercise helped me understand why so many people in the hamlet had told me not to fast: to belong to that immense community was a privilege which they had to re-earn every year, and the effort made them doubly conscious of the value of its boundaries.

In the evenings, after the prayers, the hamlet would be full of life and laughter. Where at other times of the year the lanes and paths were generally empty by eight o' clock, they were now full of bustle and activity: children going from house to house, chanting and demanding gifts, and people visiting their families and staying up late, gossiping and joking with their friends.

The night before I left for my trip to Cairo and Alexandria, I went to see Shaikh Musa to say goodbye. He and his family were resting after breaking the day's fast. They had eaten well and Shaikh Musa had just returned from the mosque. He was sitting on a mat in his bedroom, puffing on his shusha, a home-made hookah, making up for all the tobacco he had had to deny himself during the day.

He was in high spirits. 'Welcome, ya Amitab,' he said. 'How are you, come and sit here, beside me.'

As soon as I'd sat down he pointed at a young man sitting across the room and said: 'Do you know who that is?'

The room was lit only by the glow of a single oil lamp, but I recognized the young man he had pointed to the moment I saw him. It was his younger son Hasan. He looked very much like the photograph Shaikh Musa carried in his wallet: robust, with clean, chiselled features, and a pleasant, rather shy smile. He lifted his right hand to his heart to welcome me to his house, and we shook hands and exchanged the customary greetings.

'You have brought blessings.'

'God bless you.'

'You have brought light to our house.'

'The light is yours.'

His face was sunburnt, ruddy, and he was wearing the khaki fatigues of the Egyptian army.

'He's on leave,' Shaikh Musa said. 'The army let him go for a few days so he could visit his family.'

Just then Sakkina appeared in the doorway and handed Hasan a tray with three glasses of tea on it. He took it from her without a word and she disappeared back into the kitchen. Neither she nor Hasan spoke to each other, but it struck me suddenly that they were probably of exactly the same age: as children they would have worked in the same groups in the cotton fields, picking weevils from the plants, and they would have played together in the hamlet's threshing-grounds in the evenings. I could not help wondering about the nuances of their present situation, about how they dealt with each other as stepmother and stepson.

'He got here this afternoon,' Shaikh Musa said. 'He's been travelling all morning.'

I asked Hasan where he had come from and he told me that he was posted in Mansourah, a small town a couple of hundred miles away, at the other end of the Delta. His voice sounded tired and when he had finished speaking he leant his head back against the wall.

'He's not well,' Shaikh Musa explained. 'He's got a pain in the head.'

I saw then that he had a bandage tied around his forehead. I had not noticed it before for it was largely hidden by his thick, dark hair.

'He comes home for a day and look what happens to him,' Shaikh Musa said in mock outrage. 'Shouldn't the government extend his leave, at least?'

In a short while other people began to arrive. Some were relatives who had heard that Hasan was back on leave, and some were friends of Shaikh Musa's from nearby villages. I soon realized that some of them were from Nashawy, and the moment there was a break in the conversation I asked if there was going to be a feud in their village. They looked at one another in puzzlement at first, and when I recounted the story that Jabir had told me they began to laugh.

The boy had imagined it, they said. There would be no feud, even though it was true that the man called the Sparrow had died. The police had made a report, and it had been settled between the two families. The Sparrow had been a poor man, none too sound in the head, with very few relatives in the area. The man who had knocked him over was from a big and powerful family. There was no question of a feud: the elders of the two families had sat down and decided on a token payment and that was that, khalas.

Shaikh Musa, listening intently, sighed and shook his head. 'Nashawy!' he said. 'There's always some trouble there.'

It was a big, bustling place, Nashawy, with almost fourteen hundred people, fully a thousand more than Lataifa! All those people living crowded together; no wonder they had trouble.

They began to talk about Nashawy, and listening to them I wondered why I had not visited the village yet. It was just a mile or so down the road, and I would often hear the drivers of the pick-up trucks that went past Lataifa shouting 'Nashawy? Nashawy?' In my first few weeks in the hamlet I had often thought of climbing on for the ride. But now I had heard the name so often that it had begun to sound like a challenge: it had become a place that I would have to prepare for, just as I was preparing myself for Cairo.

A little later, when I got up to leave, Shaikh Musa's guests invited me to visit Nashawy, but Shaikh Musa cut them short. 'He doesn't have time now,' he said. 'He's going to Cairo, to Masr.'

He and his two sons came to the door to say goodbye. Shaikh Musa stood in the middle, holding his two grandsons by the hand, his eldest son, Ahmed, on his right and Hasan, the younger, on his left. 'Come back soon, ya mister,' he said, 'and tell us about your trip. We want to hear about it, about Masr.'

'I'll tell you about it,' I said, 'as soon as I return.'

At the end of the lane, I looked back: Shaikh Musa was still there, the picture of happiness and fulfilment, surrounded by his sons and grandsons.

'Do you know what they say about Masr?' he shouted after me. 'They say she's the umm al-duniyâ, the "mother of the world".'

10

IN THE EIGHTEENTH century, a new breed of traveller began to flock into Cairo, Europeans with scholarly and antiquarian interests, for whom Masr was merely the picturesque but largely incidental location of an older, and far more important landscape. By this time Europe was far in advance of the rest of the world in armaments and industry, and on the points of those weapons the high age of imperialism was about to be ushered in. Masr had long since ceased to be the mistress of her own destiny; she had become a province of the Ottoman Empire, which was itself enfeebled now, allowed to keep its territories only by the consent of the Great Powers. The Indian Ocean trade, and the culture that supported it, had long since been destroyed by European navies. Transcontinental trade was no longer a shared enterprise; the merchant shipping of the high seas was now entirely controlled by the naval powers of Europe. It no longer fell to Masr to send her traders across the Indian Ocean; instead, the geographical position that had once brought her such great riches had now made her the object of the Great Powers' attentions, as a potential bridge to their territories in the Indian Ocean.

Over the same period that Egypt was gaining a new strategic importance within the disposition of European empires, she was also gradually evolving into a new continent of riches for the Western scholarly and artistic imagination. From the late seventeenth century onwards, Europe was swept by a fever of Egyptomania: sphinxes and pyramids began to appear in houses and gardens throughout the continent; several operas were written around themes from ancient Egypt; a succession of Popes became interested in the placing of Rome's obelisks, and none other than Sir Isaac Newton took it upon himself to prove that Osiris, Bacchus, Sesostris and Sisac were but different names for the same deity. Concurrent with this growing interest, the study of Egyptian antiquities passed from being an esoteric and quasi-mystical pursuit into a freshly-charted field of scholarly enterprise, and in the service of the new science several travellers undertook journeys of discovery into Egypt.

It was against this background that the first report of the Geniza was published in Europe. In 1752 or '53, a Jewish traveller, Simon Van Geldern, an ancestor of the German poet Heinrich Heine, visited the Synagogue of Ben Ezra, in Babylon. The visit appears to have been an unremarkable one: all that Van Geldern had to say of it was that he had 'looked around' the Geniza and paid five coins. Effectively, the event passed unnoticed. At that time European scholarly interest was focused on the Egypt of the ancients; the Synagogue of Ben Ezra was too much a part of Masr to merit attention.

By the end of the eighteenth century, Egypt had become the scholarly counterpart of those great landmasses that were then being claimed and explored by European settlers: unknown to herself, she was already well on her way to becoming a victim of the Enlightenment's conceptions of knowledge and discovery. In fact, the first detailed plan for the conquest of Egypt was conceived not by a soldier but by a philosopher, Karl Liebniz, as early as 1670. More than a hundred years later, when Napoleon conceived of his invasion of Egypt, it was partly on the model of a scientific expedition.

In the decades immediately after Napoleon's invasion of 1798, Egypt attracted the husbandry of the Western academy in a way that no other place ever had. Yet all through this period, despite the concentrated efforts being expended on the soil around it, the Geniza remained entirely unnoticed: it was then still a part of a living tradition, and the conquering scholars had little interest in the dishevelled and unglamorous inhabitants of contemporary Masr.

More than a hundred years passed after Simon Van Geldern's visit with no public notice being taken of the Geniza at the Synagogue of Ben Ezra. By the time the next reports were published, Masr had passed into the control of the British, and her position on the route to India had become her curse, the proximate cause of her annexation. The visit that first brought the Geniza to the attention of the scholarly world occurred in 1864, and then, soon enough, events began to unfold quietly around it, in a sly allegory on the intercourse between power and the writing of history.

In the summer of 1864, when the construction of the Suez

Canal was well under way and Egypt was being readied, once again, to become the stepping-stone to India, a scholar and collector of Judaic antiquities by the name of Jacob Saphir paid several visits to the Synagogue of Ben Ezra while passing through Egypt. The synagogue was still greatly venerated by the Jewish inhabitants of Cairo, and travellers were often directed to it as a site worthy of pilgrimage.

On his visits, Saphir had the Geniza pointed out to him from a distance and was told that it contained many worn and tattered old books. But when he asked to look into the chamber he met with a flat refusal. There was a snake curled up at the entrance, the officials of the synagogue told him, and it would be extremely dangerous to go in. Their refusal made Saphir all the more determined to investigate, and he returned to the Synagogue after obtaining permission to enter the chamber from the head of the Rabbinical court. The officials were not impressed, and they told him, laughing: 'Can a man risk his life for nothing? He won't even live out the year!' They relented only when Saphir assured them that he knew how to charm snakes, and promised them a reward.

As Saphir found it, the Geniza was full to a height of two and a half storeys; it was open to the sky on top, and strewn with rubble and debris within. He left after spending two exhausting days inside, without encountering 'any fiery serpents or scorpions', and taking only a 'few leaves from various old books and manuscripts'. Upon closer examination, none of those fragments proved to be of any value, but describing his visit in his memoirs, Saphir added the rider: 'But who knows what is still beneath?'

His account appeared in 1866, arousing interest within a small circle of scholars, and lending credence to rumours that a potential treasure trove of documents was waiting to be uncovered in Cairo.

The Synagogue of Ben Ezra was probably visited again, soon afterwards, by a man who eventually put together one of the largest collections of Hebrew manuscripts in the world. He was a Crimean Jew of the Karaite sect, Abraham Firkowitch, a collector renowned as much for his unscrupulousness as for his fine judgement. The collection he assembled over his lifetime is now in the State Public Library in St. Petersburg. The manuscripts were bought in two lots: Firkowitch sold the first one himself, and the second was acquired soon after his death in 1874. The second lot alone contains about fifteen times as many Biblical manuscripts as there are in the British Museum. The German scholar Paul Kahle, who devoted the better part of a lifetime to the study of Firkowitch's collection, estimated that in all the libraries of Europe, taken together, there were not even as many as a third of the number of Biblical manuscripts as there were in this one collection in St. Petersurg. It is known that many of these documents were from the Cairo Geniza, but as to which they were there is no way of knowing because Firkowitch never revealed his sources. He had obtained many of his documents by swindling synagogue officials in various parts of the Middle East, and it was his practice to conceal his collecting methods behind a veil of secrecy.

If there is an irony today in the thought that a Jewish collector, not so very long ago, would have seen reason to steal manuscripts from his fellow Jews in Palestine in order to take them to Russia, it is not one that would have been apparent to Firkowitch: he was merely practising on his co-religionists the methods that Western scholarship used, as a normal part of its functioning, throughout the colonized world.

Over the next few years more and more Geniza documents began to change hands. Already in the 1880s substantial quantities were being carried away to Palestine, Europe and the USA—by collectors who were often still unaware of the very existence of the Geniza. Towards the end of that decade, in 1888, a Jewish Briton, who was to play an important part in the dispersal of the Geniza, happened to spend Yom Kippur in the company of some of the prominent Jewish families of Cairo. His name was Elkan N. Adler, and upon his return to London he published an account of his visit in the *Jewish Chronicle*. He took issue there with those of his fellow British Jews who passed through Cairo and showed no interest in its Jewish community. For his own part he declared himself to be very well-satisfied with his experience. 'It is not often,' he wrote, 'that a European has the opportunity of joining the aborigines in celebrating their feasts.'

In the course of his visit Adler had developed an acquaintance with a family that held a position of enormous influence within the city's Jewish community; their name was Cattaoui and they were to play a critical part in the subsequent history of the Geniza. The Cattaouis are thought to have come to Egypt by way of Holland and like most of the leading Jewish families of Cairo in the late nineteenth century, they were Sephardic rather than 'Oriental' Jews. By this time the indigenous Jews of Cairo, those whose relationship with the Synagogue of Ben Ezra was most direct, were a small and impoverished minority within the community. The Cattaouis had themselves once lived in a Jewish enclave of Cairo, but they were one of the first families to come out of the ḥâra. They had gone on to establish a prosperous banking firm with offices in Cairo, Alexandria and Paris, and at the time of Adler's visit they were by far the most powerful family within the community.

The founder of the clan, Yaʿqub Cattaoui, was the first Egyptian Jew to be granted the title of 'bey', and in the early 1880s he was also made a baron of the Habsburg Empire. After this, mindful of their standing as Austrian aristocrats, the family often styled itself 'von Cattaoui'. Little did the Barons von Cattaoui realize that they were to be instrumental, one day, in providing Elkan Adler with an opportunity to observe an aboriginal feast.

In his account of his stay in Cairo, Adler mentioned the private synagogue of the Cattaouis and their adjoining residence, a magnificent palace that had once belonged to a Pasha. He also included a small anecdote about the current head of the family, Moses Cattaoui.

About six years before Adler's visit, the British had been confronted by an armed uprising led by Ahmed Arabi Pasha, a popular figure, venerated in Egypt to this day. The Egyptians were defeated in 1882, and in the aftermath of the war the British assumed direct control of the country's administration. Soon afterwards the British ambassador in Constantinople, Lord Dufferin, was sent to Cairo to fashion a plan for the 're-habilitation' of the country. The Cattaouis made their mansion available to him for the length of his stay, and in recognition of this service, Queen Victoria later sent Moses Cattaoui her portrait—a token which he treasured, writes Adler, 'with no little pride'.

Adler was given a glimpse of a remarkable document in the Cattaouis' strong-room: the eight-hundred-year-old decree issued by the Caliph, giving possession of the Synagogue of Ben Ezra to its congregation. He also paid a visit to Fustat and was horrified to learn that the Synagogue was soon to be torn down and rebuilt. But otherwise the visit made no great impression on him: his inquiries about the Geniza elicited nothing of significance, and he came to the conclusion that 'nowadays no Hebrew MSS of any importance are to be bought in Cairo.' When he wrote his account of his journey, the Geniza did not so much as earn a mention.

Within a couple of years, just as Adler had been told, the old structure of the Synagogue of Ben Ezra was indeed torn down and the building that stands on the site today was put up in its place. The Geniza must have been disturbed in the process of demolition, for the rapid dispersal of its contents appears to have begun at about that time. The officials of the synagogue and the notoriously canny antiquities dealers of Cairo were clearly well aware that those documents could command good prices on the international market, and through their efforts a large number of documents made their way at this time to libraries in Paris, Frankfurt, London, Vienna and Budapest. The Bodleian Library at Oxford also managed to acquire a large collection of Geniza manuscripts in these years, through the efforts of two members of its staff who were quick to recognize their value.

At Cambridge, on the other hand, the manuscripts went virtually unnoticed. The expert in Hebrew documents in Cambridge then was Dr Solomon Schechter, a scholar of great distinction and a forceful, charismatic man, who also happened to be blessed with a natural warmth of spirit and a great deal of charm. He was sent several documents from the Geniza by a learned Rabbi, the scholarly Solomon Wertheimer of Jerusalem. In a few years Schechter's name was to become more closely linked with the Geniza than any other, but until well into the 1890s he was of the opinion (like many other scholars) that these 'Egyptian fragments' were of little real importance. Rabbi Solomon Wertheimer wrote him several letters begging him to forward the documents to Oxford if he saw no value in them, but his pleas went unheeded: Doctor Schechter had not yet found the time to unpack them from their boxes.

At about this time Elkan Adler must have realized that he had been wrong in his initial assessment, for he returned to Cairo in what was to prove the decisive year in the life of the Geniza, 1896. He took with him letters from his brother, Herman Adler (who was later to become the Chief Rabbi of the British Empire), and was received with great cordiality by the Chief Rabbi of Cairo, Rafaïl ben Shimon ha Cohen, and by his warders, who were none other than the senior members of the Cattaoui family. Between them, they granted Adler permission to enter the Geniza and to carry away a certain quantity of documents of his choice. He was personally conducted to Fustat by the Rabbi Rafaïl and, after spending three or four hours immersed in the chamber, he took away a sackful of documents. The material he gathered that day is now spread over several libraries, and a part of it forms the nucleus of the important collection of the Jewish Theological Seminary of New York.

That very same year, 1896, two Presbyterian women, Agnes S. Lewis and Margaret D. Gibson, returned to England after a visit to Egypt, carrying a small collection of Geniza documents. The women were sisters, identical twins with scholarly inclinations, whose large personal fortunes allowed them to travel widely in the Middle East. They had acquired a good deal of experience in manuscripts and antiquities in the course of their wanderings, and on this occasion they were convinced that some of the documents they had brought back with them were of considerable value.

Back in Cambridge, they picked out two fragments that seemed particularly interesting and took them to Solomon Schechter, the Reader in Talmudics. Schechter agreed to look at them, but chiefly out of politeness, for he was still sceptical about the value of the 'Egyptian fragments'. But it so happened that he was taken completely by surprise. One of the documents immediately caught his interest, and next morning, after examining it in his office, he realized that he had stumbled upon a sensational discovery. In great haste, Schechter sent out a note from the University Library:

Dear Mrs Lewis,

I think we have reason to congratulate ourselves. For the fragment I took with me represents a piece of the original Hebrew of Ecclesiasticus. It is the first time that such a thing was discovered. Please do not speak yet about the matter till tomorrow. I will come to you tomorrow about 11 p.m. and talk over the matter with you how to make the matter known.
In haste and great excitement,

Yours sincerely,
S. Schechter.

Schechter's note is dated 13 May 1896. On that very day, Mrs Lewis sent an announcement of the discovery to the prestigious London journal, *The Academy*. The letter was published three days later, under the title, 'Discovery of a Fragment of Ecclesiasticus in the Original Hebrew' and it began: 'All students of the Bible and of the Apocrypha will be interested to learn that, among some fragments of Hebrew MSS which my sister Mrs.

Gibson and I have just acquired in Palestine a leaf of the Book of Ecclesiasticus has been discovered to-day by Mr S. Schechter, lecturer in Talmudic to the University of Cambridge.'

In his own preliminary report published in a learned journal called the *Expositor* later the same year, Schechter announced that he had found a part of the original text of Ecclesiasticus (The Book of Wisdom) by Jesus Ben Sirah, which was known to have been written in about 200BC: the original Hebrew had been lost centuries earlier and the book had survived only in Greek translation. 'If it could be proved,' he wrote, 'that Sirach, who flourished in about 200BC composed his work, as some believe, in the Rabbinic idiom…then between Ecclesiasticus and the books of the Old Testament there must lie centuries, nay there must lie, in most cases, the deep waters of the Captivity…'

Neither of the announcements mentioned the Geniza of Fustat as the source of the document: the discovery had so excited Schechter that he had already begun thinking of travelling to Cairo to acquire whatever remained of the documents. Secrecy was essential if the plan was to succeed. He quickly succeeded in enlisting the support of Doctor Charles Taylor, the Master of St John's College, Cambridge. Taylor was a mathematician but he took a keen interest in Rabbinic studies and he persuaded the University to exercise its considerable influence on Schechter's behalf. Schechter left in December 1896, taking with him a letter of recommendation for the Chief Rabbi of Cairo from Herman Adler, then the Chief Rabbi of England, and a 'beautifully ribboned and sealed credential' from the Vice-Chancellor of Cambridge, addressed to the president of the Jewish community of Cairo.

The times could not have been more propitious for Schechter's visit. The British administration in Egypt was then presided over by Sir Evelyn Baring, later Lord Cromer. Known to his subordinates as Over-Baring, he had served in various administrative posts in India and Egypt, and had found little reason to be enthusiastic about the abilites of their modern inhabitants. So little did he think of Egyptians that once, upon hearing a famous Egyptian singer singing a song that went 'My love is lost, O! People find him for me', he is known to have commented that it was typical of Egyptians to expect to have somebody else look for their loves. He expressed his opinions trenchantly in an essay entitled 'The Government of the Subject Races': 'We need not always inquire too closely what these people, who are all, nationally speaking, more or less in statu pupillari, themselves think is best in their own interests…it is essential that each special issue should be decided mainly with reference to what, by the light of Western knowledge and experience…we conscientiously think is best for the subject race.'

Under Lord Cromer's supervision British officials were moved into key positions in every branch of the country's administration. Thus, by the time Schechter arrived in Cairo, a beribboned letter from the Vice-Chancellor of Cambridge University was no mere piece of embossed stationery: it was the backroom equivalent of an imperial edict.

Schechter was fortunate in that Cromer himself took an interest in the success of his mission. The precise details of what transpired between Schechter and British officialdom and the leaders of Cairo's Jewish community are hazy, but soon enough the Chief Rabbi of Cairo and Joseph M. Cattaoui Pasha came to a decision that seems little less than astonishing, in retrospect. They decided to make Solomon Schechter a present of their community's—and their city's—heritage; they granted him permission to remove everything he wanted from the Geniza, every last paper and parchment, without condition or payment.

It has sometimes been suggested that Schechter succeeded so easily in his mission because the custodians of the Synagogue of Ben Ezra had no idea of the real value of the Geniza documents —a species of argument that was widely used in the nineteenth century to justify the acquisition of historical artefacts by colonial powers. In fact, considering that there had been an active and lucrative trade in Geniza documents for several years before Schechter's visit, the beadles and petty officials of the Synagogue could not have been ignorant of their worth. And impoverished as they were, it is hard to believe that they would willingly have parted with a treasure which was, after all, the last remaining asset left to them by their ancestors. In all likelihood the decision was taken for them by the leaders of their community, and they were left with no alternative but acquiescence. As for those leaders, the motives for their extraordinary generosity are not hard to divine: like the élites of so many other groups in the colonized world, they evidently decided to seize the main chance at a time when the balance of power—the ships and the guns— lay overwhelmingly with England.

Schechter, however, took nothing for granted: all the while that he was working in Fustat he took care to cultivate the leaders of the Jewish community in Cairo. He was a man of considerable wit, and he described his relations with the Chief Rabbi and his family with characteristic pithiness in his letters to his wife. Of his manner of dealing with the Rabbi's brother, who had become his advisor, he wrote: 'I flirted with him for hours, and am taking Arabic lessons three times a week. You see how practical your old man is.' He also decided to take the Chief Rabbi to the Pyramids which, remarkably, he had not seen: 'It will cost me about ten shillings, but that is the only way to make yourself popular.' The Rabbi was so charmed that in a later letter Schechter was moved to remark: 'The Rabbi is very kind to me and kisses me on the mouth, which is not very pleasant...'

Other members of the community did not merit quite the same degree of cordiality. Of the custodians of the synagogue, Schechter wrote, in a letter home: 'For weeks and weeks I had to swallow...the annoyance of those scoundrel beadles whom I have to Baksheesh.' Describing his experiences at leisure later, he was to write: 'The whole population within the precincts of the Synagogue were constantly coming forward with claims on my liberality—the men as worthy colleagues employed in the same work [of selection] as myself...the women for greeting me respectfully when I entered the place, or for showing me their deep sympathy in my fits of coughing caused by the dust. If it were a fête day, such as the New Moon or the eve of Sabbath, the amount expected from me for all these kind attentions was much larger, it being only proper that the Western millionaire should contribute from his fortune to the glory of the next meal.'

It must be counted as one of the remarkable features of that age that it could induce Schechter, an otherwise kindly and humane man, himself a member of a family of impoverished Romanian Hasidim, to use a species of language that would have been immediately familiar to any British colonial official. Yet Schechter was writing of his own co-religionists, and moreover of the very group who had sustained the Geniza for almost a thousand years, and whose extraordinary achievement he was then engaged in appropriating. Lord Cromer would probably have expressed himself in more forthright language, but he would have been in complete sympathy with a view of the world in which the interests of the powerful defined necessity, while the demands of the poor appeared as greed.

Schechter had to work for several weeks inside the Geniza chamber, sorting out its contents with the help of the 'scoundrel beadles'. The documents inside were of many different kinds and only a small portion of them had a religious content, properly speaking. But the people who used the Geniza would not have countenanced the modern distinction between the 'secular' and the 'religious': for them there was little that fell outside the scope of God's work, no matter whether it had to do with marriage, prayer or porterage contracts. The Geniza did, in fact, contain innumerable Scriptural and rabbinic documents of great importance, Biblical manuscripts in particular. But it was neither a religious library nor an archive: it was a place where the members of the congregation would throw all the papers in their possession, including letters, bills, contracts, poems, marriage deeds and so on. Often the same piece of paper would contain several different writings, for paper was expensive in the Middle Ages, and people were thrifty in its use. These bits and pieces were thrown haphazardly into the Geniza, and over the centuries the people who occasionally cast their hands into the chamber disarranged them even more. To complicate matters further, large quantities of printed matter and books were also deposited in the Geniza from the sixteenth century onwards.

Schechter eventually decided to leave behind the printed fragments and take only the written ones. He filled about thirty sacks and boxes with the materials and with the help of the British Embassy in Cairo he shipped them off to Cambridge. A few months later he returned himself—laden, as Elkan Adler was to put it, 'with the spoils of the Egyptians'.

In 1898 the manuscripts that Schechter had brought back

from Cairo were formally handed over to the University Library, where they have remained ever since, well-tended and cared for, grouped together as the Taylor-Schechter Collection. The collection contains about a hundred and forty thousand fragments and is the largest single store of Geniza material in the world. It is in this collection, spread over a few dozen documents, that the stories of Abraham Ben Yiju and his slave are preserved —tiny threads, woven into the borders of a gigantic tapestry.

Other hoards of documents, very similar to the Geniza material, were discovered in the Jewish cemetery in Fustat at the turn of the century and then again a decade or so later. Within a few years they too had reached Europe and America, a large part of them going into private collections.

By the First World War, the Geniza had finally been emptied of all its documents. In its home country however, nobody took the slightest notice of its dispersal. In some profound sense, the Islamic high culture of Masr had never really noticed, never found a place for the parallel history the Geniza represented, and its removal only confirmed a particular vision of the past.

Thus, having come to Fustat from the far corners of the known world, a second history of travel carried the documents even further. The irony is that for the most part they went to countries which would have long since destroyed the Geniza had it been a part of their own history. Now it was Masr, which had sustained the Geniza for almost a millennium, that was left with no trace of its riches: not a single scrap or shred of paper to remind her of that aspect of her past.

It was as though the borders that were to divide Palestine several decades later had already been drawn, through time rather than territory, to allocate a choice of Histories.

11

I CAME BACK to Lataifa a week before the end of Ramadan. In my bag I had a few gifts—an illuminated copy of the Qur'an for Shaikh Musa, a leather wallet for Jabir, a ball for the boys' soccer team, and so on. I arrived standing in the back of a pick-up truck, at a time of evening when the boys and young men of the hamlet were always to be found sitting beside the main road, talking with their friends. Some of them ran towards me as soon as I climbed out of the truck. I waved, but to my surprise they neither smiled nor waved back. I noticed that their faces were unusually solemn, and suddenly I was stricken with apprehension.

'Something terrible has happened while you were away, ya mister,' said the first boy to reach me.

'What?'

'You remember Shaikh Musa's son, Hasan?' he said.

'Yes.'

'He's dead; he died a few days ago.'

'He was buried just the other day,' one of the other boys said. 'There was a big ceremony and everything. You missed it.'

Later that evening I went to see Shaikh Musa, carrying the present I had bought for him in Cairo. I wasn't sure whether this would be the right moment to give it to him, but I took it along anyway, because I didn't want to turn up empty-handed at his house.

I was met at the door by his son Ahmed. He was wearing a crumpled jallabeyya and he looked exhausted, with dark circles under his eyes. I shook his hand and uttered the customary phrases of mourning. Whispering the responses, he led me into the guest-room.

Shaikh Musa was sitting in a corner. The room was dark; all

the windows were shut and the lamp had not been lit. He rose to his feet with some difficulty and mumbled the usual words of greeting: 'Welcome, how are you,' and so on, just as he would have if I had dropped in for a casual chat about cotton farming. I said the conventional words of consolation and then tried to add something of my own. 'It's terrible news,' I said. 'I was very shocked…'

He acknowledged this only with a gesture and for a while the three of us sat in silence. As my eyes grew accustomed to the dark I saw that he was unshaven, with several days stubble showing white against his dark skin. He seemed to have aged terribly since I had last seen him: he looked as though he'd shrivelled and withered; his jallabeyya had suddenly outgrown him.

When I handed him the package I had brought with me he acknowledged it only with a slight inclination of his head. Ahmed took it from him, mumbling a word of thanks, and a moment later he left the room.

After we had been alone for a while, Shaikh Musa said softly: 'He was ill when you saw him; you saw how he had that pain in his head that night. It got a little better so he went back to his camp. But then it took a turn for the worse and he had to go into the military hospital. Ahmed visited him there, and I would have gone as well, but Ahmed came back and said that it was all right, he would be well soon, the doctors had said not to worry. And then one night, we had news that he had died. It was very late, the time of the suhur, but we hired a truck from the next village and I and one of my brothers set off at once for Mansourah. When we got there we found that his officers and fellow soldiers were sitting up, keeping vigil beside his body. The army even gave us a car to bring the body back, and the officers and soldiers came too, so that they could attend his funeral.'

In an Antique Land

'What happened to him?' I asked. 'What sort of illness was
it?'

A look of puzzlement came into his eyes as he turned to look
at me. 'He was ill,' he said. 'He had a pain in his head; you saw
how his head was bandaged.'

My question seemed cruel and I did not persist with it. We
sat in silence for a while, and then his two young grandchildren
came into the room with their schoolbooks and an oil lamp.
They opened their books to study, but in a few minutes
something distracted them and they began to play instead. To
my relief I saw a slight smile appear on Shaikh Musa's face.

'If you had been here at the time,' he said, 'you would have
seen his funeral and the mourning-reception afterwards. So
many people came to mourn with us...'

'If only I'd known,' I said. 'I'd have come back at once.'

He looked down at his feet and fell silent. I wanted to tell
him my big news, that Dr Issa had arranged for me to leave
Abu-'Ali's house, to move out of Lataifa, to Nashawy. But the
moment did not seem appropriate, and in a while I got up to
leave.

'He was so young,' Shaikh Musa said. 'And his health was
always so good.'

He rose to his feet, and when his face was level with mine I
saw that he was weeping. 'Al-duniya zayy kida,' he said
helplessly. 'The world is like that...' He went quickly back
inside after seeing me out, and I turned and walked away.

So it happened that I never kept the promise I had made to
tell him about Masr.

12

I LEFT EGYPT in 1981, and it was not until seven years later that circumstances permitted me to begin a serious inquiry into the story of the Slave of MS H.6: in the ten years that had passed since I first came across Goitein's brief reference to Abraham Ben Yiju and his Slave, my path had crossed theirs again and again, sometimes by design and sometimes inadvertently, in North Africa, Egypt and the Malabar, until it became clear that I could no longer resist the logic of those coincidences.

I started upon the Slave's trail hoping that I would be able to ask for guidance from Goitein himself: I took encouragement from an article published in India, in 1963, in which he had tried to interest Indians in the Geniza. But I soon discovered, to my great disappointment, that he had died in 1985, at the age of eighty-five. The only alternative left was to start by going through Goitein's work and tracking the Slave through references to Abraham Ben Yiju.

The blitheness of that beginning did not long survive the discovery of the enormity of that task. The complete bibliography of Goitein's writings runs into a seventy-page book, with a twenty-two page supplement. It contains a total of 666 entries in Hebrew, German, English and French. His writings were published in Europe, America, Israel, Tunisia, India and Pakistan, and they included pieces in popular magazines, a Hebrew play and, of course, innumerable books and articles. At the age of thirty Goitein had started single-handed upon the kind of project for which university departments usually appoint committees: an edition of the *Ansâb al-Ashrâf*, (The Noble Lineages), a 2,500 page work by the ninth-century Arab historian, al-Balâdhuri. His interest in the Geniza had begun with a visit to Budapest in 1948 and had continued through the rest of his life. His monumental study, based on his Geniza research, *A Mediterranean Society*, was acclaimed as a landmark in medieval scholarship as soon as the first of its five volumes appeared in 1967. It was to establish him as possibly the greatest of the Geniza scholars, the pioneering researcher without whose labours an inquiry into the lives of Ben Yiju and the Slave of MS H.6 would not be possible today.

Scanning through the relevant parts of Goitein's oeuvre, I discovered that his interest lay, on the whole, in the broad sweep of history, so that the references to individuals, such as Ben Yiju, were scattered randomly through his writings like the windblown trail of a paperchase. Some of those references led to the work of other scholars, such as E. Strauss, who had first edited the letter of MS H.6. Others pencilled in the outlines of Ben Yiju's career, in passing, while pointing in two further directions: on the one hand to certain specific Geniza documents, and on the other to one of Goitein's own unfinished works, a project which he had named 'the India Book'.

The references to this work began in the 1950s not long after Goitein first started working with the Geniza documents. His researches had led him to a large number of letters and other manuscripts referring to the trade between the Indian Ocean and the Mediterranean. He soon conceived of a plan to publish them as a collection, under the title of *The India Book*, but as his work proceeded he found ever-increasing quantities of material, and the project was continually deferred, while other aspects of his research took precedence. *The India Book* was never abandoned however: he announced that the book would contain about three hundred documents, and in 1964 he even published the catalogue numbers of those documents, including those that referred to Ben Yiju, as a guide to other researchers. But despite his announced intentions, the book was still unfinished when he died in 1985, in Princeton.

The road now led directly to Princeton University, where Goitein had taught for many years: I was told that his colleagues and students in the Department of Near Eastern Studies had compiled an archive of his papers there. Eventually I went to visit the archive myself but a disappointment awaited me there: I found that access to most of his papers on the India trade was restricted because an edition of his notes for the projected *India Book* was in preparation, although it was unlikely to be published within the next several years. From the papers that I was allowed to see, I had the impression that Goitein had in fact already published most of his information regarding Ben Yiju's life in scattered bits and pieces, for much of the material was already familiar from my earlier reading.

At the end of the visit it was clear to me that there was only one way forward now, and that was to go to the Geniza documents themselves, directly to Ben Yiju's own papers. But across that road lay a seemingly impassable barrier: the obstacle of language.

Ben Yiju's documents were mostly written in an unusual, hybrid language: one that has such an arcane sound to it that it might well be an entry in a book of Amazing Facts. It is known today as Judæo-Arabic; it was a colloquial dialect of medieval Arabic, written in the Hebrew script.

Judæo-Arabic evolved after Muslim armies, recruited mainly from the Arabian peninsula, conquered most of the Middle East and North Africa in the seventh century. The language of the conquerors soon came to supplant the other languages of the empire, including Aramaic, the language then generally in use among the Jews of those regions. But of course, Jews continued to use Hebrew for religious purposes and, in time, when they started writing in their newly adopted tongue, it was in the sanctified alphabet of their Scriptures.

From this odd smelting came an alloy that had its own distinct sheen and texture, with little resemblance to the language written by Muslim Arabs. Written Arabic, in its usual form, is the literary variety of the language and is more or less standard throughout the Arab world, from Morocco to Iraq. Spoken Arabic, on the other hand, varies so much from region to region that the speech of an Iraqi is almost incomprehensible to a Moroccan. A great gulf separates the two registers of Arabic, the formal, literary language, and the slangy, regional dialects: for all practical purposes they are separate languages, with their own distinct vocabularies and grammars.

Judæo-Arabic, determinedly contrary, was not like either form of Arabic: unlike the dialects, it was a written language, and unlike written Arabic, it had the vocabulary and grammar of the spoken language. It was in a way something much simpler than either form of Arabic: a representation of colloquial speech in writing. But since colloquial Arabic has always varied between regions, Judæo-Arabic too tended to take on somewhat different colours in different parts of the Arab world. The language of the Geniza documents, for example, has a strong flavour of North African Arabic, since so many members of the community were from that region.

But although Judæo-Arabic was much closer to the spoken language than literary Arabic, it was not uniformly colloquial. The people who used it would often try to introduce Arabic classicisms into their written language, with varying degrees of success. Often they would use words and spellings which would have startled well-educated Muslim Arabs, but which they took to be elegant usage. Eight centuries later, those odd solecisms often have an awkward, endearingly human grace, where the correct form would seem merely formal or stilted.

At the same time, everyone who wrote Judæo-Arabic had a thorough knowledge of the Hebrew Scriptures, and though they were not usually able to use Hebrew as a language of expression, they were well able to quote in it. Thus their prose is studded with Hebrew proverbs and long passages from the bible, as well as legal and religious terms from the archaic language Aramaic.

When I first read about it, Judæo-Arabic sounded bafflingly esoteric: it is not easy, after all, to see oneself sitting down to leaf through a collection of eight-hundred-year-old documents, written in a colloquial dialect of medieval Arabic, transcribed in the Hebrew script, and liberally strewn with Hebrew and Aramaic. At its easiest, Arabic is very difficult for a foreigner, and such knowledge as I had of it was mainly of the dialect spoken around Lataifa: a broad, peasant tongue, so earthy that my accent would often earn sniffs from waiters in Cairo restaurants and provoke shopkeepers to ask to see my money before they reached for their shelves. Those experiences had given me something of the fellah's diffidence about his language: it would never have occurred to me that this simple, rustic dialect could be of any use in so rarified a domain of erudition as the reading of twelfth-century Judæo-Arabic manuscripts.

Worse was still to come, for I soon discovered that there was no accepted method of learning to read the manuscripts except through a long apprenticeship with one of the handful of scholars who had made a lifetime's speciality of the subject. The only other means was to take copies of those documents that had been published, and to compare them with the actual folio pages—

smudged, worn eight-hundred-year-old bits of paper—until such time as one's eyes grew expert in deciphering the script.

At that point I almost gave up, but just then, when all the tunnels on the road seemed finally to have closed, a short conversation with one of the foremost experts in the field, Mark Cohen, a one-time student of Goitein's, and custodian of his archive at Princeton, gave me pause. The language was not as difficult as it seemed, Mark Cohen told me; Hebrew characters were easy to learn, and once the writing had been deciphered, the Arabic itself was fairly simple. It was the deciphering of the documents, rather than the language itself, that was the hard part: the language would not present a particular problem to someone who knew colloquial Arabic. The palæography, on the other hand, the deciphering of the texts, was often extremely difficult, yet many students had been known to grow quickly adept at it. Of course, I would never be equipped to produce authoritative editions of Geniza texts, but it was perfectly possible, if I worked hard at the palæography and learnt to decipher and transcribe the documents, that I would be able to deal with them well enough to follow the stories of the Slave of MS H.6 and Abraham Ben Yiju.

Mark Cohen's encouragement made up my mind: I decided I couldn't give up without trying.

To my surprise I found that he was right, that the Hebrew script was indeed much easier to decipher than cursive Arabic since the letters stood apart, each by itself. Soon enough, I made other surprising discoveries. I found that some of the usages of the dialect of Lataifa were startlingly close to those of the North African Arabic spoken by Ben Yiju; that far from being useless the dialect of Lataifa and Nashawy had given me an invaluable skill.

Over the next couple of years, as I followed the Slave's trail from library to library, there were times when the magnifying glass would drop out of my hand when I came upon certain words and turns of phrase for I would suddenly hear the voice of Shaikh Musa speaking in the documents in front of me as clearly as though I had been walking past the canal, on my way between Lataifa and Nashawy.

NASHÂWY

1

IN DECEMBER 1988, when I was at last hot upon the Slave's trail, I went back to visit Lataifa. It was almost eight years since I had left Egypt.

It was cold and wintry the day I left Cairo, with rain hanging down in thin sheets from a cloud-corded sky. By the time I reached Damanhour night had fallen and the streets were clogged with shoals of churned mud. I had wanted to get there in the afternoon, on one of the old Hungarian trains, where the seats had cushioned foot-rests and the attendants served elaborate meals on trays. I had imagined myself watching the familiar sights roll past my window while I ate my lunch, just as I used to all those years ago, when the railway's fried chicken had tasted richly of metropolitan excitement after weeks of village fare.

But by the time I reached Ramses Station it was too late in the morning: all the tickets were sold for the day.

I'd wanted to be there early, but I had spent the first part of the morning running feverishly between shops, wondering whether I had enough presents in my bag, stopping to buy a pen there and a wallet here and adding to my store of scarves, lighters and watches. That had been pretty much the pattern of my days ever since I arrived in Cairo. Every day, upon waking, I'd told myself that I would go to Lataifa that very morning, and every time I had found some excuse to put it off. No one was waiting for me, after all: I had not written ahead to tell anyone of my visit. My correspondence with Lataifa and Nashawy, once frequent, had become increasingly irregular and then ceased altogether. It was now almost three years since I had last received a letter from Egypt. I had no idea of what to expect, who was doing what, who was alive and who dead: the years in between were a chasm of darkness between me and a brilliantly floodlit corner of my memory.

Since all the trains were full, I had no option but to go over to the other side of Ramses Station and take a share-taxi with eight other people. 'The world's awash with rain,' said the man sitting next to me, as we set off: it was a bad day to go into the countryside; there'd been rain all through the week and the village roads had probably turned into swamps. The Datsun trucks probably wouldn't be able to get through; nobody could get through that kind of mud, nobody except the fellaheen, sitting on their donkeys. I had better be prepared to spend the night in Damanhour; it wasn't likely that I would be able to go any further.

But when we reached Damanhour he walked with me to the truck-stop and helped me get a place on the last truck heading in the direction of Nashawy. The driver made room for me in his cabin, but he wasn't eager to venture far into the countryside in such weather. As soon as we had set off, he said: 'I can't go as far as Nashawy. The road's a river of mud out there.'

'What about Lataifa?' I asked. 'Can you get as far as that?'

'Let's see,' he said, grudgingly. 'I don't know.'

Within a few minutes we had left the town behind and were

speeding down a narrow, deserted road. I had tried to imagine this moment for years: the drive from Damanhour to Lataifa and Nashawy. In my mind I had always seen a bright, sunlit day, the canal beside the road glittering under a blue sky while children played naked in the water and women walked towards the town balancing baskets of vegetables on their heads. The scene was so vivid in my mind that even in the imagining my stomach had often knotted in excitement. But now, travelling down that road after so many years I felt no excitement at all, only an old, familiar sensation, one that had always accompanied me on my way back from Damanhour, no matter whether I'd been away an hour or a week: the lassitude of homecoming mixed with a quiet sense of dread.

Most of the truck's passengers got down at the first stop, a small market town, a good distance from Lataifa. It was late now, well after the evening prayers, and the main street was deserted. All the shops were shut and there were no lights anywhere except for a few flickering lamps. Once we were past the town, the truck began to yaw and skid on the ridges of mud the rain had carved into the road. The villages around us were eerily dark, and as we crawled past them, packs of dogs came racing after the truck, snapping savagely at the tyres. The other passengers got off in ones and twos along the way, and soon I was alone in the cabin with the driver.

The driver was nervous now, unsettled by the darkness and the howling dogs. He lit a cigarette, holding the wheel steady with his elbow, and cast me a sidelong glance. 'Whose house are you going to in Lataifa?' he asked.

'Shaikh Musa's,' I said. 'Do you know him?'

'No,' he shook his head. 'La.' In front of us, half the road seemed to have dissolved into the canal which ran beside it.

'I don't know if we can go on for long,' said the driver. All that was visible ahead through the shimmering rain-drenched windscreen was a small patch of road lit by the headlights.

'How will you find the house in this darkness?' the driver asked. 'Everyone's asleep—no one can show you the way.'

'I know the house,' I said. 'If you stop where I tell you, I'll be able to find it.'

'How do you know the house?' He was suddenly curious. 'Aren't you a foreigner? Why are you going there all alone so late at night?'

I explained how I'd been brought to Lataifa by my Professor at the University of Alexandria, but his nerves were on edge and the story only served to arouse his suspicion.

'Why did they bring you here?' he said sharply. 'Why here, and what was it that you were doing exactly?'

I tried to reassure him as best I could, but my Arabic had become rusty in the years that I had been away, and my halting explanations only served to deepen his suspicions further.

'I'll come with you to the house you're going to,' he said, glaring into the windscreen. 'Just to make sure you find it.'

'And you will be welcome,' I said, hoping that he was not one of those people who were disposed to carry tales to the police. 'You will bring blessings with you. It's not much further now.'

Suddenly I saw Lataifa's little mosque on the left, through the driver's window. 'There,' I said, pointing ahead. 'Stop—I'll get off there.'

He stamped too hard on the brakes, inadvertently, and the truck skidded across the wet mud and came to a halt with its nose poised over the edge of the canal. Climbing out gingerly, I stepped back from the edge, squelching heavily through the mud. When next I looked up I saw a slight, ghostly figure in the distance: a boy in a jallabeyya, leaning against a wall, under an overhang, watching me. For a moment I was certain it was Jabir and I almost shouted out aloud: in the reflected glow of the headlights he seemed to have the same blunt, rounded features, as well as the ruddy complexion of all the Latifs. But it took only that moment to remind me that I was thinking of a Jabir I had known eight years ago, when the figure in the shadows would have been a seven- or eight-year-old boy.

I shifted my feet awkwardly in the mud, and then, raising my hand, I said: 'Al-salâm 'aleikum.' My tongue was suddenly heavy, weighted with an unexpected shyness.

''Aleikum al-salam,' he said, responding in full. 'Wa raḥmatullâhî wa barâkâtu.'

The truck suddenly started up again and came to a halt between us, engine roaring.

'Hey, boy,' the driver shouted. 'Who's Shaikh Musa? Do you know him?'

The boy stepped forward and looked into the driver's window. 'Yes,' he said, in the gruff, surly voice which the boys of the village kept for townspeople.

'Where's his house?'

'There.' The boy pointed down the lane.

'Good, let's go,' said the driver. He stepped out of the truck and kicked his feet, to dislodge the long tentacles of mud that had attached themselves to his shoes.

'Come on, yalla,' he said, in irritation. 'I want to talk to this man, this Shaikh Musa.'

Halfway down the lane the boy fell in beside me. 'I know you,' he said, smiling in surprise. 'You used to come to our house when I was little and you used to walk in the fields when we were out picking cotton.'

113

I looked at him carefully, trying to remember his name, but of course, he'd been a child when I had last seen him, and at that time I was myself of an age when I had hardly noticed children. Before I could ask him his father's name he came to a stop and gestured at Shaikh Musa's door. The house was in complete darkness. I could not see so much as a chink of light behind the door or between the shutters of the windows. The boy saw me hesitating and gave me a nudge, pointing at the door.

Scraping the mud carefully off my shoes, I went up to the door and knocked. A long time seemed to pass before a voice answered, asking: 'Who's there?' It was a woman's voice and it seemed to echo all the way down the lane.

'Ana,' I said stupidly, my legs oddly unsteady, and that very instant Shaikh Musa's voice began to roar—'Amitab, ya Amitab, ya doktór, where have you been?'—and for all the time it took his wife to undo the latch he kept repeating: 'Amitab, ya Amitab, where have you been?' When the door was open at last we brought our hands together with a great resounding slap and shook them hard, first one, and then both together, and all the while he kept saying—'where have you been all this time? where were you?'—but there were tears in his eyes now, as there were in mine, and so it was not until months afterwards that it occurred to me to wonder how he had recognized my voice when all I had said in answer to his wife's question was 'It's me'.

The driver stepped up to Shaikh Musa and shook his hand. 'So you know him?' he asked with a nod in my direction, smiling a little sheepishly.

'Yes,' Shaikh Musa laughed. 'Yes, we all know him here.'

'That's all right then,' the driver said, turning to leave. 'I just wanted to make sure that he reached you safely.'

'Come in and have some tea with us,' Shaikh Musa shouted

after him, but he was already gone, stamping noisily down the lane.

Shaikh Musa's wife ushered us into the guest-room, out of the rain, showing us the way with a kerosene lamp. 'You sit here and talk,' she said. 'I'll bring you some tea and food in a couple of minutes.'

Placing the lamp on a window-sill, she gave its sooty glass chimney a rub with her sleeve. 'We hardly bother to clean our lamps any more,' she said, 'we have electricity now. It's just fate that you should arrive in the middle of a power cut.'

'Everything's changed in all these years that you've been away,' said Shaikh Musa. 'All this time I used to say to myself, the doktór will come back one day, he will come back soon, everyone comes back to Masr; they have to, because Masr is the Mother of the World.'

His wife gave the lamp a final scrub and opened the door. 'Do you know?' she said, as the cold wind whistled in, shaking the flame. 'He used to ask about you every day. "Where's the doktór al-Hindi? Where is he? What is he doing?" Every day he used to ask.'

There was a long moment of silence when she left the room. Shaikh Musa sat on the divan with a leg crossed under him, watching the flame with a gently quizzical smile: except for a few wrinkles at the corner of his mouth, he was completely unchanged.

Then, raising his eyes, he pointed to a framed photograph hanging on the wall, an enlargement of the picture of his son Hasan that he had always carried in his wallet. 'I had this big one made in Damanhour,' he said. 'In a studio near the railway station.'

He had hung it beside his own picture, taken when he was a

young man serving his draft in the army. They were very alike, father and son, both in uniform, Shaikh Musa in a peaked cap and Hasan in combat fatigues.

'You were away in Masr when he died,' he said. 'When you came back the mourning ceremony was already over.'

He looked down at the floor, fingering his worry-beads with the slow, deliberate gesture that had become inseparably linked with him in my memory.

'All the officers came,' he said. 'The officers and all the soldiers in his unit. They all came and we had a Quran-reader from Damanhour. But by the time you came back it was all over.'

Then, unaccountably, his eyes lit up and he jumped to his feet and opened the door. 'Wait a moment,' he said, and hurried out of the room. He was back in a few minutes, carrying an ornamented box in his hands. Setting it reverently upon the divan he turned to me: 'Do you know what this is?'

I was unsure for a moment, but then suddenly I remembered.

'It's the Quran al-Sharif you brought for me from Masr,' he said. He opened the lid and took a long look at the cover.

'It was after Hasan's death,' he said. 'You came back from Masr, and afterwards you said you were leaving Lataifa and going away to Nashawy.'

2

EVEN AFTER I had gone to live in Nashawy, eight years before, it was always Shaikh Musa I came to visit when I had questions to ask. Shaikh Musa had known Nashawy well once, when he was younger, and his memory was still crammed with stories about its inhabitants: when we talked he would sometimes surprise himself by recalling an incident or a detail from fifteen or twenty years ago. Thinking back later, it often seemed to me that we had created a village of our own during those conversations, between the two of us.

Most of his memories dated back at least a decade, for with his advancing years, the one and a half miles to Nashawy had come to seem like an increasingly formidable distance and he rarely went there except to attend an old friend's funeral or a relative's wedding. The only reason why he was still able to keep up with Nashawy at all was because so many people came to visit him in his own house. That was why he enjoyed our conversations as much as I did: he liked to hear the news and keep in touch.

It was in the early days, when I first moved to Nashawy, that I was most regular in my visits to Shaikh Musa in Lataifa. He would ask me questions about who I'd met and what I'd been doing, and then he would give me advice about the people I would do best to avoid and who I ought to seek out. It was he, for instance, who first told me about Imam Ibrahim.

They were both of the same age, he told me, but you wouldn't believe it now if you saw them together, Imam Ibrahim looked so much older. Not many people knew of him now, because he lived in seclusion and didn't go out very much, but as a young man, his name had been well-known throughout the area: people had said of him that he had the gift of baraka.

It so happened that Imam Ibrahim belonged to one of the two founding families of Nashawy, a lineage called Abu-Kanaka. The other was the Badawy: they were the first two families to come and settle in the area. They had not been there very long, for Nashawy was not an old village by Egyptian standards: in fact, only a few generations ago the land around it had been a part of the great desert to the west. It was only after the Mahmudiya Canal was completed in 1820, linking Cairo and Alexandria, that the area was brought under the plough. But even then it was a wilderness for a long time, without people or settlements.

Then one day, two young men had set off westwards from a village in the interior, looking for land and a good new place to settle. One of those men was of Bedouin origin: his ancestors had once wandered as far afield as Libya and Tunisia, but in time, tiring of the nomadic life, they had abandoned the desert for the sown. They had settled in the Delta, where for many generations their descendants worked on the land as fellaheen, until all that remained to remind them of their Bedouin past was the name of their lineage—al-Badawy.

The other young settler was from a lineage of barbers and healers, a family called Abu-Kanaka whose members were well known throughout the region for their zeal in religious matters and for their skill in the arts of healing. The Abu-Kanaka youth who set out on that westward journey had a fine reputation, despite his tender years: all the world knew him to be a model of goodness and piety, as well as a skilled and knowledgeable healer.

So the two young men had set out from their native village, and after a long and difficult journey they reached the area around Nashawy. There was nothing there then, no houses or canals or fields, but the Abu-Kanaka youth had declared that he could feel in his heart that the land had baraka and they had decided to settle there. Soon the young Badawy man acquired some land and began to raise crops. As the years passed more and more of his kinsmen came out from their native village and they too bought land and built houses in Nashawy. Before long the village was so full of Badawy families that they came to be known as the pre-eminent lineage of the village, the 'aṣl al-balad'. Later people of many other lineages settled in Nashawy, but right until the Revolution of 1952 it was the Badawy who owned most of the land and it was always a Badawy who was the chief official, the 'omda of the village.

The young Abu-Kanaka man, on the other hand, bought no land at all: he earned his living by healing and cutting people's hair, as his family had always done—a humble man, with a modest house and a small family. But at the same time, his renown as a good person and a man of religion continued to grow, and when at last a mosque was built in Nashawy, he was made the Imam, the caretaker and the leader of the prayers. Such was the respect in which he was held that his son inherited the position after him and his lineage held it ever afterwards. When he died he was universally mourned and the people of the village built him a special grave, right next to the canal. Later, he even came to be acknowledged as the guardian saint of the village.

When he was a young man, Shaikh Musa said, there were many who thought that Imam Ibrahim Abu-Kanaka had taken after his famous ancestor. He had shown remarkable skill in curing the sick, for example; there was a shelf in his house that was lined with texts on medicine, and everyone knew that he was very learned in the classical arts of healing. He had soon acquired a reputation as a healer who could do miracles with his herbs and roots, and he had had patients from all the surrounding villages. He had also become known for his learning in the scriptures, and at one time he had been much sought after for his opinions on points of theology and matters

119

of religious law and jurisprudence.

'You must make sure to meet him,' said Shaikh Musa. 'He's well read in history and religion and many other things and there's a lot you could learn from him.'

But when I asked how I might meet Imam Ibrahim, Shaikh Musa's answer was a sigh and a doubtful shake of his head. He hadn't seen the Imam around for the last so many years, he said, and he heard reports that he kept very much to himself nowadays and rarely went anywhere or met anyone. He had a great many troubles on his head, people said, because he had made an unfortunate second marriage in middle age, and had been tormented by domestic difficulties ever since. His son had now taken over many of his duties, and for the most part he kept to himself, living more or less in seclusion.

'But you must try to meet him,' said Shaikh Musa. 'Ask the other people you meet in Nashawy: they'll be able to tell you about him...'

3

LATER, ON SEVERAL occasions, Shaikh Musa made a point of asking me whether I had talked to anyone about Imam Ibrahim. But as it turned out, when I did eventually have something to tell him, he was taken by surprise: he was not quite prepared for how differently people of a younger generation looked upon the world, even in a place so close to home as Nashawy.

One of the people I had talked to recently was a young

teacher called Ustaz Sabry. Shaikh Musa had never met him himself, but like everyone else in the area he had heard of him, for Ustaz Sabry was rapidly becoming quite a well-known figure in the surrounding villages.

'People say he's an impressive talker,' said Shaikh Musa, pursing his lips. 'But I've also heard it said that he's one of those men whom we call Too-Much-Talk in these parts—has something to say about everything.'

'I can tell you this,' I said, 'he knows a lot. He's read a great deal, and he's one of the best-informed people I've ever met.'

'You must be right,' said Shaikh Musa. But a look of doubt descended on his face as he puffed at his shusha.

Ustaz Sabry had taken me by surprise the very first time I met him.

I had been introduced to him by the headmaster of the school he taught in, the primary school in Nashawy. The headmaster was a friendly, pleasant man in his early forties who had been elevated to his post largely because his father had been headmaster before him. He played the part he had inherited with conscientious diligence but he was at heart too gentle a man to enjoy the authority that came with it. I once watched him caning a boy with a ruler: he had applied himself to the task with such an evident lack of relish that the boy had never once lost his smirk.

In me I think the headmaster hoped to find a source of sympathy for his daily vexations, a connection with the student-world in Alexandria that he had once inhabited himself. In any event, he always went out of his way to be kind to me, inviting me frequently to his house and always sending word the moment a letter addressed to me went astray and ended up on his desk.

It was on one such occasion, when I'd been asked to go to his office to collect a letter, that I first met Ustaz Sabry.

The mid-morning break was in progress when I arrived at the school, and a number of teachers had drifted into the head-master's office to take refuge from the hurricane of screaming children that was whirling through the corridors. I knew several of the teachers already, and the headmaster introduced me to the rest, one by one. Most of them were from Damanhour and other nearby towns, and they were all smartly dressed, the men in jackets and ties and the women in skirts and white nylon scarves. I had been surprised at first, to see how they always arrived in Nashawy looking perfectly turned out, proper effendis, with every hair in place despite the dusty ride from Damanhour; I discovered later that it was their privilege to travel in the drivers' cabins of the trucks that ran through the area—the villagers had given them the right of sanctuary from their lowly dust.

Going around the room, shaking hands, we came to a man who did not seem to belong with the others. He was dressed in a grimy, ink-stained jallabeyya, a barrel-bodied man in his mid-thirties, with thick, liver-coloured lips, and large, watery eyes.

'This is Ustaz Sabry,' said the headmaster. 'He is from Nashawy; his family live at the far end of the village, across the canal from the government clinic. You will have a lot to discuss with him because he is writing a thesis too.'

He put a hand on Ustaz Sabry's shoulder and asked: 'What is it that you're studying exactly?'

Ustaz Sabry flashed me a smile and said something quickly about medieval Egyptian history. His voice had the precise, resonant pitch of that of a man accustomed to addressing large gatherings and when he turned to me and asked what my subject was, I found to my surprise that he spoke in the simple fellah dialect of Nashawy. All the other teachers had educated city accents.

'Anthropology,' I answered, and he responded immediately with another question: 'Social or physical?'

'Social,' I said, and he nodded, smiling: 'Yes, good; that's a bit like history or philosophy, isn't it? Much better than all those bones and skeletons.'

The headmaster was pleased by this exchange. 'I knew you would have a lot to talk about,' he said. He gave me a slap on the back and said: 'You must go and talk to Ustaz Sabry properly. He's read so much he'll be able to tell you about many things.'

Later, after we had exchanged a few remarks about our respective subjects, Ustaz Sabry invited me to visit him at his home that evening, so we could carry on our conversation.

I set off for his house a little before the sunset prayers, and in my eagerness to get there I forgot to find out exactly where he lived. As a result I was soon lost, for Nashawy was much larger than Lataifa, with its houses squeezed close together around a labyrinth of tunnel-like lanes, some of which came to unexpected dead ends while others circled back upon themselves. At the centre of the village was a large, open square where the mosque and the ceremonial 'guest-house' stood, adjoining each other, a modest pair of buildings, neat, square and whitewashed, with the mosque's single minaret rising high above the tousled hayricks that topped the surrounding houses. After I had passed through the square a second time I swallowed my pride and turning to the long train of children who had attached themselves to me, I asked the tallest among them to lead me to Ustaz Sabry's house.

He ran ahead of me and after a couple of turnings he stopped and pointed at a carved door at the corner of two lanes. A communal water-tap stood directly opposite and the teenage girls who had gathered there looked up from their jerrycans and earthen pots as I came around the corner in a cloud of dust, with my train of children rumbling behind me. They watched as I stood in front of the house, looking undecidedly at the heavy wooden door, and soon they began to giggle and make catcalls.

'Come and talk to us, over here.'

'Why so shy, ya Hindi?'

'Wouldn't you like a drink of water?'

I turned my back upon them while the children squealed with laughter, and holding myself stiff and stony-faced I went up and knocked at the door. 'Who's there?' came the response, in a woman's voice, and from across the road one of the girls shouted: 'It's the Hindi.'

The door opened and a woman dressed in the severe black robes of an elderly widow appeared in front of me. 'Yes?' she said, frowning in puzzlement.

'Let him in,' the girls laughed. 'Or he'll run away.'

The woman's head snapped upright, eyes blazing. 'Shut your mouths, you over there,' she shouted. 'Don't you have any shame?'

The girls muttered rebelliously under their breath—'Listen to her, who does she think she is?'—but to my relief their giggles died away.

'Is Ustaz Sabry here?' I asked.

She was watching me closely now, and suddenly, clapping her hands to her thin, fine-boned cheeks, she cried: 'Why, aren't you the doktór al-Hindi? I saw you at the Thursday market last week: tell me, why did you pay fifteen piastres for that little handful of peas? Everyone was talking about it.'

I cast my mind back, but try as I might, I could not remember how much I had paid for my peas.

'You should let 'Amm Taha go to the market for you,' she said. 'Isn't he helping you in your house? He'll know what to do—he knows all about buying and selling.'

'All right,' I said, 'but I'm here now because Ustaz Sabry told me...'

'Welcome, welcome,' she said. 'Please come in, you're welcome, but Ustaz Sabry isn't in just this minute.'

'He isn't here?' I said. 'But he told me...'

Craning her head around, with a considerable effort, she shouted into the interior of the house: 'Where did Sabry go?'

There was no answer, and she turned around again to face me, so slowly that I could almost hear her joints creak. 'He should be back soon,' she said.

Then, all of a sudden her eyes focused brightly on me, and she stretched out a thin, bony finger and tapped me on the shoulder. 'Tell me,' she said. 'Is it true what they say about you? That in your country people burn their dead?'

'Some people do,' I said. 'It depends.'

'Why do they do it?' she cried. 'Don't they know it's wrong? You can't cheat the Day of Judgement by burning your dead.'

'Please,' I said. 'Do you know when Ustaz Sabry is going to be back?'

'Soon,' she said. 'Soon. But now tell me this: is it true that you worship cows? That's what they were saying at the market. They said that just the other day you fell to your knees in front of a cow, right out in the fields in front of everyone.'

'I tripped,' I said, taking a backwards step. 'I'll come back some other time: tell Ustaz Sabry.'

'You have to put a stop to it,' she called out after me as I hurried away down the lane. 'You should try to civilize your people. You should tell them to stop praying to cows and burning their dead.'

4

THE CARETAKER OF the house I had moved into in Nashawy was called Taha. He was a familiar figure around the village, and was known to everyone as Uncle; I never heard anyone address him without adding an 'Amm to his name. He was in his late fifties or thereabouts, excruciatingly thin, slack-mouthed because his lower jaw was not quite in line with the upper, and with one unmoving eye that looked away from the other at a sharp angle, in a fixed, unblinking glare.

Soon after I moved in, he and I reached an arrangement whereby he fetched me a meal from his house once a day: he did several different odd jobs and this was yet another in a long list. He usually came to my room at about midday with my meal, and one day, not long after I had missed Ustaz Sabry at his house, I told him about my abortive visit.

'Amm Taha was not surprised in the least. 'Of course he wasn't there,' he said. 'Ustaz Sabry is a busy man, and if you want to find him at his house you have to go at the right time. What time was it when you went?'

'A little before the sunset prayers,' I told him.

'That's not the time to go,' he said, with a mournful shake of his head. 'At that time he usually goes to one of his friends' houses to watch TV or else he goes to visit people in the next village.'

Startled as I was by the comprehensiveness of his information, I did not need to ask him how he knew; I had learnt already that very little happened in Nashawy without 'Amm Taha being aware of it. As a rule he collected his information in the evenings, when he went around from house to house to see if anyone had eggs or milk or anything else to sell. One of his many professions was that of vendor, and he regularly bought local products in Nashawy and took them elsewhere to sell. Eggs, milk and cheese were his staples, but he wasn't particular: he would just as willingly take a bunch of carrots, or a cauliflower that had escaped the pot the night before, or even a fattened chicken or a rabbit.

Every other day or so, he would gather his gleanings together, load them on his donkey-cart, and drive down the dirt road to Damanhour or to one of the weekly markets in the nearby villages. The profits were meagre and they depended largely on the quality of his information: on whether or not he knew whose cow was in milk and who needed ready cash for their daughter's wedding and would accept a punitive price for a chicken. In other words 'Amm Taha's takings as a vendor hung upon his success in ferreting out some of the most jealously guarded of household secrets: in discovering exactly how matters stood behind the walls and talismans that guarded every house from the envy of neighbours and the Evil Eye. As it happened, 'Amm Taha was unusually successful in his profession because it was mostly women who were the guardians of those secrets, and many amongst them talked to him as they would not have to any other man—in large part, I think, because he did everything he could to let it be known that he was a poor, harmless old man, still childless despite many years of marriage, and too infirm to undertake the sort of exertion that results in procreation.

''Amm Taha keeps an eye on everything,' people would say, 'because one of his eyes looks to the left, while the other watches the right.' 'Amm Taha did nothing to contradict this, nor did he discourage those who claimed to detect an element of the supernatural in his prescience.

Once, 'Amm Taha happened to be in my room when a hoopoe flew in through an open window. The sight of the bird seemed to work an instant transformation in him and he began to race around the room, slamming shut the doors and windows.

'Stop that,' I shouted while the frightened bird flapped its wings against the walls, leaving a trail of droppings on my desk. 'Stop, what are you doing, ya 'Amm Taha?'

'Amm Taha paid no attention; he was half in flight himself, leaping nimbly from the bed to my desk and back, with his hands hooked like talons and the sleeves of his jallabeyya flapping wildly, an albatross swooping on its prey. He knocked the bird to the floor with a wave of his jallabeyya, and after breaking its neck with an expert twist of his hands, he slipped it into his pocket, as matter-of-factly as though it were a ten-piastre note.

I was astonished by this performance for I had often heard people say that hoopoes were 'friends of the fellaheen' and ought not to be harmed because they helped the crops by killing worms. He must have sensed my surprise for he explained hurriedly that it wasn't anything important, it was just that he particularly needed some hoopoe's blood that day.

'Hoopoe's blood?' I said. It was clear that he would rather

have dropped the subject, but I decided to persist. 'What will you do with it?'

'I need it for a spell,' he said brusquely, 'for women who can't bear children.' One of the hoopoe's wings had somehow emerged from his pocket and its tip was hanging out now, like the end of a handkerchief. He tucked it back carefully, and then, after a moment of silence, he cast his eyes down, like a shy schoolgirl, and declared that he didn't mind telling me that he was a kind of witch, a sâhir, and that he occasionally earned a bit of extra money by casting the odd spell.

It was a while before I could trust myself to speak, partly for fear of laughing, and partly because I knew better than to comment on the impressive range of his skills: I had discovered a while ago that he was very sensitive about what was said about the many little odd jobs he did to earn money—so much so that he had actually fallen ill a few days after we worked out our agreement.

Our paths had first crossed when I was negotiating to rent a set of rooms in an abandoned house, soon after moving to Nashawy. The rooms were part of a house that had been built by the old 'omda, the headman or chief official of the village, a decade or so before the Revolution of 1952. The 'omda was then the largest landowner in the village and the house he built was palatial by local standards, a villa of the kind one might expect to see in the seafront suburbs of Alexandria, with running water, electric lights and toilets. But he died soon after it was completed and the house was locked up and abandoned; his children were successful professionals in Alexandria and Cairo, and they had no interest whatever in their ancestral village. Only one of them even bothered to visit Nashawy any more, a chain-smoking middle-aged woman who occasionally drove down from Alexandria to collect the rent from the few acres that remained with the family after the Revolution. It was she who agreed to let me rent the rooms her father had built for his guests, on the outer side of the main house—a large bedroom with an attached toilet and a little kitchen. The floorboards in the room had long since buckled and warped and the plaster had fallen off the walls, yet the room was comfortable and there was a cheerful feel to it, despite the gloomy shadows of the abandoned house and the eerie rattles it produced at night, when the wind whistled through its unboarded windows and flapping doors.

It was the same woman who had led me to 'Amm Taha: one of his many jobs was that of caretaker. She had suggested that I pay a part of his wages and make an arrangement with him so that he could bring me food cooked by his wife—the kitchen attached to the guest-room was too small for daily use. The matter had been quickly settled and for the first few days after I moved in he arrived at midday, as we had agreed, bringing a few dishes of food with him. But then one afternoon he sent word that he wasn't well, and when he didn't turn up the next day either I decided to go and see what had happened.

His house was in the most crowded part of the village, near the square, where the dwellings were packed so close together that the ricks of straw piled on their roofs almost came together above the narrow, twisting lanes. It was a very small house, a couple of mud-walled rooms with a low, tunnel-like door. 'Amm Taha called out to me to enter when I knocked, but so little light penetrated into the house that it took a while before I could tell where he was.

He was lying on a mat, his thin, crooked face rigid with annoyance, and he began to complain the moment I stepped in:

he was ill, too ill to go anywhere, he didn't know what was going to happen to all his eggs, he had had to send his wife to the market because he hadn't been able to go out for two days.

'But what's happened, ya 'Amm Taha?' I asked. 'Do you know what's wrong?'

His good eye glared angrily at me for a moment, and then he said: 'What do you think has happened? It's the Evil Eye of course—somebody's envied me, what else?'

I looked slowly around the room at the ragged mats and the sooty cooking utensils lying in the corners.

'What did they envy?' I said.

'Can't you see?' he said irritably. 'Everyone's envious of me nowadays. My neighbours see me going to the market every other day, and they say to themselves—that Taha, he has his business in eggs and then he sells milk too, sometimes, as well as vegetables; why, he even has a donkey-cart now, that Taha, and on top of all that, he has so many other little jobs, he's ever so busy all day long, running around making money. What's he going to do with it all? He doesn't even have any children, he doesn't need it.'

He sat up straight and fixed his unmoving eye on me. 'Their envy is burning them up,' he said. 'They're all well-off, but they can't bear to see me working hard and bettering my lot. Over the last few days they've seen me going off to your house, carrying food, and it was just too much for them. They couldn't bear it.'

I began to feel uncomfortable with the part I had been assigned in this narrative: I was not sure whether I was being included amongst the guilty. 'But ya 'Amm Taha,' I said, 'isn't there anything you can do?'

He nodded impatiently; yes, of course, he said, he had already been to the government clinic that morning and they'd given him an injection and some tablets; and now a woman who lived a few doors away was going to come and break the spell—I could stay and watch if I wanted.

The woman arrived a short while later, a plump, talkative matron who seemed more disposed to chatter about the wickedness of their neighbours than to perform her duties. But 'Amm Taha was in a bad temper and he quickly cut her short and handed her a slip of paper, telling her to hurry up if she wanted her fee. She flashed me a smile, and then shutting her eyes she began to stroke his back with the slip of paper, murmuring softly. At times when her voice rose I thought I heard a few phrases of the Fâtiḥa, the opening prayer of the Quran, but for the most part her lips moved soundlessly, without interruption.

After a few minutes of this she opened her eyes and declared plaintively: 'You haven't yawned once, ya 'Amm Taha. You're fine, nobody's envied you.'

This excited a squall of indignation from 'Amm Taha. 'I haven't yawned, did you say?' he snapped. 'How would you know, with your eyes shut?'

'I know you didn't yawn,' she insisted. 'And if you didn't yawn while I was reciting the spell, it means you haven't been envied.'

'Oh is that so? Then look at this,' said 'Amm Taha. Opening his mouth he leaned forward, and when his nose was a bare inch away from hers he produced a gigantic yawn.

She fell back, startled, and began to protest: 'I don't know, ya 'Amm Taha, if you'd really been envied I'd be yawning too. And I haven't yawned at all—can you see me yawning?'

'You're not doing it properly,' he said. 'That's all. Now go on, yalla, try once more.'

132

She shut her eyes and began to run the slip of paper over his back again, and this time within a few minutes they were both yawning mightily. Soon it was over, and she leant back against the wall, swelling with pride at her success, while 'Amm Taha began to pump his kerosene stove so he could brew us some tea.

'Do you know who it was who envied you?' I asked.

They exchanged a knowing glance, but neither of them would tell me who it was. 'God is the Protector,' 'Amm Taha said piously. 'It doesn't matter who it was—the envy's been undone and I'm fine now.'

The next morning, sure enough, he was back at work, collecting eggs and driving his cart to Damanhour.

Having known of 'Amm Taha's gifts for a while now, I was confident that he would be able to tell me exactly when Ustaz Sabry would be at home.

I was not disappointed.

'Go there this evening,' he said. 'An hour or so after the sunset prayers, and you can be sure you'll find him in.'

5

SURE ENOUGH, USTAZ Sabry was at home when I went to his house that evening: he was sitting in his guest-room surrounded by some half-dozen visitors. He was talking in his clear, powerful voice, holding a shusha in his hands, while the others sat around the room in a circle. A couple of the visitors were dressed in shirts and trousers and looked like college students while the others were fellaheen who had dropped by to spend

133

some time talking at the end of the day.

Ustaz Sabry exclaimed loudly when he saw me at the door, and asked me why I hadn't come earlier, he had been expecting me several days ago. Since his mother had clearly failed to mention my earlier visit, I began to tell him myself, but I had already forfeited Ustaz Sabry's attention: he had launched upon an introduction for the benefit of his visitors.

I was a student from India, he told them, a guest who had come to Egypt to do research. It was their duty to welcome me into their midst and make me feel at home because of the long traditions of friendship between India and Egypt. Our countries were very similar, for India, like Egypt, was largely an agricultural nation, and the majority of its people lived in villages, like the Egyptian fellaheen, and ploughed their land with cattle. Our countries were poor, for they had both been ransacked by imperialists, and now they were both trying, in very similar ways, to cope with poverty and all the other problems that had been bequeathed to them by their troubled histories. It was a difficult task and our two countries had always supported each other in the past: Mahatma Gandhi had come to Egypt to consult Sa'ad Zaghloul Pasha, the leader of the Egyptian nationalist movement, and later Nehru and Nasser had forged a close alliance. No Egyptian could ever forget the support that his country had received from India during the Suez crisis of 1956, when Egypt had been subjected to an unprovoked attack by the British and the French.

One of the men sitting across the room had been shifting impatiently in his seat while Ustaz Sabry made his speech; a small, wizened, prematurely aged man, with a faraway look in his deeply-lined eyes. His name was Zaghloul, I later learnt, and he was a self-taught weaver, who spun his own woollen yarn and wove it on a rudimentary loom.

Now, Zaghloul had a question to ask, and as soon as he found an opportunity he said, in a breathless rush: 'And in his country do they have ghosts like we do?'

'Allah!' Ustaz Sabry exclaimed. 'You could ask him about so many useful and important things—religion or politics—and instead you ask him about ghosts! What will he think of you?'

'I don't know about all that,' Zaghloul said stubbornly. 'What I want to know is whether they have ghosts in his country like we do.'

'What ghosts?' Ustaz Sabry exploded. 'These ghosts you talk about, these 'afârît, they're just products of your own imagination. There are no such things, can't you see? What's the use of asking him about ghosts, what can he tell you? People imagine these things everywhere; in India just as here, there are people who think they see ghosts, and in England and Europe too there are people who point to certain houses and say, "This house is haunted, the ghost of Lord So-and-So walks here at night." But all these things are purely imaginary—no such beings exist.'

'Imaginary!' cried the weaver. 'What do you mean imaginary? How can something be imaginary if someone sees it with his own eyes, right in front of his face?'

'Have you ever seen such a thing?' Ustaz Sabry shot back.

A dreamy look came into the weaver's faraway eyes. 'No,' he said, 'but listen to me, I'll tell you something: my father saw a female ghost once, an 'afrîta, at night as he was walking past the graveyard. He never went that way at night again, by God. Why, and just the other day my neighbour's wife saw a ghost running down the road near the canal, wrapped in a blanket. I can even tell you whose ghost it was; but only if you want to know.'

'Who was it?' someone asked.

'It was Fathy, the Sparrow,' he announced triumphantly. At once, two of the men sitting next to him recoiled in horror, and began to whisper the Fatiha and other protective prayers.

'Do you mean,' I said, 'the man who was killed at the mowlid in Nakhlatain—a few months ago?'

'Yes,' said Zaghloul, 'on God's name, it was him, the Sparrow, who was knocked off a swing and killed at the mowlid. They're saying his ghost has come back to haunt us because his kinsmen were too weak to start a feud or to get the murderer's lineage to pay the proper blood-money.'

At this Ustaz Sabry and one of the college students immediately took issue with him. There was no question of a blood feud, Ustaz Sabry said. The man's death had been proved to be accidental—there had been a police inquiry and the matter had been settled. Feuds and vengeance killings were things of the past; nowadays it was the government's job to deal with crimes and murders.

'The world is wide,' said Zaghloul, 'and with prayers to the Prophet, God have mercy on him, I'll tell you something and you give it mind: something wasn't right about how the whole business of the Sparrow's death was handled. The elders of the killer's family should have gone to the elders of the Sparrow's family, and said to them: Let us sit together and read the Quran and reach an agreement, insha'allah. And while they were sorting things out, the killer should have sought sanctuary somewhere else. But instead there he was, walking freely about, showing no respect for the dead man's rights.'

'But it was an accident,' said Ustaz Sabry. 'The matter went to the police and it was settled, and that was that, khalas.'

'God fortify you, ya Ustaz,' the weaver said, deferential but obstinate. 'You know many things we don't, but something must be wrong, otherwise why is the Sparrow's ghost appearing to so many people?'

Ustaz Sabry clapped his hands to his temples in despair.

'This happens every time,' he said to me. 'Whenever there's an accidental death the talk turns to ghosts and jinns. A few years ago the whole village was gripped by a panic when a boy fell off a roof and died, during the Nashawy mowlid.'

'Does the doktór al-Hindi know about our mowlid?' Zaghloul said eagerly, with a glance in my direction. 'That is a story he should be told.'

Later, when I got to know Zaghloul better, I discovered that besides being very fond of stories, he had a manner of telling them that was marvellously faithful to the metaphorical resonances of his chosen craft. I would often come upon him out in the fields, squatting on his haunches, with his eyes fixed on his hands in an absent, oddly melancholy gaze, spinning yarn, and waiting for someone to talk to. He was, in fact, much better at telling stories than at weaving, for the products of his loom tended to look a bit like sackcloth and never earned him anything more than a generous measure of ridicule. Zaghloul himself had no illusions about the quality of his cloth: he was overcome with shock, for instance, when I asked him to make me a couple of scarves to take back as mementoes. 'You're laughing at me,' he said, 'you want to use my cloth to show your people that the fellaheen of Egypt are backward and primitive.'

His wife was even more astonished than he, especially when she discovered that I intended to pay for the scarves. 'Can't you take him too?' she said, bursting into laughter. 'To show him off to your people?' Later, I discovered that there was a festering bitterness between them that sometimes exploded into ugly quarrels; Zaghloul would threaten to divorce her and marry again, while she retaliated with the taunt—'Do you think anyone would marry you, you shrivelled old man? You're the old man of the village, the 'ajûz al-balad, no one will have you.' It was probably because of these scenes that Zaghloul spent an inordinate amount of time out on the fields, and was always glad to have an audience for his stories.

'The doktór doesn't know the story of Sidi Abu-Kanaka,' Zaghloul announced to the room, and then, leaning back on the divan he took a deep, satisfied puff of his shusha and began at the beginning.

The story was an old one, he said; even when he was a child there were very few people alive who had witnessed the events of that time, and they too had never seen Sidi Abu-Kanaka in the flesh: he had died long before they were born. But everyone knew of him of course, for he had achieved great renown in his lifetime. He was universally mourned when he died and the villagers had even built him a special grave in their cemetery.

Many years later, long after Sidi Abu-Kanaka's death, when the land around Nashawy had become green and thickly populated, the government decided that the time had come to build a canal to serve the farmers of the area. The work began soon enough and the canal proceeded quickly, past Lataifa, all the way down the road, and everyone was glad, for the area had long needed better irrigation. But when the canal reached Nashawy the villagers discovered that a calamity was in the offing, for if it went ahead as the engineers had planned, it would go directly through their cemetery. Everybody was horrified at the thought of disturbing the dead and the elders of the village went to see the government authorities to beg them to change the route. But their complaints only made the effendis impatient; they shut their doors upon the village shaikhs, saying that the canal would have to go on in a straight line, just as it was drawn in the plan.

So the villagers had watched with heavy hearts as the canal ploughed through their graveyard. Then one morning the workmen, to their utter astonishment, came upon a grave that would not yield to their spades; they hammered at it, for days and days, all of them together, but the grave had turned to rock, and no matter how hard they tried they couldn't make the slightest dent in it. When all their efforts failed, the engineers and the big effendis tried to do what they could, but it was to no purpose—they still weren't able to make the least impression on the tomb. At last, realizing that their efforts were in vain, they spoke to the village shaikhs, and upon learning that it was the tomb of Sidi Abu-Kanaka that had thwarted them, they went to his descendants and begged them to open the vault if they could.

'By all means,' the Sidi's grandson said, 'we are at your service,' and at his touch the tomb opened quite easily. Then all the people who had gathered there saw for themselves, what they would never have believed otherwise: that the Sidi's body was still whole and incorrupt, and that instead of being affected by the decay of time, it was giving off a beautiful, perfumed smell.

Everyone who was there was witness to the event and nobody, not even the effendis, could deny the miracle that Sidi Abu-Kanaka had wrought. And so it happened that the canal was made to take a slight diversion there, and on that plot of land the people of the village built a maqâm for the Sidi. The Sidi, in turn, extended his protection over Nashawy and kept its people from harm. Once, for instance, when a gang of armed thieves set out to attack Nashawy the Sidi summoned up a miracle and surrounded the village with a deep, impassable moat. In the years that followed, time and time again, he gave the villagers proof of his benevolence with miracles and acts of grace.

'This is the story that people tell here,' Ustaz Sabry said to me, as I scribbled furiously in my notebook. 'You see how the fellaheen can thwart the government when they choose…'

Yet, although everyone in the village revered the Sidi, there was no mowlid to honour his name; Nashawy's annual mowlid commemorated a saint from the settlement's parent village, far in the interior. Then one year there was a terrible accident at the Nashawy mowlid. A boy who had climbed on to the roof of a house to get a better view of the chanting of the zikr, lost his footing on the straw and fell off, breaking his neck. The people of the village were so horrified that they ran back and shut their doors, and the streets of the village were deserted, night after night, while everyone cowered at home. There were many who interpreted these events as a sign that the village ought to begin celebrating a mowlid in honour of Sidi Abu-Kanaka.

There was so much fear in Nashawy in those days, said Ustaz Sabry, that one night he and some of the other teachers decided that they ought to do something to counter the panic that had overtaken the village. What they did was this: they formed small groups, together with the other educated people in the village, and every night after the sunset prayers they walked through the lanes crying the name of God out loud, and calling upon the fellaheen to come out of their houses. Nobody joined them the first night, but over the next few days more and more people came out, until finally every man was out in the lanes shouting 'Allahu Akbar'. Thus the villagers got over their fear and Nashawy slowly returned to normal.

Later the teachers got together and decided that the time had come to call a halt to the extravagances of the mowlid. The celebration of mowlids for local saints was not a part of the true practice of Islam, Ustaz Sabry argued; such customs only served to encourage superstition and religious laxity. Besides, the fellaheen wasted a lot of money on the mowlid each year, money they had worked hard to earn, and which they would have done better to spend on fertilizers and insecticides.

For a few years after that, the villagers celebrated Sidi Abu-Kanaka's mowlid, but on a much reduced scale. But then there was further disagreement about the saints and their mowlids and in the end the Imam and many others declared that things being as they were, it was better not to hold a mowlid at all.

'Is that Imam Ibrahim you're referring to?' I said.

'Yes,' said Ustaz Sabry, in surprise. 'Have you met him? He hardly goes out at all nowadays.'

'No,' I said, 'I haven't met him. But I've heard a lot about him; people say that he was once famous as a "man of religion" in this area.'

One of the college students, a lean, wiry youth with deep-set eyes, cast a startled glance in my direction. 'Nowadays people laugh at his sermons,' he said. 'He doesn't seem to know about the things that are happening around us, in Afghanistan, Lebanon and Israel.'

Ustaz Sabry shrugged. 'He's from another time,' he said. 'What he knows about religion is what he learnt from his father in the village Qur'an school, the kuttâb.'

'He doesn't know anything about today's world,' said the student. 'When you deliver the Friday sermons, ya Ustaz Sabry, it's so inspiring—everyone feels they should do something about all that's happening in the world around us.'

Ustaz Sabry threw him a nod of acknowledgement. 'It's the times that are different,' he said. 'When Imam Ibrahim was a young man it was very hard for people like him to go to college or university and they didn't have many dealings with the big cities. How were they to learn about the real principles of religion?'

'But I've heard Imam Ibrahim reads a lot,' I said. 'And that he's very knowledgeable about traditional kinds of medicine.'

'Yes,' conceded Ustaz Sabry, 'that is true, no doubt about it. He's read many of the classical texts and he's very knowledgeable about plants and herbs and things like that—or so they say.'

Zaghloul interrupted him with a sudden outburst of laughter. 'Those leaves and powders don't work any more,' he said. 'Nowadays everyone goes to the clinic and gets an injection, and that's the end of it.'

'But Imam Ibrahim's learnt to give injections too,' Ustaz Sabry said, 'just like all the other barbers.'

'Except that he sticks in the needle like it was a spear,' said the weaver.

In the laughter that followed I got up to leave, for it was late now, and I had a long day's notes to write out. Ustaz Sabry rose to see me out and invited me to come back again soon, so we could have another talk. At the door he turned and asked the two college students to accompany me.

'It's dark outside,' he said, overruling my protests. 'You won't be able to find your way back; you city people always get lost in villages. These two boys, Nabeel and Isma'il, will take you to your room.'

6

'I HEARD SOMETHING about those friends of yours,' Shaikh
Musa suddenly exclaimed, while we were sitting in his guest-
room talking about everything that had happened in the years I
had been away. 'You know those two fellows you used to talk
about so much, Nabeel and Isma'il—I heard something about
them.'

'Yes?' I said. 'What was it?'

'Someone told me, I can't remember who,' he said. 'It was
many years after you went back to India.'

He paused to think, scratching his chin while I waited
impatiently.

'I heard they were going to Iraq,' he said at last. 'They had
gone to Cairo to make the arrangements.'

'Nabeel and Isma'il!' I said. 'Are you sure you're thinking of
the right names?'

'Yes,' said Shaikh Musa. 'I would sometimes ask about them
when I met people from Nashawy: how they were, what they
were doing. Things like that. Didn't you know they were going?'

'No,' I said. I could only shake my head, in stupefaction: it
had never occurred to me that Nabeel might have left Egypt
and gone abroad.

It was several years now since I had last heard from Nabeel.
He and I had corresponded regularly for a while after my
departure, but then I had changed address several times in New
Delhi, while he had gone off to do his stint in the army, and
one way or another our correspondence had been ruptured and
never resumed. In the intervening years I had assumed that he
and Isma'il had become employees of the Agriculture Ministry,
just as they had always intended to.

When I first met them, that night at Ustaz Sabry's house, they were still students at an agricultural training college in Damanhour. They had only a short while to go and once in possession of their degrees they would each be entitled to a job in the Agriculture Ministry. They knew it would be several years before they actually got those jobs—they would have to serve their drafts in the army first, and then there would be a long wait while the Ministry tried to find places for them (no easy matter since it had to cope with thousands of new graduates every year). Still they were very sure in their minds that the eventual security would be well worth the wait, and they had both decided long before that they would send their papers in to the Ministry as soon as they had served their time in the army.

It was no coincidence that their visions of the future were so similar: they were best friends as well as cousins; their mothers were sisters, strong-willed, resourceful women who had always told their children that only by hanging closely together would their families be able to make their way in a harsh and hostile world.

They had both hoped that they would be sent to Nashawy or some other village co-operative nearby once they got their jobs in the Agriculture Ministry. In Nashawy, as in the rest of Egypt, landowning farmers had been organized into a co-operative soon after the Revolution of 1952. The co-op was staffed by a small complement of Agriculture Ministry employees, who advised the fellaheen on technical matters. These officers were a significant force in the village, almost as much so as the schoolteachers, for although their profession lacked the moral authority that went with teaching, it gave them much more real power: it was they, for instance, who dealt with the vitally important (and potentially lucrative) business of distributing government-subsidized fertilizers and insecticides.

In general the officers of the co-operative preferred to exercise their powers from a magisterial distance: they held themselves apart from the fellaheen, and would consort with no one in the village except a few schoolteachers. Inevitably their aloofness lent them a certain glamour in the villagers' eyes: schoolboys kept a close eye on their styles of dress, ambitious mothers subtly courted the bachelors amongst them, and everyone except the teachers deferred to their views on subjects such as politics and religion.

Like many of their peers, Nabeel and Isma'il had wanted to become officers in the Nashawy co-op ever since their boyhood. They usually spoke of that ambition in terms of convenience: of how they would save money by living at home, how they would be able to help their families and look after their parents, how their mothers wanted them to be in the village so they could start thinking of suitable marriages and so on. But behind that matter-of-fact reasoning there was a rich and glossy backdrop of remembered images: memories from a time when they had gathered around the doors of the co-op and eavesdropped on the officers, talking about the great world outside, until they were chased away with yells—'Get going you kids, you sons of bitches, get out of here.' Over the years, it had become their dearest ambition to see themselves installed behind those very desks.

'I think Nabeel and Isma'il left for Iraq soon after they did their draft,' Shaikh Musa said. 'I thought they would have written to you.'

He shook his head, smiling. 'They were fine young fellows, real jad'ân,' he said. 'I only heard good things about them;

everyone always spoke well of those two.'

But Shaikh Musa had taken a different view at first. He had been shocked to hear that Isma'il had spoken dismissively of Imam Ibrahim. 'Those students!' he had exclaimed indignantly. 'They think they know everything.' It was hard for him to accept that the public life of the area had changed almost beyond recognition since his own youth.

For Isma'il it was Ustaz Sabry who was a figure of respect, not Imam Ibrahim: he talked of him at length when he and Nabeel accompanied me back to my room that night when I first met them. There was no one in the village he admired more, he said; no one from whom he had learned as much, nobody he so dearly wished to emulate. It was Ustaz Sabry, for instance, who had first thought of raising money for the Afghans: in a speech at the mosque, he had talked of how Muslims were being slaughtered by Communists in Afghanistan, and the men of the village were so moved they raised quite an impressive sum of money for the mujahideen. On another occasion, in a speech on superstitions and mistaken beliefs he had eloquently condemned the custom that women observed, of leaving offerings at the graves of dead relatives. He had described the practice as unlawful and contrary to the spirit of Islam, and his speech was so powerful and convincing that the men went straight home from the mosque, and forbade the womenfolk to do it again. He and the other teachers had even succeeded in uniting the villagers against a man who was known to perform exorcism rituals for women, secret Ethiopian rites called Zâr: a large group of men had gone to confront him and they had told him to put an end to his doings.

When Ustaz Sabry put his mind to it, said Isma'il, he could always prevail upon others, because no one was more skilled in disputation than he. Friends who had served in the army with him told a story about an argument he had once had with an East German, a Communist military expert who was attached to their unit. The German had been in Egypt many years and spoke Arabic well.

'Do you believe in God?' the German had asked, and when Ustaz Sabry answered yes, he certainly did, the German replied: 'So then where is he, show me?'

Ustaz Sabry countered by asking him a question in turn. 'Tell me,' he said, 'do you believe that people have a spirit, the spirit of life itself?'

'Yes,' the German answered, so then Ustaz Sabry said to him: 'Where is this spirit, can you show it to me?'

'It is in no one place' the German replied, 'it is everywhere—in the body, the head…'

'And that,' Ustaz Sabry said, 'is exactly where God is.'

The German knew he was beaten, but he wasn't willing to admit defeat. 'I don't believe in God,' he insisted, 'we Communists think of religion as the opium of the masses.'

'You can believe what you please,' Ustaz Sabry had told him, 'but you will see that the people of your own country will soon sicken of your atheistic beliefs, just as we have in Egypt.'

It was a story that was often repeated.

Ustaz Sabry and the other young teachers had completely changed Nashawy, said Isma'il; they were constantly active, constantly battling against ignorance. Now they had even hatched a plan to start a consumers' co-operative that would sell essentials like rice, sugar, oil and suchlike at rock-bottom prices, so that the people of Nashawy would no longer have to put up with the sinful profiteering of the village's shopkeepers. In time, with the help of God, they would succeed in rooting out all exploitation and unbelief from the village, and people would see for themselves where the path of true Islam lay.

Nabeel had said very little while Isma'il was talking, apart from murmuring a few noises of assent. Later I discovered that this was not unusual: Isma'il usually did the talking when the two of them were together. There was a kind of complementarity between them, a close-stitched seam of differences which became ever more visible when they were in each other's company. Nabeel was the quiet, reflective one, not shy, but serious and earnest, never saying anything or committing himself without a good deal of prior thought. Isma'il, on the other hand, was like a bird—or so his family said—giving voice to every passing thought and always ready with a joke or a pun. You could see the difference between them from a long way off: Nabeel was stocky, with a square, tidy face, while Isma'il was short, wiry and aquiline; when Nabeel walked through the village it was with a steady, considered kind of gait, but Isma'il, in contrast, walked with quick, jaunty steps, and always seemed to be in a hurry to get where he was going.

When I came to know the cousins better, I understood that the differences between them were no less a product of their upbringing than the ties that held them together: it was true that their mothers were sisters, and very alike in many ways, but their fathers were quite unlike one another, and the difference in their characters had left a profound mark on the children. Isma'il's father belonged to a humble lineage of small tradesmen, but he was a hard-working, cheerful man, a good provider who had succeeded in handing on something of his own optimistic spirit to his children. Nabeel's father, Idris, on the other hand, was a member of the largest and most powerful lineage in the village, the Badawy. But, of course, not all the

Badawy were alike in their material circumstances, and it so happened that Idris belonged to one of the clan's most impoverished branches. He himself had almost nothing in the world apart from the house he and his family lived in, a dilapidated complex of three mud-walled rooms grouped around a tiny courtyard. His forefathers had owned a fair bit of land once, but they had somehow contrived to lose it, and ever since, their descendants had been forced to make their living in the lowliest possible way, by working as labourers on other people's land, for daily wages.

Idris had been presented with a rare opportunity to improve his circumstances when he was allotted some land after the Revolution of 1952. But at about that time, quite by chance, he also managed to find employment as a village watchman, a post that carried a monthly salary. To his way of thinking, it was infinitely more respectable to be a mowazzaf, a 'salaried employee', than a fellah, sweating in the mud, so he decided to take the watchman's job. It would have been hard for him to work the land anyway, he had reasoned, because his oldest son was just an infant then, and he wasn't strong enough to farm a couple of feddans on his own. So he let the land go, and over the following years, eking out an existence on his watchman's salary, he had watched regretfully while the other recipients of Reform land slowly gained in prosperity and built themselves bigger and better houses.

Yet Idris bore no grudges and counted it an achievement that he had succeeded in becoming a mowazzaf even if his job was a humble one and his wages negligible. Once, he showed me the gun he had been issued in his capacity as a watchman: he was hugely proud of it and kept it locked in a trunk under his bed. It was a British-made Enfield, of considerable antiquity, not far

149

removed from a blunderbuss in fact. When he stood it on the floor it looked like an up-ended cannon, reaching higher than his shoulder and dwarfing him, with his frail, stooped frame and his tendril-thin wrists. I had difficulty in believing that he had ever been able to raise that redoubtable weapon to his chin, much less fire it, but he assured me I was wrong, that he had indeed used it on several occasions in the past. The last time admittedly was some fifteen years ago, when he let fly at some thieves who were escaping through a cornfield: the thieves got away but a large patch of corn was flattened by the blast.

Idris was not personally unhappy with his lot for he counted it an honour to be paid a monthly salary by the government. Nabeel, on the other hand, hated his family's poverty, and loyal though he was to his father, he considered a watchman's job demeaning, unworthy of his lineage. He had always been treated as a poor relative by his more prosperous Badawy cousins, and he had responded by withdrawing into the defensive stillness of introspection. But there was a proud streak in him and, even more than Isma'il, he was determined to escape his poverty and improve his family's condition.

Fortunately for Nabeel, his mother, through a mixture of determination and good sense, had succeeded in providing him and his younger brothers with the necessary means for bettering their lot. She had taken her oldest son, 'Ali, out of school at an early age, and sent him out to work in the fields. Realizing that her family's best hope lay in educating the other children, she had somehow contrived to keep the family going, with the help of 'Ali's meagre earnings, while Nabeel and his younger brothers went through school and college. But she was acutely aware all along that it was 'Ali's sacrifice that had given the others the possibility of a better future, and to show her gratitude, she set about arranging his marriage as soon as it became clear that, God willing, nothing could now prevent Nabeel from graduating.

Nabeel and Isma'il told me about 'Ali's forthcoming wedding at our very first meeting, when they walked with me from Ustaz Sabry's house to my room. I asked them in when we reached my door, and while I made tea Isma'il talked at length about the forthcoming wedding.

'Ali was going to marry Isma'il's sister, Fawzia (who was, of course, his first cousin)—now, apart from being best friends and cousins, he and Nabeel would also be linked by marriage! It was the best kind of union, he said: the bride and groom were cousins and had known each other all their lives; they were of the same age and they had virtually lived in each other's houses since the day they were born. There would be no outsiders involved, everything would be kept within the family and arranged between relatives, so there would be none of those problems that went with bringing a stranger into one's household.

'We will sing and dance for the bride and groom,' said Isma'il. 'You must come: it will be a sight that you will remember.'

'I shall be honoured to come,' I said. 'It will be a privilege.'

Nabeel in the meanwhile had been running his eyes silently around my room, looking from my clothes, hanging on pegs, to my paper-strewn desk and the pots and pans stored in the tiny space that served as a makeshift kitchen. He seemed to become wholly absorbed in his scrutiny while Isma'il talked and I busied myself with the tea; he looked at everything in turn with a deep and preoccupied concentration, running his hands over his jallabeyya.

Suddenly, as I was spooning tea into my kettle, he spoke up, interrupting Isma'il.

'It must make you think of all the people you left at home,' he said to me, 'when you put that kettle on the stove with just enough water for yourself.'

There was a brief pause and then Isma'il said quickly: 'Why should it? He has us and so many other friends to come here and have tea with him; he has no reason to be lonely.'

'It's not the same thing,' said Nabeel. 'Think how you would feel.'

The conversation quickly turned to something else, but Nabeel's comment stayed in my mind; I was never able to forget it, for it was the first time that anyone in Lataifa or Nashawy had attempted an enterprise similar to mine—to enter my imagination and look at my situation as it might appear to me.

It took me some time to absorb the fact that Nabeel and Isma'il were gone now: for a while I found it hard to believe what Shaikh Musa had told me. In the many years that had passed since I last met them, I had grown accustomed to thinking of the two cousins as officers in the co-op; I had even tried to imagine what their responses would be when I walked through the door.

'Nabeel came with me to the station the day I left Nashawy,' I told Shaikh Musa. 'He said that by the time I returned he would have his job and be settled in Nashawy.'

'Do you know why they left?' I asked. 'Was there any specific reason?'

Shaikh Musa shrugged. 'Why does anyone leave?' he said. 'The opportunity comes, and it has to be taken.'

TO THE YOUNG Ben Yiju, journeying eastwards would have appeared as the simplest and most natural means of availing himself of the most rewarding possibilities his world had to offer.

His own origins lay in Ifriqiya—in the Mediterranean port of Mahdia, now a large town in Tunisia. His family name 'ibn Yijû'—or Ben Yijû, in Hebrew—was probably derived from the name of a Berber tribe that had once been the protectors, or patrons, of his lineage. The chronology of his childhood and early life is hazy, and nothing is known exactly about the date or place of his birth. Working backwards from the events of his later life, it would seem that the date of his birth was somewhere towards the turn of the century, in the last years of the eleventh or the first of the twelfth. Since his friends sometimes referred to him as 'al-Mahdawî' it seems likely that he was born in Mahdia, which was then a major centre of Jewish culture, as well as one of the most important ports in Ifriqiya.

A contemporary of Ben Yiju's, the Sharîf al-Idrîsî, a distinguished Arab geographer, developed a personal acquaintance with Mahdia at about the time that Ben Yiju would have been growing up there. He had a few sharp words to say about the quality of its water, but otherwise he found much to admire in the town: it had pretty buildings, nice promenades, magnificent baths, and numerous caravanserais; its inhabitants were generally good-looking and well-dressed and 'altogether Mahdia offered a view of something wonderful'.

Of Ben Yiju's immediate family, only two brothers, Yûsuf and Mubashshir, and one sister, Berâkhâ, figure in his later correspondence. Nothing at all is known about his mother, and very little about his father, apart from his name and a few incidental details. He was called Peraḥyâ (spelt Farḥîa in Arabic), and he was a Rabbi, a respected scholar and scribe. He may have dabbled in business, like most scholars of his time, but the family's circumstances seem to have been modest, and in all likelihood his principal bequest to his sons lay in the excellent education he provided them with.

Abraham Ben Yiju was certainly well enough educated to have become a scholar himself and he was very well versed in doctrinal and religious matters. His personal inclinations, however, appear to have tended towards the literary rather than the scholastic: he was an occasional poet, and he wrote a clear, carefully crafted prose, with some arresting images hidden under a deceptively plain surface.

But for all that, when it came to a choice of career the opportunities offered by the eastern trade must have seemed irresistible to the young Ben Yiju, reared as he was in a community that had made a speciality of it. And once he had launched upon it, that career would have followed a natural progression, leading him from Ifriqiya to Fustat, and then to Aden, the port that sat astride the most important sea-routes connecting the Middle East and the Indian Ocean.

Ben Yiju's papers leave no room for doubt that he did indeed move to Aden, probably for a considerable length of time, in the 1120s, or maybe even earlier. The exact dates and duration of his stay may never be known, however, because not a single scrap of material dating from that period of his life has survived: apart from a few pinpricks of light, refracted back from the letters he received in India, those years are shrouded in dark obscurity.

However, it is clear enough from his later correspondence that his early years in Aden played a formative part in his life. It was probably there, for example, that he made the acquaintance of a man who was to become first his mentor and then his partner in business, a wealthy and powerful trader called Maḍmûn ibn al-Ḥasan ibn Bundâr.

Madmun ibn Bundar, like his father before him, was the Nagîd or Chief Representative of merchants, in Aden. He was thus the head of the city's large and wealthy Jewish community, as well as the superintendent of the port's customs offices—a man of great substance and influence, a key figure in the Indian Ocean trade, whose network of friends and acquaintances extended all the way from Spain to India.

Several of Madmun's letters figure in Ben Yiju's correspondence: crisp and straightforward in style, they are written in the prose of a bluff, harried trader, with no frills, and many fewer wasted words than was usual at the time. The letters are often spread over a number of different folio sheets, some written in his own hand, and some by scribes. Madmun himself wrote a terrible hand, a busy, trader's scrawl, forged in the bustle of the market-place. Often the carefully calligraphed copies produced by his team of scribes end in swathes of his own hasty handwriting: there is a freshness and urgency about them which make it all too easy to see him snatching the letters away to add a few final instructions while the ships that are to carry them wait in the harbour below.

Ben Yiju almost certainly knew of Madmun long before he left Egypt, and his friends and relatives are sure to have armed him with letters of introduction when he set out for Aden. Madmun, for his part, had probably been warned of the newcomer's impending arrival by his own networks of information, and he may well have been favourably disposed towards him even before he reached Aden. For a young man in Ben Yiju's circumstances there could have been no more fortunate connection than to have the Chief Representative of Merchants as his patron: fortunately for him he appears to have made a favourable impression on Madmun, and it was probably in his warehouse that he first learned the rudiments of the Indian Ocean trade.

Madmun's earliest extant letters date from after Ben Yiju's departure from Aden, when he was engaged in setting up in business in the Malabar. From the tone and content of those early letters it would seem that Ben Yiju's relationship with Madmun at that time fell somewhere between that of an agent and a junior partner. The letters are full of detailed instructions, and beneath the surface of their conventionally courteous language there is a certain peremptoriness, as though Madmun were doubtful of the abilities and efficiency of his inexperienced associate. But at the same time it is amply clear from Madmun's warm but occasionally irascible tone that he regarded Ben Yiju with an almost parental affection. His familiarity with his tastes and habits suggests that he may even have taken the young Ben Yiju to live in his household, regarding him as a part of his family, in much the same way that artisans sometimes made their apprentices their presumptive kin.

Indeed, Ben Yiju appears to have been warmly welcomed by the whole of Madmun's close-knit social circle in Aden. His two other principal correspondents there were both related to Madmun. One of them, Yûsuf ibn Abraham, was a judicial functionary as well as a trader: a man of a somewhat self-absorbed and irritable disposition, on the evidence of his letters. The other was Khalaf ibn Ishaq—the writer of the letter of MS

H.6, and possibly the closest of Ben Yiju's friends in Aden.

The fortunes of each of these men were founded on the trade between India and the Middle East but their part in it was that of brokers and financiers rather than travelling merchants. At one time or another they too had probably travelled extensively in the Indian Ocean, but by the time Ben Yiju met them they were all comfortably settled in Aden, with their days of travel behind them.

There was no lack of travellers in their circle, however: at least two of Madmun's friends deserve to be counted amongst the most well-travelled men of the Middle Ages, perhaps of any age before the twentieth century. The first was a prominent figure in the Jewish community of Fustat, Abû Sa'îd Ḥalfon ben Nethan'el ha-Levi al-Dimyâṭî, a wealthy merchant, scholar and patron of literature, whose surname links him to the Egyptian port of Dumyâṭ or Damietta. A large number of Abu Sa'id Halfon's papers have been preserved in the Geniza and their dates and places of writing bear witness to a pattern of movement so fluent and far-ranging that they make the journeys of later medieval travellers, such as Marco Polo and Ibn Battuta, seem unremarkable in comparison. From year to year he was resident in different countries and continents, travelling frequently between Egypt, India, East Africa, Syria, Morocco and Spain. He was also a close friend and patron of one of the greatest of medieval Hebrew poets, Judah ha-Levi, who dedicated a treatise to him and composed a number of poems in his honour. Abu Sa'id Halfon regularly corresponded and did business with Madmun and Khalaf, and although there is no record of a direct exchange of letters between him and Ben Yiju, there can be no doubt that they were well acquainted with each other.

The second of the great travellers of Madmun's circle was

Abû-Zikrî Judah ha-Kohen Sijilmâsî. As his name suggests, Abu Zikri Sijilmasi had his origins in the desert town of Sijilmasa in Morocco, but he later emigrated to Fustat and rose to prominence within the Jewish community there, eventually becoming the Chief Representative of Merchants. He too travelled far afield, between Egypt, Aden, southern Europe and India. References in Ben Yiju's correspondence show that he frequently encountered Abu Zikri Sijilmasi and his brother-in-law, a ship-owner called Maḥrûz, in Mangalore. So close were the links between the three of them that on one occasion, when Abu Zikri Sijilmasi was captured by pirates off the coast of Gujarat, Ben Yiju penned him a letter on behalf of Mahruz, urging him to travel quickly down from Broach to Mangalore.

It was probably no coincidence, since merchant families have always tightened the bonds of trade with a tug of kinship, that Abu Zikri's Sijilmasi's sister happened to be married to Madmun. It could well be that it was Abu Zikri who, out of allegiance to a fellow North African, gave Ben Yiju the introduction which secured his entry into Madmun's circle.

Circumstances were thus propitious for Ben Yiju's introduction into Madmun's privileged circle in Aden. Still, it needs to be noted that if Ben Yiju succeeded in finding ready acceptance within the society of the wealthy merchants of Aden, despite his comparatively humble standing as a young apprentice trader, it must have been largely because of his individual gifts. His distinction of mind is evident enough in his letters, but he must have had, in addition, a certain warmth or charm, as well as the gift of inspiring loyalty—qualities whose attribution is none the more doubtful for being a matter of conjecture since their indisputable proof lies in the long friendships enshrined in his correspondence.

The circle which the young Ben Yiju was received into in Aden was one that had place for literary talent as well as business acumen. At the time of his stay there were several gifted Hebrew poets living and writing in Aden. It was an ambience that must have been attractive in the extreme to a man of Ben Yiju's tastes, with his inclination for poetry and his diligence in business. That, combined with the warmth of his welcome into an exclusive society, must have made Aden an extraordinarily congenial place for this young trader with a literary bent.

Yet, curiously enough, at some point before 1132 Ben Yiju moved to the Malabar coast and did not return to Aden for nearly two decades.

At first glance there appears to be nothing unusual about Ben Yiju's departure, for of course, merchants involved in the eastern trade travelled frequently to India. But there are two good reasons why this particular move appears anomalous, a deviation from the usual pattern of traders' travels.

The first is that merchants involved in the eastern trade, like Abu Sa'id Halfon and Abu Zikri Sijilmasi for example, generally travelled back and forth at regular intervals between the ports of the Indian Ocean and the Middle East. While there are a few other instances in the Geniza of traders living abroad for long periods of time, none of them quite matches the continuous duration of Ben Yiju's stay—he does not seem to have travelled back to Aden or Egypt even once in the nineteen or twenty years that he was in India. Indeed, it would seem that when the need arose he preferred to send his slave—the slave of MS H.6—to Aden to transact his business there, while he himself remained in Mangalore.

The second reason for suspecting that there may have been

something out of the ordinary in Ben Yiju's departure from Aden lies in a cryptic letter that is now in the possession of the Taylor-Schechter collection in Cambridge. This particular piece of paper is quite large, about eleven inches long and more than five inches wide, but it is still only a fragment—a scrap which Ben Yiju tore from a longer sheet so he could scribble on its back. The little that remains of the original letter is badly damaged and much of the text is difficult to decipher. Fortunately the scrap does contain the name of the letter's sender: it is just barely legible and it serves to link the fragment with this story for it proves that the writer was none other than Madmun ibn al-Hasan ibn Bundar, of Aden.

For most of its length, the letter is perfectly straightforward: following the conventional protocols of their correspondence Madmun refers to Ben Yiju as 'my master' and to himself as his 'servant'. He begins by acknowledging a shipment of areca nuts, mentions the sale of a quantity of pepper, and lets Ben Yiju know that certain goods have been safely delivered to his two other associates in Aden.

The puzzling part of the letter comes towards the end, and it consists of a short, six-line passage. It reads thus:

'Concerning what he [my master] mentioned [in his letter]: that he has resolved to return to Aden, but that which prevents him [from returning] is the fear that it would be said that he had acted rashly. His servant spoke to [the king] al-Mâlik al-Sa'îd concerning him...and took from him his guarantee as a safeguard against his return, insha'allah. So he [my master] has nothing to fear: [the king] will resolve everything in his court in the country of India. And if, God forfend, he were to lose...what he has and his children were part of that [loss]...'

The rest is lost; it was upon this tantalizingly incomplete line that Ben Yiju's hands fell when he was tearing up the letter. No other document contains any mention of whatever matter it was that Madmun was referring to in his letter: unless the rest of the letter is discovered some day nothing more will ever be known of it.

Despite its brevity and the suddenness of its termination, there is one fact the passage does serve to establish beyond any doubt. It proves that Ben Yiju's departure for India was not entirely voluntary—that something had happened in Aden that made it difficult for him to remain there or to return.

The passage provides no direct indication of what it was that had happened. The most obvious possibility is that the matter had to do with a debt or a financial irregularity. But on the other hand, it is hardly likely that the ruler of Aden would take an interest in a purely civil dispute, as the letter suggests. In any case, if it were only an unpaid debt that prevented Ben Yiju's return to Aden, he and his friends would surely have settled the matter quickly and quietly, without recourse to the ruler.

The passage, such as it is, provides little enough to go on, and the careful discretion of Madmun's language has wound a further sheet of puzzles around an affair that is already shrouded in mystery. For instance, the word Madmun uses to describe the safeguard offered by the ruler of Aden is one of those Arabic terms that can spin out a giddying spiral of meanings. The word is dhimma, whose parent and sister words mean both 'to blame' as well as the safeguards that can be extended to protect the blameworthy.

Used as it is here, the word could mean that the ruler of Aden had agreed not to prosecute Ben Yiju for a crime that he had committed, or been accused of. Or it could mean that he had pledged to protect him from certain people whose enmity Ben

161

Yiju had cause to fear. By Arab tradition this was the kind of guarantee that was extended to a man who had killed someone: it was intended to protect him and his relatives from a vengeance killing so that they could raise the murdered man's blood-money.

That implicit suggestion, along with the hint that the matter somehow implicated Ben Yiju's children as well as himself, is all there is to suggest that Ben Yiju may have fled to India in order to escape a blood feud.

For all we know, it could just as well have been a matter of unpaid taxes.

8

SHAIKH MUSA HAD never heard of Khamees the Rat before I mentioned his name.

He pursed his lips when I asked him, and began to finger his beads, thinking hard, but after a while, loath to admit defeat, he gave a peremptory shake of his head and exclaimed: 'The Rat? Al-Fâr? What sort of name is that? Are you sure you heard it right?'

It was a nickname, I said, his relations called him that because of the way he talked, because he gnawed at things with his tongue like a rat did with its teeth.

But in fact I didn't really know how he had got the name: for all I knew it could have been his appearance that bestowed it upon him. It was easy to imagine his thin face and bright, darting eyes putting his cousins in mind of a rodent, years ago,

162

when he was a boy; even now, in his mid-twenties with two marriages behind him, something of that resemblance still remained, a certain quickness of movement and a ferile, beady-eyed wit.

'His land is near Zaghloul the weaver's,' I added, for it was often details like that which helped Shaikh Musa make connections. But this time, despite his best efforts, the name eluded the tripwires of his memory.

'Nashawy is a big place,' he said at last, philosophically. 'Which family are they from, do you know?'

The Jammâl, I said, and when I saw the faint curl that came upon his lips it struck me suddenly that of course, that was the reason why Shaikh Musa did not know Khamees—his lineage. People like the Latifs and the Badawy tended to look down their noses at the Jammal; they were unmannerly in their ways, the Badawy would whisper, uncouth in behaviour and wild in temperament, and it was best to keep them at a distance. But they were always careful to lower their voices when they said those things: the Jammal were both very numerous and very pugnacious, and everyone knew that their men would be out in the lanes at the least provocation, eager to fight for their honour.

It stuck in the throats of Nabeel and his Badawy kin that the Jammal had been the biggest gainers from the redistribution of land that had followed the Revolution of 1952: their hostility was now spiced with envy, because from being the poorest people in the village, mere labourers and sharecroppers, many of the Jammal had gone on to become landowning fellaheen, with several feddans of land to their name. Now the Badawy could no longer afford to be so haughty as they once were, and when they received a proposal of marriage from one of the more prosperous Jammal families, they were often all too quick to accept. But still, for people like Shaikh Musa the majority of the Jammal still fell outside the boundaries of respectability, despite the dramatic changes of the last few decades.

Suddenly I recalled another, more promising detail, one that was sure to sound an echo in Shaikh Musa's memory. 'You may know Khamees's sister,' I said. 'She was married not far from you, in Nakhlatain, but she left her husband a few months ago and moved back to Nashawy with her children.'

'Oh my eyes!' Shaikh Musa cried. 'The tall sweet-looking one, who had two little boys—is that the woman you mean?'

Yes, I said, exactly. That was her, tall and sweet-looking; her name was Busaina and she was Khamees's sister.

It was thanks to 'Amm Taha that I knew those details about her: if it were not for him, the self-contained world of Nashawy's women would have been even more firmly closed for me than it was for other men, since unlike them, I had no female relatives in the village to keep me abreast of that parallel history.

I had asked 'Amm Taha about Busaina the very first day I met her, out in the fields during the rice harvest, with Khamees and the rest of her family. I hadn't even known who she was then, for only the mens' names were mentioned, as always. But while we were talking, someone had pointed to the child in her arms and announced with a laugh that there was Khamees's son. As far as I knew no one joked about things like that, so naturally I had concluded that they were married.

'Amm Taha had corrected me the moment I described her. No, he had explained, with his dry, coughing laugh; that wasn't Khamees's wife I had seen, it couldn't have been if she were holding a baby because Khamees didn't have any children. He had been married off at the age of fifteen, several years ago, and having failed to father any children, he had taken a second wife recently, but with no result. The marriage had caused quite a scandal because his first wife had walked off in a rage, shouting to the world that it was his fault that he was childless, not hers. And after all that trouble, the marriage had made no difference —several of Khamees's brothers had families now, but despite being the oldest and the longest married, he remained without child, and was often the butt of their jokes.

'So that couldn't have been his wife you saw,' 'Amm Taha said, wagging a finger in my direction. 'That was probably his sister, Busaina, who's just come back to Nashawy with her children.'

Busaina had been married off years ago to a man from Nakhlatain, not far from Lataifa. But although she had given her husband two fine, healthy children, the two of them had never really got on. They had quarrelled all the time, over this and that, and in the end things had come to such a pass that her husband had announced that he was going to marry again. She told him plainly at the time that she'd leave him if he did, and sure enough, when she heard rumours that he'd been talking with another girl's father, she picked up her things, her pots, pans and furniture, and moved back to Nashawy with her children. So now she was back in her father's house, along with Khamees and all her other brothers and their children.

'It was bound to happen,' Shaikh Musa said. 'She wouldn't listen to anyone. She and her husband used to quarrel all day long because she had to have her way in everything.'

He shook his head ruefully, running a hand over his white-stubbled chin.

'It was because of her origins,' he said. 'The Jammal are all like that, difficult and quarrelsome, and it's best to keep them at a distance.'

He did not look at me, but there was an air of disapproval about him that warned me not to tell him about my first meeting with Khamees and his family.

It was Zaghloul the weaver who had made the introductions. It was the time of the rice harvest, late autumn, and he had spotted me walking through the fields, notebook in hand, and had shouted across: 'Come here, ya doktór—come and eat with us, over here.'

He was sitting with a group of people on a tree-shaded knoll which served to house a couple of wooden water-wheels. He, and the other men in the group were seated cross-legged around a huge tin tray; I could tell from the number of dishes in front of them that they were eating a generous midday meal of the kind that always accompanied a harvest. The women who had brought the food out to the fields were squatting beside them, doling out servings of rice, cheese, salâṭa and fish.

One woman had withdrawn a little from the rest of the group; she was sitting apart, leaning against a tree, with a scarf thrown carelessly over her shoulders, holding a baby to her breast. She looked up as I made my way across the newly-harvested rice fields, fixing me with a clear, inquiring gaze, and when the scarf slipped inadvertently off her breast she straightened it without the slightest show of confusion or shyness. She had a wide, oval face, with well-defined features, and eyes that were brilliantly forthright and direct.

When I reached the knoll Zaghloul stretched out a hand to me, laughing uproariously. 'These men were scared when they saw you walking down the path,' he said, 'because of that notebook in your hands. They thought you were an effendi from Damanhour who'd come to check whether anyone's evading military service.'

He cast a glance at the sheepish grins on the faces around him, his small wizened face crumpling up with mirth.

'So I told them,' he said, 'why no, that's not a military inspector; he's not an effendi or even a veterinarian—that's the doktór from al-Hind, where they have ghosts just like we do.'

'Ahlan!' said the man sitting next to him, a sharp-faced young fellah in a brown jallabeyya. 'Ahlan! So you're the doktór from al-Hind?'

'Yes,' I said, 'and you?'

'He's a rat,' someone answered, raising a gale of laughter. 'Don't go anywhere near him.'

His name was Khamees, said Zaghloul, laughing louder than the rest, Khamees the Rat, and the others sitting there were his brothers and cousins. Their land ran next to each others', he explained, so they always worked together as a group. It was Khamees's family's land they were working on today; it would be his own tomorrow and so on, until they all finished harvesting their rice, in one short week of hard work and good eating.

'Why are you still standing, ya doktór?' cried Khamees. 'You've come a long way and you won't be able to get back to your country before sundown anyway, so you may as well sit with us for a while.'

He moved up, smiling, and slapped the earth beside him. He was in his mid-twenties, about my age, scrawny, with a thin mobile face, deeply scorched by the sun. Almost in spite of myself, I felt instantly at home with him: he had that brightness of eye and the slightly sardonic turn to his mouth that I associated with coffee-houses in Delhi and Calcutta; he seemed to belong to a familiar world of lecture-rooms, late-night rehearsals and black coffee.

He leant back to look at me now, as I seated myself, summing me up with his sharp, satirical eyes.

'All right, ya doktór,' he said, once I had settled in beside him with my legs crossed. 'Tell me, is it true what they say, that in your country you burn your dead?'

The moment he said it the women in the group clasped their hands to their hearts and cried in breathless horror: 'Ḥarâm! Ḥarâm!' and several of the men began to mutter prayers, calling upon the Lord to protect them from the devil.

My heart sank: this was a question I encountered almost daily, and since I had not succeeded in finding a word such as 'cremate' in Arabic, I knew I would have to give my assent to the term that Khamees had used: the verb 'to burn', which was the word for what happened to firewood and straw and the eternally damned.

'Yes,' I said, knowing that I would not be able to prevent the inevitable outcome. 'Yes, it's true; some people in my country burn their dead.'

'You mean,' said Khamees in mock horror, 'that you put them on heaps of firewood and just light them up?'

'Yes,' I said quickly, hoping he would tire of the subject.

It was not to be. 'Why?' he persisted. 'Is there a shortage of kindling in your country?'

'No,' I said, 'you don't understand.'

There was a special word, I tried to explain, a special ceremony, certain rites and rituals—it wasn't like lighting a bonfire with a matchstick. But for all the impression my explanation made, I may as well have been silent.

'Even little children?' said Khamees. 'Do you burn little children?'

Busaina spoke now, for the first time. 'Of course not,' she said, in disbelief, hugging her baby to her breast. 'They wouldn't burn little dead children—no one could do that.'

'Yes,' I said, regretfully. 'Yes, we do—we burn everyone.'

'But why?' she cried. 'Why? Are people fish that you should fry them on a fire?'

'I don't know why,' I said. 'It's the custom—that's how it was when I came into the world. I had nothing to do with it.'

'There's nothing to be surprised at, really,' Zaghloul said wisely, gazing at the horizon. 'Why, in the land of Nam-Nam people even eat their dead. My uncle told me: it's their custom—they can't help it.'

'Stop jabbering, ya Zaghloul,' Busaina snapped at him, and then turned her attention back to me.

'You must put an end to this burning business,' she said to me firmly. 'When you go back you should tell them about our ways and how we do these things.'

'I will,' I promised, 'but I don't know if they'll listen. They're very stubborn, they go on doing the same thing year after year.'

Suddenly Khamees clapped his hands with an exultant cry. 'I'll tell you why they do it,' he said. 'They do it so their bodies can't be punished upon the Day of Judgement.'

The others keeled over with laughter while he looked around in triumph, his eyes astart with the thrill of discovery. 'Don't you see?' he said. 'It's really clever—they burn the bodies so there'll be nothing left to punish and they won't have to answer for their sins.'

'No, no, that's not true,' I said, obscurely offended by this imputation. But no sooner had I begun to argue than I realized that Khamees's interpretation was not intended as a slur: on the contrary he was overcome by a kind of appalled admiration at the wiliness of 'my people'—as far as he was concerned we were friends now, our alliance sealed by this daring cosmic confidence trick.

'All right then,' said Zaghloul, silencing the others with a raised hand. 'The people in your country—do they have a Holy Book, like we do?'

'Yes,' I said, pausing to think of an answer that would be both brief and undeniably true. 'Yes, they have several.'

'And do you have a Prophet, like we do?'

I answered with a quick nod, and having had enough of this conversation, I tried to turn it in a more agronomic direction, by asking a question about phosphates and rice-growing. But Zaghloul, as I was to discover later, had all the patient pertinacity that went with the weaver's craft and was not to be easily deflected once he had launched upon a subject.

'And who is your Prophet?' he said, ignoring my question. 'What is his name?'

I had no option now but to improvise; after a few moments of thought, I said: 'Al-Buddha.'

'Who?' cried Khamees. 'What was that you said?'

'Al-Buddha,' I repeated feebly, and Zaghloul looking at the others in stupefaction, said: 'Who can that be? All the world knows that Our Prophet, the Messenger of God, peace be on him, was the last and final Prophet. This is not a true prophet he is speaking of.'

Khamees leant over to tap me on my knee. 'All right then, ya doktór,' he said. 'Tell us something else then: is it true what they say? That you are a Magûsî, a Magian, and that in your country everybody worships cows? It is it true that the other day when you were walking through the fields you saw a man beating a cow and you were so upset you burst into tears and ran back to your room?'

'No, it's not true,' I said, but without much hope: I knew

from experience that there was nothing I could say that would effectively give the lie to this story. 'You're wrong. In my country people beat their cows all the time; I promise you.'

'So tell us then,' said someone else. 'In your country do you have military service, like we do in Egypt?'

'No,' I said, and in an effort to soften the shock of that revelation I began to explain that there were more than 700 million people in my country, and that if we'd had military service the army would have been larger than all of Egypt. But before I could finish Busaina interrupted me, throwing up her hands with a cry of despair.

'Everything's upside down in that country,' she said. 'Tell us, ya doktór: in your country do you at least have crops and fields and canals like we do?'

'Yes,' I said, 'we have crops and fields, but we don't always have canals. In some parts of my country they aren't needed because it rains all year around.'

'Ya salâm,' she cried, striking her forehead with the heel of her palm. 'Do you hear that, oh you people? Oh the Protector, oh, the Lord! It rains all the year around in his country.'

She had gone pale with amazement. 'So tell us then,' she demanded, 'do you have night and day like we do?'

'Shut up woman,' said Khamees. 'Of course they don't. It's day all the time over there, didn't you know? They arranged it like that so they wouldn't have to spend any money on lamps.'

After the laughter had died down, one of Khamees's brothers pointed to the baby who was now lying in the shade of a tree, swaddled in a sheet of cloth.

'That's Khamees's baby,' he said, with a grin. 'He was born last month.'

'That's wonderful,' I said: I had no idea then that he had

171

made me party to a savage joke at Khamees's expense. 'That's wonderful; Khamees must be very happy.'

Ignoring his brother, Khamees gave a cry of delight. 'The Indian knows,' he said. 'He understands that people are happy when they have children: he's not as upside down as we thought.'

He slapped me on the knee, grinning, and pushed forward his brother 'Eid, an exact miniaturized version of himself, no taller than his waist.

'Take this fellow with you when you go back, ya doktór, take him with you: all he does here is sit in the cornfields and play with himself.'

Stretching out a hand he squeezed the back of the boy's neck until he was squirming in discomfort. 'What would happen,' he said to me, 'if this boy 'Eid knocked on the door of your house in India and said: Is anyone there?'

'Someone would open the door,' I said, 'and my family would look after him.'

Khamees pulled a face: 'You mean they wouldn't set him on fire so that he wouldn't have to answer for his sins? What's the point of sending him then?'

Everyone else threw their heads back to laugh, but Busaina leaned across and patted my arm. 'You had better not go back,' she said, with an earnest frown. 'Stay here and become a Muslim and marry a girl from the village.'

Zaghloul was now rocking back and forth on his heels, frowning and shaking his head as though he had given up all hope of following the conversation.

'But tell me, ya doktór,' he burst out. 'Where is this country of yours? Can you go there in a day, like the people who go to Iraq and the Gulf?'

'You could,' I said, 'but my country is much further than Iraq, thousands of miles away.'

'Tell me something, ya doktór,' he said. 'If I got on to my donkey (if you'll pardon that word) and I rode and rode and rode for days, would I reach your country in the end?' He cocked his head to peer at me, as though the prospect of the journey had already filled him with alarm.

'No, ya Zaghloul,' I said, and then thinking of all the reasons why it would not be possible to travel from Egypt to India on a donkey, something caught fire in my imagination and I began to talk as I had never talked before, in Lataifa or Nashawy, of visas and quarantines, of the ribbon of war that stretched from Iraq to Afghanistan, of the heat of the Dasht-e-Kabir and the height of the Hindu Kush, of the foraging of snow leopards and the hairiness of yaks. No one listened to me more intently than Zaghloul, and for months afterwards, whenever he introduced me to anyone, he would tell them, with a dazzled, wondering lilt in his voice, of how far away my country was, of the deserts and wars and mountains that separated it from Egypt, and of the terrible fate that would befall one if one were to set out for it on a donkey.

To me there was something marvellous about the wonder that came into Zaghloul's voice when he talked of travel: for most of his neighbours travel held no surprises at all. The area around Nashawy had never been a rooted kind of place; at times it seemed to be possessed of all the busy restlessness of an airport's transit lounge. Indeed, a long history of travel was recorded in the very names of the area's 'families': they spoke of links with distant parts of the Arab world—cities in the Levant, the Sudan and the Maghreb. That legacy of transience had not ended with their ancestors either: in Zaghloul's own generation dozens of men had been 'outside', working in the shaikhdoms of the Gulf, or Libya, while many others had been to Saudi Arabia on the Hajj, or to the Yemen, as soldiers—some men had passports so thick they opened out like ink-blackened concertinas. But of course, Zaghloul and Khamees were eccentrics in most things, and in nothing so much as this, that for them the world outside was still replete with the wonders of the unknown. That was why our friendship was so quickly sealed.

9

FOR BEN YIJU the journey from Egypt towards Aden and India would have begun with a four-hundred-mile voyage down the Nile.

The trip could have taken as long as eighteen days since it meant sailing against the current; the same journey, in the other direction, could sometimes take as little as eight. The first leg of the eastward journey ended usually at one of several roadheads along the southern reaches of the Nile. In the twelfth century the largest and most frequently used of these was a place called Qus, now a modest district town a little north of Luxor. An Andalusian Arab, Ibn Jubaîr, who travelled this leg of the route some sixty years after Ben Yiju, spent a few weeks there while waiting for a camel caravan, for the next stage of his journey. He noted in his account that the town was admirably cosmopolitan, with many Yemeni, Ethiopian and Indian merchants passing through—'a station for the traveller, a gathering place for caravans, and a meeting-place for pilgrims.'

On Monday, 6 June 1183, he and his companions took their baggage to a palm-fringed spot on the outskirts of the town where other pilgrims and merchants had gathered to join a caravan. Their baggage was weighed and loaded on to camels, and the caravan set off after the evening prayers. Over the next seventeen days they progressed slowly through the desert, on a south-easterly tack, camping at night and travelling through the day. A well-marked trail of wells helped them on their way, and all along the route they passed caravans travelling in the opposite direction so that the barren and inhospitable wastes were 'animated and safe'. At one of the wells Ibn Jubair tried to count the caravans that passed by, but there were so many that he lost count. Much of their cargo consisted of goods from India; the loads of pepper, in particular, were so many 'as to seem to our fancies to equal the dust in quantity'.

It was a long, arduous journey, but there were ways of easing its rigours—for example, special litters called shaqâdîf, the best of which were made in the Yemen, large, roomy constructions, covered with leather inside, and provided with supports for a canopy. These litters were usually mounted in pairs, one balancing the other, so that two people could travel on each camel in relative comfort, shielded from the heat of the sun. Ibn Jubair remarked that 'whoso deems it lawful' could play chess with his companion while travelling, but as for himself he was on a pilgrimage, and being disinclined to spend his time on pursuits of questionable lawfulness, he spent the journey 'learning by heart the Book of Great and Glorious God.'

On 23 June, the caravan reached its destination, a Red Sea port on the coast of what is now northern Sudan. Fifty-three days had passed since Ibn Jubair had left Masr.

The port he had reached, 'Aidhâb, is one of the mysteries of

175

the medieval trade route between Egypt and India. It was a tiny outpost, a handful of reed shacks and a few newly built plaster houses, marooned in a fierce and inhospitable stretch of desert. The area around it was inhabited by a tribe which regarded the merchants and pilgrims who passed through their territory with suspicion bordering on hostility. The sentiment was amply reciprocated by travellers like Ibn Jubair: 'Their men and women go naked abroad, wearing nothing but the rag which covers their genitals, and most not even this. In a word they are a breed of no regard and it is no sin to pour maledictions upon them.' Nothing grew in the harsh desert surroundings; everything had to be imported by ship, including water, which tasted so bitter when it arrived that Ibn Jubair found it 'less agreeable than thirst'. It was in every way a hateful, inhospitable place: 'A sojourn in it is the greatest snare on the road to [Mecca]... Men tell stories of its abominations, even saying that Solomon the son of David ...took it as a prison for the 'ifrît.'

Yet this little cluster of huts wedged between desert and sea was a busy, thriving port. Ibn Jubair himself, for all his dislike of the place, was among the many travellers who marvelled at the volume of Aidhab's traffic: 'It is one of the most frequented ports of the world, because of the ships of India and the Yemen that sail to it and from it, as well as the pilgrim ships that come and go.'

For about five hundred years Aidhab functioned as one of the most important halts on the route between the Indian Ocean and the Mediterranean. Then, suddenly, in the middle of the fifteenth century its life came to an end: it simply ceased to be, as though it had been erased from the map. The precise cause of its demise is uncertain, but it is possible that the port was destroyed on the orders of the then Sultan of Egypt. In any case, all that remains of it today are a few ruins and a great quantity of buried Chinese pottery.

A curious fragment, a piece of twelfth-century paper, links Abraham Ben Yiju to this doomed port. It contains an angry accusation against him, the only one of several such letters that has survived. It was not however sent to Ben Yiju himself. Cannily, the writer addressed it to the man who was in the best position to exercise an influence on Ben Yiju—his friend and mentor, the Nagid of merchants in Aden, Madmun ibn Bundar.

Madmun appears not to have taken the complaints very seriously at first, but the old man's sense of injury was deep enough to make him extraordinarily persistent. He wrote to Madmun again and again, and finally, in about 1135, when Ben Yiju had been in India at least three years, Madmun cut off a part of one of the letters and sent it on to Ben Yiju in Mangalore, along with a letter of his own.

Madmun's letter is a long one, one of the most important he ever wrote. It is only towards the end of it that he makes a cryptic reference to the note of complaint from Aidhab. 'The carrier of this letter,' he writes, 'will deliver to you a letter from Makhlûf al-Wutûm, which he sent from 'Aidhâb, and of which I already have more than 20…He is old and has become feeble-minded. He is reaching the end of his life and doesn't know how to go on.'

By an extraordinary coincidence it so happens that the letter has survived and is currently lodged, like Madmun's own, in the library of the University of Cambridge. It is written on a fragment of paper of good, if not the best, quality, more than a foot in length, and about four inches wide. The paper is considerably weathered and discoloured; it is torn at the top, and there is a small hole in it that looks as though it has been caused by a burn. But the writing, which extends all the way down both sides, is clear and can be read without difficulty: it is written in a distinctively Yemeni hand. The complaint is worded thus:

> Shaikh Abraham ibn Yijû bespoke the porterage of 5 bahârs from me. But every time I see him he crosses words with me, so that I have become frightened of him. Each time he says to me: Go, get out, perish…a hundred times…[My master Maḍmûn] deals with me according to his noble character and custom…I spoke previously to the ship-owner about this matter, and he told me I should turn to you…[I ask] of your Exalted Presence to act in this matter, until you reclaim the [money]…Stand by me in this, and strengthen your heart, O my lord and master…and extend your help to me…

Nothing else is known either about the writer of this letter or where the two men met. In any event the old man clearly felt that Ben Yiju owed him a large sum of money for transporting goods of the weight of five bahars. As it turned out he eventually even succeeded in persuading Madmun of his claims. Madmun's dismissive comments about the old man are probably nothing more than a gesture to spare Ben Yiju's feelings: he is hardly likely to have forwarded the letter all the way to Mangalore if he thought the old man's complaints to be entirely unfounded.

There is one last piece of evidence that bears upon the incident. It occurs in a later letter from Madmun to Ben Yiju. It consists of a brief entry on the debit side of Ben Yiju's account with Madmun. It says : 'For the affair of Shaikh Makhlûf, three hundred dînârs exactly.'

Evidently, Madmun was able to persuade Ben Yiju to pay off his insistent creditor.

10

AS IT TURNED out, Busaina had a hand in the events that led to my first meeting with the Imam—or a finger, more accurately, for it was largely by accident that she happened to embroil me in a conversation with the Imam's son at the village market.

It was no accident that the Imam's son, Yasir, happened to be there that morning, for by tradition his family had always had a special role to play in the Thursday souk. The market was held in the open threshing-ground beside the tomb of his ancestor, Sidi Abu-Kanaka, in exactly the same place as the saint's annual mowlid: in a way the mowlid and the market were a twinned pair, for although one was a weekly and the other an annual, one a largely secular and the other an avowedly spiritual event, by virtue of their location they both fell within the immediate sphere of the Sidi's blessings, and his benign presence stood surety for the exchanges of the market-place just as much as it guaranteed the sanctity of the mowlid. For that reason, it fell to his descendants, as the executors of his spiritual estate, so to speak, to collect a share of the proceeds of the market for the village. The organizing committee of the village mosque had authorized Yasir to sell tickets to every trader who came to the market, so that everyone who profited from the Thursday souk would also make a small contribution to the general betterment—towards the upkeep of the Saint's tomb, the maintenance of the village mosque and perhaps even the relief effort in Afghanistan. At one time the Imam had collected the proceeds himself, but with advancing age and an increasing disinclination to spend his time on workaday business, he had delegated more and more of his responsibilities to his son, and now it was Yasir who made the rounds of the market on Thursday mornings.

Yasir was a pleasant, cheerful-looking person, and although our acquaintance had never proceeded beyond a few polite words, he always called out a friendly greeting when we passed each other in the lanes of the village. He was in his early forties or so, a tall, deep-chested man who, like his father, always wore a large, white turban—a species of headgear that was as distinctive of men who practised specialized trades as lace caps were of educated men, or woollen 'tageyyas' of the fellaheen. Like the old Imam, Yasir had learnt to cut hair and do everything else that went with the hereditary trade of his lineage, but while the Imam had never had much of a taste for barbering, Yasir, on the other hand, had taught himself to take a good deal of satisfaction in his craft. In his later years the Imam had driven away nearly all his customers; his increasing contempt for his profession eventually lent his razor so furious an edge that a time came when few men were willing to sit still with that agitated instrument hovering above their naked throats and bared armpits. But then, at just the right moment, Yasir had stepped in, and much as though he were the aberrantly conscientious son of a decaying industrial family, he had turned the business around and made it profitable.

In the years when the Imam had allowed his clients to drift away, several men had taken to barbering to make a little extra money. There were some half-dozen barbers in Nashawy now, who went from house to house, cutting their clients' hair and doling out injections for fifteen piastres a shot. But Yasir had started with an advantage over them in that he was the only man of his age in the village who could legitimately claim to have been born with the scissors in his fist. Upon coming to manhood he had made the best of his head-start by setting up a small barber-shop, the first in the entire area.

'Amm Taha had pointed it out to me once as we walked past. It was a simple enough affair; a little room with a couple of chairs, a wooden desk on which he kept his scissors and razors, a mirror hanging on one of the mud walls, and a few pictures for decoration, including a poster from a cinema theatre in Damanhour, of Raj Kapoor in *Sangam*.

There were those who had warned against the venture, 'Amm Taha said, for new-fangled ideas didn't generally go down well in Nashawy. There was the case of Shahata Bassiuni's café, for example: everyone had said it was a good idea to begin with, especially the young mowazzafeen who missed the coffee-houses they had got used to while studying in the city. So Shahata Bassiuni went ahead and set up a few iron tables and chairs, bought some narguilahs for those who wanted to smoke, and laid out a couple of chess and backgammon sets. As far as he was concerned, he was in business. But in the end all that came of it was that a few young layabouts took to spending their days hanging around his shop, ordering nothing and filching the chess pieces. A couple of times fights broke out too, and eventually, for the sake of his own peace of mind, Shahata Bassiuni had shut the place down.

'Amm Taha had laughed gleefully at the end of the story, giving me a suggestive little glance, to let it be known that if he had conspired with the dark powers that had taught Shahata Bassiuni his lesson, he would neither admit nor deny it. But even 'Amm Taha was willing to grant that Yasir had made a success of his barber-shop; so willing, in fact, that I was not surprised when Yasir began to whisper prayers to protect himself from envy upon encountering 'Amm Taha's eye as we walked past his shop.

Yasir's was now the only barber-shop in the area around Nashawy; the next one lay at a full truck-ride's distance, half-way to Damanhour. Over the past few years many men from nearby villages and hamlets had started coming to Yasir's shop—not just his father's old clients but even educated people like Ustaz Sabry, who could just as easily have gone to shops in the city. But despite his best efforts, Yasir had not yet succeeded in enticing college students like Nabeel or Isma'il into his shop; this was one instance in which they were not willing to follow Ustaz Sabry's lead. They would readily grant that Yasir was a perfectly good barber, more than adequate for the fellaheen and village folk but, as for themselves, they went on saving their coins in ones and twos, waiting for their monthly visit to the one shop in Damanhour which could be trusted to execute the styles they liked best.

Yasir's shop was in the front room of the small house that he and his family shared with his mother, the Imam's first wife. His mother had moved into the house when Yasir was just a boy, soon after the Imam took a second wife. The Imam was distraught with grief at the time, even though they'd only moved to the other side of the village square—Yasir was his only son and the thought of being separated from him was more than he could bear. In the end, taking pity on him, Yasir's mother allowed him to visit her house once a day, at the time of the midday meal. The arrangement stuck and ever afterwards Imam Ibrahim had walked over to their house once a day, after the noon-time prayers, to share his midday meal with his son and his grandchildren.

Yasir usually began work early in the morning, not long after the sunrise prayers and, depending on the flow of customers, he worked through till the midday prayers, when he went home to eat with his father. On Thursdays, however, his day was interrupted by the souk: he would close his shop for the morning, and with his ticket-book under his arm he would go out and plunge into the crowd of people swirling past his ancestor's tomb. Soon his white turban would be lost in the flood of colour that poured through the market-place on Thursdays: the flashing red of the butcher's tarpaulin, the cloth-sellers' bolts of parrot-green, scarlet and azure, the fish glittering on plastic sheets and the great black umbrella that hung slantwise over the man who repaired stoves. On other days the dun shades of the village's mud walls seemed thirsty for a touch of colour; Thursday mornings were the moments when that need was abundantly and extravagantly slaked.

The professional traders and vendors were usually the first to set up their stalls. They would begin to arrive early in the morning in their little donkey-carts, the fishmongers, the butchers, the fruit-sellers, the cloth-merchants, the watchmaker and a score of others of less determinate callings. The amateurs would follow a little later, women for the most part, swathed heavily in black, carrying wicker baskets loaded with tomatoes, carrots and cauliflowers, depending on the season. The moment they set foot in the market-place they would begin to call out greetings to their friends, to cousins from other villages and sisters who had married into faraway hamlets; they would spread out little sheets of plastic in the dust and pile them high with vegetables or fruit or whatever it was that they had gathered on their plots that morning and then, squatting behind their heaped wares, they would revive the innumerable interrupted relationships the market sustained from week to passing week.

The younger girls would do their best to be there too, slipping quietly out of their houses after their fathers and brothers had gone out to work on the fields; they would wander around the souk in groups, their hands around each others' waists, talking and laughing, and when they encountered a group of young men they would flounce past, holding their noses high, amidst explosions of bantering laughter.

On this particular Thursday the crowd had thinned by the time I went down to the market; it was already ten o'clock now, and most people had done their shopping earlier, while the vendors' wares were still fresh. Now, the time of day was beginning to show on the vegetables; the lettuce and watercress had wilted and the tomatoes were beginning to blister. Soon the prices would begin to tumble, when the women became impatient to set off for their homes in time to give their children their midday meals.

'What are you doing here?' a voice demanded as I stooped over a pile of knobbly carrots. 'Didn't I tell you to ask me if you wanted anything from the market?'

Looking up in surprise, I saw two diminutive women standing over me, their frowning faces framed by heavy black robes. The smaller of the two was Ustaz Sabry's mother, and her eyes darted from my face to the carrots in my hand as she leant over to look at me.

'What will you do with those carrots?' she shot at me, glaring, as though she had chanced upon a dark secret.

'I'll eat them,' I answered.

'How?'

'I may eat them raw,' I said, 'or I may cook them if I feel like it.'

'Cook them?' she said, frowning. 'What will you cook them on? Have you got a stove?'

'Yes.'

'What sort of stove do you have?'

'A kerosene stove.'

'A kerosene stove! And what do you cook on your kerosene stove?'

'Many things—rice for example; I cook rice.'

'How do you cook your rice?' she said, smiling sweetly. 'Do you cook it with milk?'

'Yes,' I declared recklessly, anxious to establish my self-sufficiency. 'Sometimes I cook it with milk.'

'But how?' she said. 'Don't you know you have to have an oven to cook rice with milk?'

She shook her head sadly as I floundered for an answer. 'What will you do with your stove when you go?' she demanded.

'Why don't you give it to me?' said the other woman.

'No he won't,' said Ustaz Sabry's mother, casting her a significant look. 'It's no use asking: old Taha must have his eyes on it already.'

She began to stroke my arm with a maternal weariness. 'Tell me my son,' she said, 'when are you going back home? Isn't your holiday over yet?'

Summoning my dignity as best I could, I told her I was not on holiday; what I was doing was work, serious work (secretly I had begun to have doubts on that score, but I wasn't going to admit them to her). I still had a lot of work to do, I insisted, and it would be several more months before I was finished.

'Your poor mother,' she said. 'She must miss you so much.'

Still stroking my arm she flashed her friend a smile.

'He is very fond of cows,' she told her. 'He often goes down to the fields to take pictures of cows.'

Her friend nearly dropped her cauliflowers as she spun around to look at me, her mouth falling open in amazement.

'Yes,' said Ustaz Sabry's mother, nodding knowledgeably. 'He goes down to the fields whenever he hears the cows are out. He goes with his camera and he takes pictures of cows—and sheep and goats and camels.'

'And people too,' I added reproachfully.

She pursed her lips as though that were a subject on which she would prefer to reserve judgement. Her eyes in the meanwhile had fastened upon a distant cabbage, but before shuffling off to bargain for it she gave my arm a final parting pat. 'You must come to us whenever you want anything,' she said. 'Sabry so much likes to talk to you—why, just the other day he said to me, the people of Egypt and India have been like brothers for centuries. You must consider yourself one of our family.'

I turned back to the carrots as she went off to hunt down her cabbage, but no sooner had I begun to pick through the pile than I was interrupted once again.

'Over here, ya doktór,' a voice called out to me. 'Come over here.' It was Busaina, sitting cross-legged behind her own plastic sheet, waving a bunch of green coriander.

'Here, ya doktór,' she said. 'Come and buy some things from over here so I can say khalas and make my way home.'

My very first glance at the collection of vegetables in front of her told me that they were the most miserable in the market: a few fraying heads of lettuce, some ragged bunches of watercress and a heap of soggy onions mixed with a few other scraps. Unlike the other piles in the row, hers didn't consist of remnants from the morning's sales: it was so large that it was clear that she had sold hardly anything at all.

It had happened to her before, 'Amm Taha told me later; her vegetables were often untouched at the end of the morning. It wasn't her salesmanship that was to blame—she was, if anything, a real professional, the only woman in the market who actually made a living by selling vegetables. Her problem was that her vegetables did not come directly from the fields— she gathered them in bits and pieces, going from house to house and buying leftovers. It wasn't often that she could bring vegetables from her own family's land, for there were so many people in their household that they rarely had anything to sell. When they did, it was her brothers' wives who usually brought them to the market; that was their privilege as the wives of the house, and Busaina, as a sister, had to fend for herself.

Her family had welcomed her back after she left her husband, and according to the custom of the village they had given her all the support they could, and would go on doing so, even if her husband did not meet his obligation to send money for the children. But she for her part had begun to look for work the moment she arrived, for she wasn't willing to let her children be raised as dependants in her brothers' household. She had known, when she left her husband, that she was entering upon virtual widowhood, for although she was still in her twenties it was almost a certainty that, as the mother of two young children, she would not be able to marry again. Having renounced wifely domesticity, she had become doubly ambitious for her sons and had begun to work long hours carrying her basket around all the markets in the nearby villages.

'What am I going to do, ya doktór?' she said, flicking the flies off her vegetables with a loud, full-throated laugh. 'I'll have to throw these things into the canal—maybe the catfish will want to eat them.'

Her hilarity increased when I picked out a bunch of watercress and held out a twenty-five piastre note. 'I'll save some of that for my son's wedding,' she said, and her shoulders shook as she handed me my change.

A few minutes later, when I was bargaining over a bunch of grapes with a travelling fruit-vendor from Damanhour, I was taken by surprise to hear her voice, shouting angrily over my shoulder.

'Say that again, boss,' she challenged the fruit vendor. 'I want to hear you say that again. Fifty piastres for that rotten bunch—is that what you want to charge him?'

The vendor stood his ground, but a sheepish look came over him as he began to explain that it wasn't his fault, things were getting more and more expensive day by day, and he had to come all the way from Damanhour in his donkey-cart. 'And besides,' he ended lamely, his voice rising to a high-pitched whine, 'they're good grapes, you just try them and see.'

'"Good grapes",' mimicked Busaina. 'So if they're so good why don't you keep them yourself?'

'Wallahi,' swore the vendor, pointing a finger heavenwards. 'I'm not asking too much—that's exactly what it costs.'

'I go to the market every day,' said Busaina. 'Don't try to fool me. I know, you're having fun at his expense.'

'But he's from the city,' the vendor protested. 'Why shouldn't he pay city prices—since he'll only take them back with him?'

'He lives here now,' said Busaina, 'he's not in the city any more.' She snatched the grapes out of my hand and thrust them back on to his cart. 'Thirty piastres, not a girsh more.'

'Never,' said the vendor, with an outraged yell. 'Never, never—I'd rather divorce my wife!'

'Why don't you do it?' shouted Busaina. 'You'll see: she'll clap her hands and cry "Praise God".'

That was when Yasir appeared, just as an audience was beginning to collect around us. Through his adjudication Busaina was vindicated and order restored, and after she had gone triumphantly back to her pile of vegetables, Yasir and I had a long conversation which ended with his offering to take me to meet his father, Imam Ibrahim, at any time of my choosing.

11

TAKING YASIR AT his word I stopped at his shop one morning, several days later. He was busy with a client, but he immediately laid down his razor and offered to lead me to his father's house, on the far side of the village square.

He had let Imam Ibrahim know that I wanted to talk to him, he said, so my visit would not be unexpected. He would have liked to stay himself, to listen to me talking to his father, but of course he couldn't leave his shop for long.

'But come and eat with us this afternoon,' he said with a smile, leading me across the square. 'Come after the midday prayers. My father will be there too, insha'allah, so we can sit together and discuss all kinds of matters.'

The Imam's house was directly opposite the mosque, squeezed in amongst a maze of low huts, each crowned with a billowing head of straw. Yasir rapped hard on his heavy, wooden door and after making sure that someone was stirring inside, he hurried back towards his shop, with another quick reminder about eating at his house at midday.

I listened for a while, and then knocked again, gingerly. A moment later the door swung open, and the Imam was standing directly in front of me. He was dressed in a mud-stained blue jallabeyya, with his turban knotted haphazardly around his head; a tall man, and somehow bigger than he had seemed at a distance, deep-chested and burly, with a broad pair of shoulders and long, busy fingers that kept fidgeting with his buttonholes and sleeves. There was something unkempt about his appearance, a look of mild disarray, yet his short white beard was neatly trimmed, and his brown eyes were bright with a sharp and impatient intelligence. Age had been harsh on him, but there was still an unmistakable energy about the way he carried himself; it was easy to see that he had long been accustomed to swaying audiences through the sheer force of his presence.

'Welcome,' he said, inclining his head. His tone was stiffly formal and there was no trace of a smile on his face.

Standing aside, he waved me through and once I was in he pulled the door shut behind him. I found myself in a small, dark room with mud walls that sloped and bulged like sodden riverbanks. The room was very bare; it held a bed, a couple of mats, and a few books and utensils, all uniformly covered with a thin patina of grime.

'Welcome,' said the Imam, holding his right hand stiffly and formally over his heart.

'Welcome to you,' I said in response, and then we began on the usual litany of greetings.

'How are you?'

'How are you?'

'You have brought blessings.'

'May God bless you.'

'Welcome.'

'Welcome to you.'

'You have brought light.'

'The light is yours.'

'How are you?'

'How are you?'

He prolonged the ritual well past its usual duration, and as soon as we had exhausted the list of salutations, he pulled out a kerosene stove and began to pump it in preparation for brewing tea. At length, after lighting the stove and measuring the tea and water, when conversation could no longer be forestalled, he turned to me stiffly and said: 'So you're the doktór al-Hindi?'

Yes, I said, and then I explained that I had come to talk to him about his methods of healing, and, if he wished, about his ancestors and the history of his family. He was taken by surprise; he stirred the kettle silently for a while and then began again on the ritual of greetings and responses, as though to pre-empt any further discussion.

'Welcome.'

'Welcome to you.'

'You have brought light.'

'The light is yours.'

We went slowly through the list of greetings and at the end of it, determined not to be shaken off, I repeated again that I was greatly interested in learning about folk remedies and herbal medicines, and I had heard that no one knew more about the subject than he. I had thought that he might perhaps be flattered, but in fact his response was one of utter dismay.

'Who told you those things?' he demanded to know, as though I had relayed an unfounded and slanderous accusation. 'Who was it? Tell me.'

'Why, everyone,' I stammered. 'So many people say that you know a great deal about remedies; that is why I came to you to learn about herbs and medicine.'

'Why do you want to hear about my herbs?' he retorted. 'Why don't you go back to your country and find out about your own?'

'I will,' I said. 'Soon. But right now...'

'No, no,' he said impatiently. 'Forget about all that; I'm trying to forget about it myself.'

Reaching over, he poured out two glasses of tea and, after handing me one, he emptied the other in a couple of mouthfuls. Then, falling to his knees, he reached under his bed and brought out a glistening new biscuit tin.

'Here,' he said, thrusting the open box in front of me. 'Look!'

Half a dozen phials and a hypodermic syringe lay inside the box, nestling in a bed of soiled cotton wool. His eyes shone as he gazed at them: this is what he had been learning over the last few years, he said, the art of mixing and giving injections —he had long since forgotten about herbs and poultices. There was a huge market for injections in the village; everyone wanted one, for colds and fevers and dysentery and so many other things. There was a good living in it; it was where the future lay.

He seemed to change as he talked; he did not seem like an old man any more; he was rejuvenated, renewed by the sight of his needle and syringe, lying in their box like talismans of times yet to come.

I knew then that he would never talk to me about the remedies he had learned from his father; not merely because he was suspicious of me and my motives, but also because those medicines were even more discredited in his own eyes than they were in everyone else's; the mere mention of them was as distasteful to him as talk of home to an exile. The irony was that he, who was no more than a walking fossil, a relic of the past, in the eyes of Nabeel and his generation, was actually on fire with a vision of the future.

'Let me show you,' he said, and picking up his syringe, he reached for my arm, eager to demonstrate his skills. I snatched my sleeve away, edging backwards, protesting that I wasn't ill and didn't need an injection, perhaps later, one day when I wasn't feeling well. He squinted at me, narrowing his eyes, and then, packing his syringe away, he rose to his feet.

'I have to go to the mosque right now,' he said. 'It's time for the midday prayers. Perhaps we can talk about this some other day, but right now I'm busy and I have to go.' He ushered me quickly out of the house, and then, at the steps of the mosque, he gave my hand a perfunctory shake and ran up the stairs, vanishing before I could tell him that he was not quite rid of me yet, and that we would be eating together at his son's house a short while later.

When we met again at Yasir's house, an hour or so later, he seemed more affable and not in the least bit put out to see me. We sat down around a tray in the guest-room, with Yasir's children playing around us. Afterwards, mellowed by the food, holding one child on his knee and another on his shoulder, he began to talk about his own, distant boyhood. He told stories I had often heard before from the older people in the village: of how, in the old days, everybody in the village, children included, would walk every morning to an estate that belonged to a rich Pasha from Alexandria, and of how they had worked through till sunset for a couple of piastres, sweating in the cotton fields under the gaze of armed overseers whose whips would come crashing down on their shoulders at the slightest sign of fatigue or slackness. Those were terrible times, he said, before Jamal 'Abd al-Nâṣir and the Revolution of 1952, when the Pashas, the King and their 'kindly uncles', the British army, had had their way in all things and the fellaheen had been forced to labour at their orders, like flies, working without proper recompense. Why, even in Nashawy, for a full score of years before the Revolution, the village had been ruled like a personal fiefdom by the old 'omda, a Badawy headman (the very man whose house I was living in) who had considered everything and everyone in the village his personal property. No one had been safe from his anger, and no one had dared stand up to him.

Yasir's children began to laugh; reared as they were, in free schools, with medical care abundantly and cheaply available, stories of those times had the mythical quality of a dark fairytale. But Yasir, who was a boy at the time of the revolution and was just old enough to remember those days, had turned sombre, as people of his age always did when they heard their elders talk of the past.

'Alḥamdu'lillah,' said Yasir, 'God be praised, all that was long ago, and now Egypt is a free country and we are all at liberty to do as we please.'

If I had not lived in Nashawy I might well have wondered whether he was being entirely serious in using those sonorous,

194

oddly parliamentary phrases. But now, having been there, I understood very well that he meant exactly what he said, although it was not the whole range of classical liberal freedoms that he had in mind. He was really referring to the deliverance from forced labour that the Revolution of 1952 had ensured: to the fellaheen their most cherished liberty was that which had been most cruelly abused by the regimes of the past—their right to dispose freely of their worktime. It was a simple enough dispensation, but one for which every fellah of an age to remember the past was deeply and unreservedly grateful.

In a while Yasir's mother, the Imam's first wife, brought in a tray of tea, and after the glasses had been handed around, she sat with us and began to talk about her daughter and how, after her marriage, she had settled in a village that was so far away that now she had nobody for company except Yasir's wife and children.

I was still thinking about the stories I had just heard, listening to her with only half an ear, and when there was a lull in the conversation, I turned to Yasir absent-mindedly, and said: 'So you have only one sister then? No brothers at all?'

There was a sudden hush; Yasir's mother gasped, and Yasir himself cast a stricken glance at his father, sitting across the room. After what seemed an age of silence, he cleared his throat and, holding his right hand over his heart, he said: 'It is all the same, my father has given me one sister and there is no reproach if he has not been blessed with any sons other than I.'

The tone of his voice told me that I had trespassed unwarily on some deeply personal grief, something that had perhaps haunted their family for years. Knowing that I had committed a solecism for which I could never hope to make amends, I kept my silence and willed myself to stay sitting, exactly as I was.

'And my father has married again,' said Yasir, in an unnaturally loud voice. 'And since he is still in the full fitness of age, he may beget brothers for me yet…'

Imam Ibrahim did not allow him to finish. He threw a single frowning glance in my direction and stalked out of the room.

12

USING HIS POWERS, 'Amm Taha foretold the events of Nabeel's brother's wedding ceremony the morning before it was held. There would be lots of young people around their house, he said: all the young, unmarried boys and girls of the village, singing and dancing without a care in the world. But the supper would be a small affair, attended mainly by relatives and guests from other villages. Old Idris, Nabeel's father, had invited a lot of people from Nashawy too, for their family was overjoyed about the marriage and wanted to celebrate it as best they could. But many of the people he had invited wouldn't go, out of consideration for the old man, to cut down his expenses— everyone knew their family couldn't really afford a big wedding. Their younger friends and relatives would drop by during the day and then again in the evening, mainly to dance and sing. They would be outside in the lanes; they wouldn't go into the house with the guests—the supper was only for elders and responsible, grown-up men.

'They'll start arriving in the morning, insha'allah,' said 'Amm Taha, 'and by the time you get there they'll all be sitting in the guest-room. They'll want to talk to you, for none of them will ever have met an Indian before.'

My heart sank when I realized that for me the evening would mean a prolonged incarceration in a small, crowded room. 'I would rather be outside,' I said, 'watching the singing and dancing.'

'Amm Taha laughed with a hint of malign pleasure, as though he had already glimpsed a wealth of discomfiture lying in wait for me in his divinations of the evening ahead. 'They won't let you stay outside,' he said. 'You're a kind of effendi, so they'll make you go in and sit with the elders and all the other guests.'

I tried to prove him wrong when I went to Nabeel's house that evening, and for a short while, at the beginning, I actually thought I'd succeeded.

By the time I made my way there, a large crowd had gathered in the lane outside and I merged gratefully into its fringes. There were some forty or fifty boys and girls there, packed in a tight semicircle in front of the bride and groom. The newly-married couple were sitting on raised chairs, enthroned with their backs against the house, while their friends and relatives danced in front of them. The groom, 'Ali, was dressed in a new jallabeyya of brown wool, a dark, sturdily built young man, with a generous, open smile and a cleft in his chin. His bride and cousin, Fawzia, was wearing a white gown, with a frill of lace and a little gauzy veil. Her face had been carefully and evenly painted, so that her lips, cheeks, and ears were all exactly the same shade of iridescent pink. The flatness of the paint had created a curious effect, turning her face into a pallid, spectral mask: I was astonished to discover later that she was in fact a cheerful, good-looking woman, with a warm smile and a welcoming manner.

A boy was kneeling beside her chair, pounding out a

deafening, fast-paced rhythm upon a tin wash-basin that was propped against his leg. Someone was dancing in front of him, but the crowd was so thick around them that from where I stood I could see little more than the bobbing of the dancer's head. Bracing myself against a wall, I rose on tiptoe and saw that the dancer was a boy, one of Nabeel's cousins; he was dancing bawdily, jerking his hips in front of the girls, while some of his friends reached out to slap him on his buttocks, doubling over with laughter at his coquettish twitching.

All around me voices were chanting the words of a refrain that invoked the voluptuous fruitfulness of pomegranates—'Ya rummân, ya rummân'—and with every word, dozens of hands came crashing together, clapping in unison, in perfect time with the beat. The spectators were jostling for a better view now, the boys balancing on each others' shoulders, the girls climbing upon the window-sills. The dance was approaching its climax when Nabeel appeared at my side, followed by his father. After a hurried exchanged of greetings, they put their arms through mine and led me firmly back towards their house.

The moment I stepped into their smoky, crowded guest-room, I knew that I was in for a long interrogation: I had a premonition of its coming in the strained boredom on the faces of the men who were assembled there, in the restlessness of their fidgeting fingers and their tapping toes, as they sat in silence in that hot, sweaty room, while the lanes around them resounded with the clamour of celebration. They turned to face me as I walked in, all of them together, some fifteen or twenty men, grateful for the distraction, for the temporary rupture with the uncomfortably intimate world evoked by the songs outside, the half-forgotten longings and reawakened desires, the memories of fingers locking in secret and hands brushing against hips in the surging crowd—all the village's young and unmarried, boys and girls together, thronging around the dancers, clapping and chanting, intoxicated with the heightened eroticism of the wedding night, that feverish air whose mysteries I had just begun to sense when Nabeel and his father spotted me in the crowd and led me away to face this contingent of fidgeting, middle-aged men sitting in their guest-room.

I looked around quickly, searching for a familiar face, but to my dismay I discovered that they were all outsiders, from other villages, and that I knew no one there, no one at all, since Nabeel and his father had gone back to their post outside to receive their guests. There were a few moments of silent scrutiny and then the man beside me cleared his throat and asked whether I was the doctor who had recently been posted to the government clinic.

A look of extreme suspicion came into his eyes when I explained my situation, and as soon as I had finished he began to fire off a series of questions—about how I had learnt Arabic, and who had brought me to Nashawy, and whether I had permission from the Government of Egypt. No sooner had I given him the answers than he demanded to see my identity card, and when I explained that I did not have a card, but I did indeed have an official letter from the Ministry of the Interior which I would gladly show him if he would accompany me to my room, his face took on an expression of portentous seriousness and he began to mutter direly about spies and impostors and a possible report to the Mukhabbarât, the intelligence wing of the police.

He was quickly elbowed away however, for there were many others around him who were impatient now, brimming with questions of their own. Within moments a dozen or so people had crowded around me, and I was busy affirming that yes, in my country there were indeed crops like rice and wheat, and yes, in India too, there were peasants like the fellaheen of Egypt, who lived in adobe villages and turned the earth with cattle-drawn ploughs. The questions came ever faster, even as I was speaking: 'Are most of your houses still built of mud-brick as they are here?' and 'Do your people cook on gas stoves or do they still burn straw and wood as we do?'

I grew increasingly puzzled as I tried to deal with this barrage of inquiries, first, by the part the word 'still' played in their questions, and secondly by the masks of incredulity that seemed to fall on their faces as I affirmed, over and over again, that yes, in India too people used cattle-drawn ploughs and not tractors; water-wheels and not pumps; donkey-carts, not trucks, and yes, in India too there were many, many people who were very poor, indeed there were millions whose poverty they would scarcely have been able to imagine. But to my utter bewilderment, the more I insisted, the more sceptical they seemed to become, until at last I realized, with an overwhelming sense of shock, that the simple truth was that they did not believe what I was saying.

I later came to understand that their disbelief had little or nothing to do with what I had said; rather, they had constructed a certain ladder of 'Development' in their minds, and because all their images of material life were of those who stood in the rungs above, the circumstances of those below had become more or less unimaginable. I had an inkling then of the real and desperate seriousness of their engagement with modernism, because I realized that the fellaheen saw the material circumstances of their lives in exactly the same way that a university economist would: as a situation that was shamefully anachronistic, a warp upon time; I understood that their relationships with the objects of their everyday lives was never innocent of the knowledge that there were other places, other countries which did not have mud-walled houses and cattle-drawn ploughs, so that those objects, those houses and ploughs, were insubstantial things, ghosts displaced in time, waiting to be exorcized and laid to rest. It was thus that I had my first suspicion of what it might mean to belong to an 'historical civilization', and it left me bewildered because, for my own part, it was precisely the absoluteness of time and the discreteness of epochs that I always had trouble in imagining.

The supper was a quick affair; about ten of us were taken to another room, at the back, where we helped ourselves to lamb, rice and sweetmeats standing around a table, and as soon as we had eaten, we were led out again and another lot of guests was brought in. I decided to take advantage of the bustle, and while Nabeel and his father were busy leading their guests back and forth, I slipped out of the guest-room and back into the lane.

It was long past sunset now, and the faces around the bridal couple were glowing under a dome of dust that had turned golden in the light of a single kerosene lamp. The drum-beat on the wash-basin was a measured, gentle one and when I pushed my way into the centre of the crowd I saw that the dancer was a young girl, dressed in a simple, printed cotton dress, with a long scarf tied around her waist. Both her hands were on her hips, and she was dancing with her eyes fixed on the ground in front of her, moving her hips with a slow, languid grace, backwards and forwards while the rest of her body stayed still, almost immobile, except for the quick, circular motion of her feet. Then gradually, almost imperceptibly, the tempo of the beat quickened, and somebody called out the first line of a chant, *khadnâha min wasaṭ al-dâr*, 'we took her from her father's house,' and the crowd shouted back, *wa abûha gâ'id za'alân*, 'while her father sat there bereft.' Then the single voice again, *khadnâha bi al-saif al-mâḍî*, 'we took her with a sharpened sword,' followed by the massed refrain, *wa abûha makânsh râḍî*, 'because her father wouldn't consent.'

The crowd pressed closer with the quickening of the beat, and as the voices and the clapping grew louder, the girl, in response, raised an arm and flexed it above her head in a graceful arc. Her body was turning now, rotating slowly in the same place, her hips moving faster while the crowd around her clapped and stamped, roaring their approval at the tops of their voices. Gradually, the beat grew quicker, blurring into a tattoo of drumbeats, and in response her torso froze into stillness, while her hips and her waist moved ever faster, in exact counterpoint, in a pattern of movement that became a perfect abstraction of eroticism, a figurative geometry of lovemaking, pounding back and forth at a dizzying speed until at last the final beat rang out and she escaped into the crowd, laughing.

'Where have you been all this while?' a voice cried out behind me. 'We have been looking everywhere for you—there's so much still to ask.'

Turning around I came face to face with the man who had demanded to see my identity card. Nabeel was following close behind, and between the two of them they led me back, remonstrating gently with me for having left the guest-room without warning.

There was a thick fog of smoke in the room when we went back in, for the wedding guests had lit cigarettes and shushas now and settled back on the divans to rest after the supper. Nabeel's father handed me a shusha of my own, and while I was trying to coax my coal into life, my interlocutors gathered around me again, and the questions began to flow once more.

'Tell us then,' said someone, 'in your country, amongst your people, what do you do with your dead?'

'They are burned,' I said, puffing stoically on my shusha as they recoiled in shock.

'And the ashes?' another voice asked. 'Do you at least save the ashes so that you can remember them by something?'

'No,' I said. 'No: even the ashes are scattered in the rivers.'

There was a long silence for it took a while before they could overcome their revulsion far enough to speak. 'So are they all unbelievers in your country?' someone asked at last. 'Is there no Law or Morality: can everyone do as they please—take a woman off the streets or sleep with another man's wife?'

'No,' I began, but before I could complete my answer I was cut short.

'So what about circumcision?' a voice demanded, and was followed immediately by another, even louder one, which wanted to know whether women in my country were 'purified' as they were in Egypt.

The word 'to purify' makes a verbal equation between male circumcision and clitoridectomy, being the same in both cases, but the latter is an infinitely more dangerous operation, since it requires the complete excision of the clitoris. Clitoridectomy is, in fact, hideously painful and was declared illegal after the Revolution, although it still continues to be widely practised, by Christian and Muslim fellaheen alike.

'No,' I said, 'women are not "purified" in my country.' But my questioner, convinced that I had not understood what he had asked, repeated his words again, slowly.

The faces around me grew blank with astonishment as I said 'no' once again. 'So you mean you let the clitoris just grow and grow?' a man asked, hoarse-voiced.

I began to correct him, but he was absorbed in his own amazement, and in the meanwhile someone else interrupted, with a sudden shout: 'And boys?' he cried, 'what about boys, are they not purified either?'

'And you, ya doktór?'

'What about you...?'

I looked at the eyes around me, alternately curious and horrified, and I knew that I would not be able to answer. My limbs seemed to have passed beyond my volition as I rose from the divan, knocking over my shusha. I pushed my way out, and before anyone could react, I was past the crowd, walking quickly back to my room.

I was almost there, when I heard footsteps close behind me. It was Nabeel, looking puzzled and a little out of breath.

'What happened?' he said. 'Why did you leave so suddenly?'

I kept walking for I could think of no answer.

'They were only asking questions,' he said, 'just like you do; they didn't mean any harm. Why do you let this talk of cows and burning and circumcision worry you so much? These are just customs; it's natural that people should be curious. These are not things to be upset about.'

13

I SOMETIMES WISHED I had told Nabeel a story.

When I was a child we lived in a place that was destined to fall out of the world's atlas like a page ripped in the press: it was East Pakistan, which, after its creation in 1947, survived only a bare twenty-five years before becoming a new nation, Bangladesh. No one regretted its passing; if it still possesses a life in my memory it is largely by accident, because my father happened to be seconded to the Indian diplomatic mission in Dhaka when I was about six years old.

There was an element of irony in our living in Dhaka as 'foreigners', for Dhaka was in fact our ancestral city: both my parents were from families which belonged to the middle-class Hindu community that had once flourished there. But long before the Muslim-majority state of Pakistan was created my ancestors had moved westwards, and thanks to their wanderlust we were Indians now, and Dhaka was foreign territory to us although we still spoke its dialect and still had several relatives living in the old Hindu neighbourhoods in the heart of the city.

The house we had moved into was in a new residential suburb on the outskirts of the city. The area had only recently been developed and when we moved there it still looked like a version of a planner's blueprint, with sketchy lots and lightly pencilled roads. Our house was spanking new; it was one of the first to be built in the area. It had a large garden, and high walls ran all the way around it, separating the compound from an expanse of excavated construction sites. There was only one other house nearby; the others were all at the end of the road, telescopically small, visible only with shaded eyes and a squint. To me they seemed remote enough for our house to be a desert island, with walls instead of cliffs.

At times, unaccountably, the house would fill up with strangers. The garden, usually empty except for dragonflies and grasshoppers, would be festooned with saris drying in the breeze, and there would be large groups of men, women and children sitting on the grass, with little bundles of clothes and pots and pans spread out beside them. To me, a child of seven or eight, there always seemed to be an air of something akin to light-heartedness about those people, something like relief perhaps; they would wave to me when I went down to the garden and sometimes the women would reach into their bundles and find me sweets. In the evenings, large fires would be lit in the driveway and my mother and her friends would stand behind huge cooking-pots, ladles in hand, the ends of their saris tucked in purposefully at the waist, serving out large helpings of food. We would all eat together, sitting around the garden as though it were a picnic, and afterwards we, the children, would play football and hide-and-seek. Then after a day or two everyone would be gone, the garden would be reclaimed by dragonflies and grasshoppers and peace would descend once more upon my island.

I was never surprised or put out by these visitations. To me they seemed like festive occasions, especially since we ate out of green banana leaves, just as we did at weddings and other celebrations. No one ever explained to me what those groups of people were doing in our house and I was too young to work out for myself that they were refugees, fleeing from mobs, and that they had taken shelter in our garden because ours was the only 'Hindu' house nearby that happened to have high walls.

On one particular day (a day in January 1964, I was to discover many years later) more people than ever before appeared in the garden, suddenly and without warning. They began to pour in early in the morning, in small knots, carrying bundles and other odds and ends, and as the day wore on the heavy steel gates of the house were opened time and time again to let more people in. By evening the garden was packed with people, some squatting in silent groups and others leaning against the walls, as though in wait.

Just after sunset, our cook came looking for me in the garden, and led me away, past the families that were huddled on the staircase and in the corridors, to my parents' bedroom, upstairs. By the time we got to the room, the shutters of all the windows had been closed, and my father was pacing the floor, waiting for me. He made me sit down, and then, speaking in a voice that could not be argued with, he told me to stay where I was. I was not to leave the bedroom on any account, he said, until he came back to fetch me. To make sure, he left our cook sitting by the door, with strict instructions not to leave his post.

As a rule I would have been perfectly happy to stay there with our cook, for he was a wonderful story-teller and often kept me entranced for hours on end, spinning out fables in the dialect of his region—long, epic stories about ghosts and ghouls and faraway lands where people ate children. He was from one of the maritime districts of East Pakistan and he had come to work with us because he had lost most of his family in the riots that followed Partition and now wanted to emigrate to India. He had learnt to cook on the river-steamers of his region, which were famous throughout Bengal for the quality of their cooking. After his coming the food in our house had become legendary amongst our family's friends. As for me, I regarded him with an equal mixture of fear and fascination, for although he was a small wiry man, he seemed bigger than he was because he had large, curling moustaches which made him somehow mysterious and menacing. When I tried to imagine the ghouls and spirits of his stories, they usually looked very much like him.

But today he had no stories to tell; he could hardly keep still and every so often he would go to the windows and look outside, prising the shutters open. Soon, his curiosity got the better of him and, after telling me to stay where I was, he slipped out of the room, forgetting to shut the door behind him. I waited a few minutes, and when he didn't come back, I ran out of the bedroom to a balcony which looked out over the garden and the lane.

My memories of what I saw are very vivid, but at the same time oddly out of synch, like a sloppily edited film. A large crowd is thronging around our house, a mob of hundreds of men, their faces shining red in the light of the burning torches in their hands, rags tied on sticks, whose flames seem to be swirling against our walls in waves of fire. As I watch, the flames begin to dance around the house, and while they circle the walls the people gathered inside mill around the garden, cower in huddles and cover their faces. I can see the enraged mob and the dancing flames with a vivid, burning clarity, yet all of it happens in utter silence; my memory, in an act of benign protection, has excised every single sound.

I do not know how long I stood there, but suddenly our cook rushed in and dragged me away, back to my parents' bedroom. He was shaken now, for he had seen the mob too, and he began to walk back and forth across the room, covering his face and tugging at his moustache.

In frustration at my imprisonment in that room, I began to disarrange the bedclothes. I pulled off the covers and began to tug at the sheets, when suddenly my father's pillow fell over, revealing a dark, metallic object. It was small, no larger than a toy pistol but much heavier, and I had to use both my hands to lift it. I pointed it at the wall, as I would my own water-pistol, and curling a finger around the trigger I squeezed as hard as I could. But nothing happened, there was no sound and the trigger wouldn't move. I tried once more, and again nothing happened. I turned it over in my hands, wondering what made it work, but then the door flew open and my father came into the room. He crossed the floor with a couple of strides, and snatched the revolver out of my hands. Without another word, he slipped it into his pocket and went racing out of the room.

It was then that I realized he was afraid we might be killed that night, and that he had sent me to the bedroom so I would be the last to be found if the gates gave way and the mob succeeded in breaking in.

But nothing did happen. The police arrived at just the right moment, alerted by some of my parents' Muslim friends, and drove the mob away. Next morning, when I looked out over the balcony, the garden was strewn with bricks and rubble, but the refugees who had gathered there were sitting peacefully in the sun, calm, though thoroughly subdued.

Our cook, on the other hand, was in a mood of great elation that morning, and when we went downstairs he joked cheerfully with the people in the garden, laughing, and asking how they happened to be there. Later, we squatted in a corner and he whispered in my ear, pointing at the knots of people around us, and told me their stories. I was to recognize those stories years later, when reading through a collection of old newspapers, I discovered that on the very night when I'd seen those flames dancing around the walls of our house, there had been a riot in Calcutta too, similar in every respect except that there it was Muslims who had been attacked by Hindus. But equally, in both cities—and this must be said, it must always be said, for it is the incantation that redeems our sanity—in both Dhaka and Calcutta, there were exactly mirrored stories of Hindus and Muslims coming to each others' rescue, so that many more people were saved than killed.

The stories of those riots are always the same: tales that grow out of an explosive barrier of symbols—of cities going up in flames because of a cow found dead in a temple or a pig in a mosque; of people killed for wearing a lungi or a dhoti, depending on where they find themselves; of women disembowelled for wearing veils or vermilion, of men dismembered for the state of their foreskins.

But I was never able to explain very much of this to Nabeel or anyone else in Nashawy. The fact was that despite the occasional storms and turbulence their country had seen, despite even the wars that some of them had fought in, theirs was a world that was far gentler, far less violent, very much more humane and innocent than mine.

I could not have expected them to understand an Indian's terror of symbols.

14

WITH THE COMING of winter the rains began and soon the lanes of Nashawy were knee-deep in cold, sticky mud and nobody ventured out of their houses if they could help it. Those were quiet days, for there was not much to do in the fields, apart from watering the winter wheat and taking the livestock out to pasture so that they could feed on freshly-cut maize and berseem. Cows and buffaloes would bear rich loads of milk during these months, if fed properly, so every family that could afford to had planted fodder crops, and those that hadn't were buying fresh feed from others. No house wanted to be without its supply of milk now, for in this season everyone relished the thought of sitting at home, away from the cold, and talking and resting through the day and eating plentifully of yoghurt, cheese and ghee.

One morning, eager for a break from the long days I had spent sitting in smoke-filled rooms, I took advantage of a sudden clearing of the skies and set out for the fields with a book. It took a while to get through the muddy lanes, but once the village was behind me it seemed well worth it. The countryside was extraordinarily beautiful at this time of year: whenever there was a clear day the wheat, clover and maize stood brilliantly green against deep blue skies, while Nashawy itself, with its huddle of earth houses, seemed like a low range of hills brooding in the distance.

I took a path that led past Khamees's land, for I often stopped by to talk to him or his brothers when I went out for a walk. They were usually to be found sitting in the spot where I had first met them, a shady knoll beside a canal, where two water-wheels stood side-by-side. One belonged to Khamees's family and the other to Zaghloul's, and they took it in turns to irrigate their fields at the times when water was released into the canal. They had planted trees there so that their cattle would have some shade while they were drawing the wheels, and since that was where they usually fed their livestock, they had also built a wooden water-trough, at one end of the clearing. It was a quiet, evocative spot, for there was a tranquil, sculptural quality to the great wooden disks of the water-wheels, lying half-buried in the leafy shade, with the tall maize standing like a green curtain against the background: in all of Nashawy there was no better place to read, especially when the wheels were turning and the water was gurgling slowly through the canals and into the fields.

Neither Khamees nor his brothers were anywhere in sight when I arrived there, but I knew that one of them had to be close by for their family's livestock was tethered beside the trough—a buffalo, a cow, and a nanny-goat with great, pendulous udders. They were chewing contentedly on freshly-cut fodder, a great pile of a kind of maize called diréwa, grown specially for feeding livestock. I knew that it would not be long before Khamees or one of his brothers appeared and, eager to make the best of the silence, I settled down quickly to read.

I had only turned a page or two when there was a sudden rustling nearby, followed by a burst of giggles, and then Khamees's youngest brother, 'Eid, shot out of the maize field, carrying a sheaf of plants. He took shelter behind the trough, grinning delightedly, and moments later two girls burst into the clearing, hot on his heels. They came to an abrupt halt upon seeing me, and after looking me over, murmured their greetings. I had seen them before and knew them to be the daughters of men who had fields nearby; they were dressed in flowered skirts and headscarves, and they must have been about sixteen or so. They could not have been more than a couple of years older than 'Eid, but the difference seemed much greater, because 'Eid was unusually small for his age—a telescopically foreshortened version of Khamees.

At first my presence seemed to make the girls unsure of themselves, but my role as a harmless fixture was well established now, and they soon forgot about me and began to chase 'Eid round and round the water-wheel until finally his jallabeyya snagged on a beam and threw him to the ground.

The girls fell upon him where he lay, tickling and teasing, tugging his ears and pinching his knees. 'What's the matter, ya

'Eid, have you forgotten what you said?' one of them said, laughing. The other scratched him on the back and began to cajole, plaintively: 'Come on, ya 'Eid, you promised, you said you'd do it, now we're not leaving until you do.'

'Eid, gasping for breath, was in no state to answer until he finally managed to free himself and climb back on to his feet.

'No,' he said, with a masterful shake of his head while the two girls stood towering over him. 'No—can't you see I'm busy?'

At this, one of the girls pinned his arms back while the other began to tickle him and just when it seemed as though he would fall over yet again, he cried out loudly in surrender: 'Stop, stop that, you girls—wait a minute.'

The girls released him, but stood where they were, watchful and ready to spring. 'You said you'd help,' one of them said. 'Now you've got to do it.'

'All right,' he said, shrugging, haughtily. 'All right, all right, all right.'

He straightened his jallabeyya with a flourish and walked away from them, strutting like a prizefighter. As soon as his back was turned the girls ran past the livestock, exploding into giggles, and after pausing for a moment they raced into the maize field, vanishing as suddenly and mysteriously as they had come.

After they had gone, 'Eid tossed his head with a show of disdain and seated himself beside me. 'Did you see how they were behaving?' he said, crossing his arms across his chest. 'Did you see? Do you see how they've filled out; how they move their bodies when they walk? I'll tell you: what those two want is to get married. That's what they want, you understand—especially the big one, the one in the green dress—she wants to get married, she really wants it.'

Picking up a maize-leaf he began to chew on the stem, gazing narrow-eyed into the distance. 'Actually it's me they want to marry,' he said, after a long pause. 'Especially the big one, the one in the green dress; she really wants me—it's obvious. But I've made up my mind; I won't have her; she's too big for me. Why, if she rolled on me, I'd be finished. There'd be nothing left.'

There was a rustling sound in the maize again, and he jumped quickly to his feet. 'There, you see,' he said, with an air of world-weariness. 'You see—they just can't leave me alone. They're back again.'

When the two girls ran back into the clearing, a moment later, he cupped his hands around his mouth and announced: 'I've told him; I've told him how much you want to marry me.'

The girls stood transfixed for a moment, and then, with loud hoots of laughter they began to chase him around the trough again, tickling and slapping him playfully.

'Of course we'll marry you, ya 'Eid...'

'We'll both marry you...'

'As soon as you grow a little...'

'When you're a man...'

In a matter of seconds he was squealing and shouting, crying out to them to stop, but the chase went on until he had been reduced again to a squirming heap in the dust. Then, leaving him lying where he was, the girls vanished once again, suddenly and mysteriously.

'It's sad,' said 'Eid, once he had picked himself up again. 'It's sad how desperately they want to marry me. I want to get married too—it's about time now—but I don't want to marry them. They're no good; they're not pretty enough for me.'

'Who do you want to marry then?' I asked.

'I know the girl I would like to marry,' he said. 'She walks past here sometimes, on her way to her father's fields. I've said a few words to her, and from the way she smiles I know she would agree. But her parents wouldn't let her, so it's no use thinking of it.'

'Why not?' I said.

'Because she's in school, studying,' he said. 'And her people are well-off, while in our family we don't have very much and often things are very hard in our house. And apart from that, her father is a Badawy, and he probably wouldn't let her marry into our family. There's nothing I can do—in the end I'll probably have to marry one of my cousins, like my parents want.'

Then, squatting beside me, he explained that he hadn't told anyone in his family about the girl he wanted to marry: it was no use hoping that anything would come of it, because there had been trouble between the Jammal and the Badawy for a long time, since long before he was born. It went back to the days of a Badawy 'omda, one Ahmed Effendi, who had owned a lot of land around the village.

'Look over there,' said 'Eid, pointing with a stick. 'Do you see the land in front of us, from there to there, almost four feddans? That was all his land, and it still belongs to his son, who lives in Cairo. Khamees and I and my brothers, we work on it as sharecroppers—it doesn't belong to us. We only get a small part of the crop, he takes all the rest. We have some land of our own, which we got during the Reforms, but that's far away and it's not half as big as this.'

Ahmed Effendi, the old 'omda, had always treated the Jammal as though they were his slaves, said 'Eid. He had made them work without payment, in his house and on the fields, and as a result, once elections were started, the Jammal voted against him. There had been fights between the two clans afterwards and for a while it was just like a feud. Ahmed Effendi would gladly have evicted his Jammal tenants, but by then the law had changed and there was nothing he could do.

Towards the end of his story, Zaghloul the weaver appeared, leading a cow and a buffalo. He listened to 'Eid while giving his livestock their feed and then he seated himself beside us. Soon, in keeping with his habit, he piled a heap of freshly-shorn wool in front of him and began to spin yarn with a hand-held spindle.

When 'Eid had finished, Zaghloul broke in to say that he remembered Ahmed Effendi well; like every other man in the village he had often had to work on his fields. At the time of the harvest Ahmed Effendi had gone around the village, from door to door, with his watchmen in tow, and he'd left a sickle on the doorpost of every house which had an able-bodied man in it. Those who didn't turn out on his fields next morning ran the risk of being being beaten by his watchmen, with whips. Ahmed Effendi had been able to get away with anything he liked because he had had friends amongst the Pashas, powerful people who had connections with the British.

'And is it true, ya Zaghloul,' asked 'Eid, agog with curiosity, 'that whenever he saw a good-looking girl he would ask for her to be sent to him?'

'Yes,' said Zaghloul. 'When his eyes fell on a girl he would say to her relatives, "I want that woman in my house for the night," and sure enough, she would go, for there was nothing anyone could do. He had only to raise his voice and you would see twenty men throwing themselves in front of him, crying "at your service Effendi".'

'And what about you, ya Zaghloul?' said 'Eid, with a grin. 'Didn't you throw yourself flat in front of him so he could use you as he liked?'

Zaghloul smiled at him good-naturedly, his eyes vanishing into the folds of his prematurely wizened face. Then he turned to look at me, twirling his spindle in his hands.

'So what has our boy 'Eid been talking about?' he said. 'Has he been talking about the girl he's staring at nowadays?'

'Eid's eyes widened in shock. 'How did you know, ya Zaghloul?' he cried in astonishment. 'How did you know about that?'

'I know about these things,' said Zaghloul.

'But how could you know? Who was it who told you?'

'I've seen the way you stare at her,' said Zaghloul. 'No one had to tell me; it's clear enough, especially since you're at that age. If you're not careful, you'll find yourself saying "I'm in love," like a student or a college-boy. Watch what you're doing and don't forget you're a fellah: "love" is not for people like us.'

'Eid didn't answer; at the mention of the word 'love' he flushed red and darted off to replenish the stock of fodder that lay in front of his livestock. Busying himself with armloads of maize plants, he pretended not to hear what Zaghloul had said.

'What do you mean?' I asked Zaghloul. 'Why can't a fellah fall in love?'

'For us it only leads to trouble,' said Zaghloul. 'Love is for students and mowazzafeen and city people; they think about it all the time, just like they think of football. For us it's different; it's better not to think of it.'

'Eid was back now, his eyes wide with curiosity. 'How do you know, ya Zaghloul?' he said. 'Did it ever happen to you?'

'Something happened to me once,' Zaghloul said quietly,

fixing his gaze upon his twirling spindle. 'It began when I was a boy, about your age, fourteen or fifteen, and it went on for five whole years. She was a girl from the city, the daughter of a relative of ours who had a job in Alexandria. Her father would come down with all of them once every summer to visit his family in Nashawy. I had known her all my life, but that summer when we were fourteen, I saw her when she came to the village, and suddenly everything changed. We would talk sometimes, for we were relatives after all, and I would try to tell her things, but I could never find the words. You know, she and her family used to sleep in a house that was in the centre of the village, a long way from where we lived. But when she was in Nashawy, I was never able to sleep. I would steal out late at night and go silently across the village, and when I reached their house, I would put my ear to the crack in her door and listen to her breathing in her sleep; it was like my life was in her breath. And that was how I lived for five years, waiting for her to come to the village for a few days in the summer so that I could listen to the sound of her breath at night, kneeling by her door. And all the while my family kept trying to get me married, and every time I'd say no, no, not yet, and in my heart I would think of her and the day when she would come back again to Nashawy.'

'Eid cocked his head to look into Zaghloul's lowered face. 'So what happened, ya Zaghloul?' he said. 'Why didn't you try to marry her?'

'My father wouldn't hear of it,' said Zaghloul. 'I told him once, to his face I told him—I want to marry that girl and none other. But he said to me: "Get that idea out of your head; you'll never marry her. We want a girl for you who can work in the fields and milk the cattle and sweep away the cow dung. She's a city girl, that one, she doesn't know how we live." I wanted to tell him that I loved her, but I knew he would slap me if I did, so I kept my peace, and later that year he arranged for me to marry a girl from the village, one of his cousin's daughters, and that was that, khalas.'

There was a tight, lopsided little smile on his shrunken face as he looked up and nodded at 'Eid.

'But I was lucky,' he said. 'At least I didn't lose my reason like some men do. If you go through Nashawy and the next village and the village after that and you ask everyone how many mad people there are and what it was that drove them mad, you'll see that there was one reason and one alone: it was love. That's what happens, ya 'Eid, that's why you have to be careful and mind what you're doing.'

'Eid rubbed his chin, frowning reflectively. 'But in the city,' he said, 'they all fall in love—in Cairo and Alexandria and Damanhour. You can see it on TV.'

'Things are different there,' said Zaghloul. 'All kinds of things happen in cities: why, do you know they have places there where women will let their bodies be used, for just a few pounds?'

He nodded sagely as 'Eid stared at him, in speechless astonishment. 'Yes,' he said, warming to his theme, 'that's right, there are houses in Alexandria where men pay five hundred pounds to spend a night with a woman—five hundred pounds, for one night!'

He paused to reflect, chewing on his lip, remembering perhaps that the sum he had just quoted was equal to the figure his harvest of cotton earned him in a year. 'Of course,' he added quickly, 'that includes food and other things—turkey, whiskey and things like that.'

'Eid, goggle-eyed in wonder, cried: 'And do they all cost that much—five hundred pounds?'

'No,' said Zaghloul, 'not all—some are as cheap as five pounds and some take just a pound and a half. But that's just for a couple of hours, or even less.'

'Where, ya Zaghloul?' said 'Eid, prodding him eagerly with his elbow. 'Where can one find these houses? Tell me.'

Zaghloul shook his head vaguely. 'My cousin worked in Alexandria,' he said, 'for a few months in the winter, and the men he worked with used to go to those places. He told me about them, but he never went himself—one can't really.'

'But where are those places, ya Zaghloul?' cried 'Eid. 'Tell me—on which street? I'd like to go and see one of those places.'

Zaghloul smiled at him gently. 'They'd make a fool of you, ya 'Eid,' he said. 'They'd feel your face, like this, and ask for five pounds. They'd stroke your chest, like this, and ask for ten. They'd reach under your jallabeyya, like this, and ask for fifty, and before they were done, you'd lose everything your father possesses.'

'We'll see about that,' said 'Eid, 'just tell me where those places are.'

They began to laugh, but soon their laughter died away, and they fell silent, squatting on their heels—tiny 'Eid, too small for his age, and bandy-legged, prematurely wizened Zaghloul—they smiled and rubbed their groins and scratched their thighs as they sat there, day-dreaming about forbidden pleasures in faraway cities.

Presently 'Eid said: 'Why do they do it, those girls? Do their families make them?'

'Yes,' said Zaghloul. 'That's what happens; their families put them up to it. They take thirty pounds a month from the owner of the house and that's that, khalas—they leave their daughters there and the owners are free to do what they like with them.'

'Eid grinned and shot him a glance. 'And how much do you charge for your wife, ya Zaghloul?' he said. 'Fifteen pounds? I'll pay it, will you let me?'

'It'll cost more than you can afford,' Zaghloul said, smiling at him, unmoved.

Then, turning to me, he added: 'Don't take offence: we fellaheen, we love to joke; "our blood is light," as people say.'

'Oh the black day!' cried 'Eid, jumping to his feet, as though he could not contain himself any longer. 'I'd really like to go to one of those places.'

He ran across to the trough, where the livestock were feeding, and put his arm around his nanny-goat. 'Look how I love her,' he shouted, planting a kiss on her face.

Later, on the way back to Nashawy, I came across Khamees, riding out to the fields on his donkey. He climbed off when he saw me, and after we had exchanged greetings and talked for a while, he asked casually: 'Did you see 'Eid on your way? Was he feeding the livestock, out by the water-wheel?'

'Yes,' I said, 'that's just where I'm coming from.'

'Was there anyone else there?' he asked, watching me closely.

'There was Zaghloul,' I said. 'We were all sitting there talking.'

'No one else?'

'A couple of girls dropped by,' I said, 'just for a minute or two.'

Khamees struck his forehead with a loud, despairing cry: 'Oh the Protector, oh the Lord! That dog 'Eid is going to bring my family to ruin. What were those girls doing? Go on, tell me.'

'Nothing,' I stammered, taken aback; it seemed wholly out of character for Khamees to be overcome by moral indignation. 'Nothing at all, they just came by for a minute…'

'Tell me something,' he said, shaking my arm. 'Tell me, try to remember—were they, by any chance, carrying away our fodder?'

It dawned on me that Khamees was right: the girls had carried away armloads of fodder every time they ran out of the clearing. The reason for their cultivation of 'Eid's friendship was suddenly clear to me.

Khamees read the answer on my face, and at once, hitching up his jallabeyya, he jumped on his donkey.

'That 'Eid is going to ruin our whole family,' he cried. 'Those girls tickle him and tease him and he ends up giving away all our fodder—the fool, he thinks they like him.'

He struck his donkey on the rump, and as it trotted away he turned around in his seat to call out to me. 'What that boy needs is a wife,' he shouted; 'we'll get him married to one of our cousins—that'll help him understand life and its difficulties.'

15

'A COUPLE OF years after you left Egypt,' said Shaikh Musa, 'I heard some news about your friend Khamees and his family, and I thought—this is something the doktór would like to know.'

He paused to prod the embers of his shusha, and settled back in his divan.

A friend of his, he said, had stopped by in Lataifa one day, on his way to Damanhour. His friend was from Nashawy, and while they were talking about the crops and the fields, who had planted what and whose cotton was doing well, his friend had told him an amazing tale—a story about a recent event in his village.

There was a parcel of land in one of the village's fields that was owned by one of the sons of the old 'omda, Ahmed Badawy Effendi, a highly-placed civil servant who lived in Cairo. It was one of the few pieces of land that had been left to the family after the Land Reforms; a tiny fraction of what they had once owned, admittedly, but still a very large area in relation to the landholdings of the ordinary fellaheen.

One morning, quite unexpectedly the civil servant's car was seen driving into Nashawy. Everyone was taken by surprise, because he very rarely came to visit the village: he was afraid of getting mud on his clothes, or so people said. But there was yet another surprise in store for the people of the village. When the car stopped and the 'omda's son stepped out, the people who were watching assumed that he would go straight to his father's old house. But no: to their utter astonishment, he headed in the opposite direction—towards a tumbledown mud hut that belonged to the fellah family that had share-cropped his land for the last so many years.

Those members of the family who were at home were astonished when they saw the 'omda's son knocking on their door: it was years since they had last seen him, for he always sent one of his minions to pick up his share at harvest-time. But they threw their doors open and welcomed him in, and it was a good hour or so before he emerged again.

No one knew exactly what the 'omda's son had said while he was in that house, but everyone agreed later that it was something like this: 'I am soon going to buy a new apartment in Cairo, insha'allah (or perhaps a car), and for that reason I need to raise a large sum of money quickly. Pray to the Prophet! I have given the matter much thought, and after speaking to my children I have decided to sell my land. So, as law and custom demands, I have come to your family first, because you have worked on that land for so long, to ask whether you can raise the money to buy it. If you can, you will be welcome to it—everything good is the work of God—but if you cannot, I must tell you that I shall put my land on the market, with God's permission.'

Now, it so happened that this family was both very poor and very large, and between all of them together they probably had no more than a couple of pounds in savings. But it was many, many years since such good land had been put up for sale in Nashawy, and they knew that they would never again be presented with such an opportunity. So they took their chance and said to him: 'Give us a month, ya Effendi, to see if we can raise the money, insha'allah, and if at the end of that time we do not succeed, you will be free to dispose of the land as you please, and we shall not stand in your way, by God.'

The moment the Effendi left, the brothers began to run around the village—even the youngest one, who was just a boy. They went from house to house, from distant cousins to far relatives, borrowing a few pounds here and a few piastres there. They sold their cattle, they sold parts of the house they lived in, they even sold their ploughshares, but on the day the Effendi came back they had the money ready and were able to take possession of the land. They were heavily in debt by this time, but still, from that day onwards they could be counted amongst the largest landowners in the village. They had realized the secret dream that every fellah inherits from his ancestors: they had succeeded in expanding their family's landholdings.

'That was six years ago,' said Shaikh Musa, 'just a couple of years after you left. It took only three or four harvests for your friend Khamees and his family to pay off their debts, and now they're so well-to-do they've built a new brick-and-cement house on their own land, outside the village.'

'What about Busaina?' I asked. 'What's become of her?'

Her life had changed too, Shaikh Musa said, but not quite so dramatically as her brothers'. She had decided to set up on her own, with her two sons, when her brothers moved to their new house. She had managed to save a fair bit of money in the meanwhile, because she had become a seasoned businesswoman, trading regularly in the market in Damanhour. With her savings she had bought a little two-room house in the centre of Nashawy, right beside the square. People said she made her two sons study late into the night, and they were both doing quite exceptionally well at school, although they were still very young.

'What about her husband?' I asked. 'The boys' father?'

Shaikh Musa laughed. 'He went away to Iraq,' he said. 'And no one's heard from him for years.'

Shaikh Musa recalled the story's ending later in the night, while talking of something else.

'I forgot to tell you,' he said cutting himself short. 'There's another piece of news about Khamees and his family: I heard it from Jabir.'

A few months ago, Shaikh Musa said, a large truck had driven past Lataifa, piled high with suitcases and cardboard boxes, of the kind that were used for television sets and such like. It took just one glance at that truck to see that somebody had returned from Iraq, or the Gulf, or some place like that, having made a lot of money. Jabir had seen the truck go past from a window in his house, and had gone off at once to make inquiries about who it was that had driven past in such state. He'd soon discovered that the returning hero was none other than Khamees's brother, 'Eid.

'Do you remember him?' said Shaikh Musa. 'You mentioned him sometimes, when you were living in Nashawy. He was a little boy then, of course, but now he's taller than any of his brothers.'

'Eid had been away in Saudi Arabia for some three or four years, and had done very well for himself, working in construction. He had come home with a colour television set, a fridge, a washing-machine, and many other things of that kind. On top of that, he had also saved a lot of money and was soon going to buy his family a new tractor.

'And not long ago,' said Shaikh Musa, 'we heard that 'Eid is soon to be married. He is going to pay a large sum of money as a marriage-payment, and he's going to have an educated wife. Can you imagine! And him a Jammal, and an unlettered fellah!'

Shaikh Musa shook his head in wonderment.

'He's marrying a Badawy girl,' he said. 'They say it's a real love-match, and the two of them have been waiting for years.'

16

THERE IS GOOD reason to believe that soon after moving—or being forced to move—to Mangalore Ben Yiju contracted a liaison which eventually led to his marriage. The evidence lies in the earliest documents that can be dated to Ben Yiju's stay in India: two unusual and intriguing fragments which can fortunately be dated without fear of inaccuracy.

The first actually specifies both the day and the place where it was drawn up, for it happens to be a legally attested deed. The second, which is closely linked to the first, is a rough draft of another legal document, written in Ben Yiju's handwriting, on one of those scraps of paper which he used for making notes.

Of the two, the first is the more important, but it has long been relatively inaccessible being lodged in a collection in the erstwhile Leningrad. Fortunately, there can be no doubt about the nature of its contents, for Goitein chanced upon it during his researches there and referred to it frequently in his later writings: it is a deed of manumission which records that on 17 October 1132, in Mangalore, Ben Yiju publicly granted freedom to a slave girl by the name of Ashu. The second fragment, which is now in the Taylor-Schechter Collection in Cambridge, is a supporting document: the draft of a deposition backing up the deed of manumission.

The date on the deed of manumission establishes it as the earliest document that can be reliably dated to the period of Ben Yiju's stay in India. It is uncertain how long he had been in Mangalore at the time of its writing; it must, at any rate, have been long enough for him to acquire slaves and set up a household. This could mean that Ben Yiju had left Aden and moved to India as early as 1130 or 1131; in any event the date must have preceded Ashu's manumission by a good few years.

It is probably not a coincidence that the first dated document from Ben Yiju's stay in India has to do with the woman who probably bore his children. Indeed, he may well have expected to contract a marital or sexual liaison soon after his arrival, for amongst the people of the Middle East, India then bore a reputation as a place notable for the ease of its sexual relations. Had Ben Yiju read the works of his contemporary, the Sharif al-Idrisi, for example, he would have discovered that in India 'concubinage is permitted between everyone, so long as it is not with married women.' A couple of centuries before Ben Yiju's lifetime, a chronicler in the Persian Gulf port of Siraf had professed shock upon hearing of the duties of Indian temple dancers. 'Let us thank God,' he had written, in pious disapproval, 'for the Qur'ân which he has chosen for us and with which he has preserved us from the sins of the infidels.' Some travellers, such as the Italian Nicoló Conti, who visited India in the fifteenth century, were struck by the number of courtesans. 'Public women are everywhere to be had,' he wrote, 'residing in particular houses of their own in all parts of the cities, who attract the men by sweet perfumes and ointments, by their blandishments, beauty and youth; for the Indians are much addicted to licentiousness.' A contemporary of his, a Persian ambassador called 'Abd al-Razzâq al-Samarqandî who travelled to the kingdom of Vijaynagar in 1442, appears to have acquired a much closer acquaintance with the customs of courtesans. Soon after his arrival in the capital, he was taken by his hosts to visit the area in which the women lived, and discovered that: 'Immediately after midday prayer they place before the doors of the chambers…thrones and chairs, on which the courtesans seat themselves…Each one of them has by her two young slaves, who give the signal of pleasure, and have the charge of attending to everything which can contribute to amusement. Any man may enter into this locality, and select any girl that pleases him, and take his pleasure with her.'

It could well be that Ben Yiju encountered Ashu on just such a visit, soon after moving to Mangalore.

The fact that Ben Yiju manumitted Ashu a short while after having acquired her custody indicates that his intentions towards her were anything but casual. Since he also appears to have celebrated her manumission with some fanfare, it is possible that he made use of the occasion to issue public notice of a wedding, or betrothal.

At any rate, before three years were over Ben Yiju was the father of a young son. The proof of this lies in a letter written to him by his mentor, Madmun, in 1135: 'I have also sent a piece of coral for your son Surûr,' wrote Madmun, listing the presents he had sent for Ben Yiju in Mangalore, along with a shipment of cargo.

There is no particular reason to connect Ashu's manumission with Ben Yiju's fatherhood yet it is difficult not to. The connection seems so obvious that Goitein, for one, was persuaded that Ben Yiju had married Ashu, and that Ashu was 'probably beautiful'.

About Ashu's origins there is only a single clue. In a set of accounts scribbled on the back of one of Madmun's letters, Ben Yiju refers to a sum of money that he owed to his 'brother-in-law', who bears the name 'Nâîr'. The lucky accident of that reference provides Ashu with a semblance of a social identity: it links her to the matrilineal community of Nairs, who still form a substantial section of the population of the southern part of the Malabar coast.

Ashu is not mentioned anywhere else in the entire corpus of Ben Yiju's documents, although her children figure in it frequently. Ben Yiju did not once refer to her in his letters or jottings, and his correspondents in Aden, who were always careful to send their good wishes to his children, never mentioned her either, not even by means of the euphemisms

---

customary in their time, and nor did they send her their greetings. This haunting effacement may in fact be proof that Ben Yiju did indeed marry Ashu, for only a marriage of that kind—with a slave girl, born outside the community of his faith—could have earned so pointed a silence on the part of his friends. Ben Yiju probably converted Ashu to Judaism before their marriage, but the conversion may have signified very little, either to Ashu or to Ben Yiju's friends and relatives. It is also possible that their liaison was modelled upon the institution of 'temporary marriage', a kind of marital union that was widely practised by expatriate Iranian traders.

There were certain marital choices open to Ben Yiju in India that may well have been more acceptable to his friends. For instance, he could well have married into the ancient sect of the Jews of Malabar—a community so well-known for its strictness in religious matters, that it had even found favour with Ben Yiju's near contemporary, the strict and learned Spanish Rabbi, Benjamin of Tudela, who wrote after his visit to the Malabar: 'And throughout the [land] including all the towns there, live several thousand Israelites. The inhabitants are all black, and the Jews are also. The latter are good and benevolent. They know the law of Moses and the prophets, and to a small extent the Talmud and the Halacha.'

Yet, since Ben Yiju chose, despite the obvious alternative, to marry a woman born outside his faith, it can only have been because of another overriding and more important consideration.

If I hesitate to call it love it is only because the documents offer no certain proof.

17

EVEN THOUGH KHAMEES never mentioned the subject himself, everyone around him seemed to know that he was haunted by his childlessness.

Once, on a cold winter's day, I dropped in to see him and found him sitting with his father in the guest-room of their house—one of the shabbiest and most derelict in the village. His father was sitting in a corner, huddled in a blanket, hugging his knees and shivering whenever a draught whistled in through the crumbling walls. He smiled when I stepped in, and motioned to me to sit beside him—a thin, frail old man with absent, wandering eyes. He had worked as a labourer in Alexandria during the Second World War, and he had met many Indians among the soldiers who had passed through the city at the start of the North African campaign. They had made a deep impression on his memory and at our first meeting he had greeted me as though he was resuming an interrupted friendship.

Now, after I had seated myself beside him, he leant towards me and ran his hands over my wool sweater, examining it closely, rubbing the material carefully between finger and thumb.

'That's the right thing to wear in winter,' he said. 'It must be really warm.'

'Not as warm as your blanket,' interjected Khamees.

His father pretended not to hear. 'I've heard you can get sweaters like that in Damanhour,' he said to me.

'You can get anything if you have the money,' said Khamees. 'It's getting the money that's the problem.'

Paying him no attention, his father patted my arm. 'I remember the Indian soldiers,' he said. 'They were so tall and dark that many of us Egyptians were afraid of them. But if you talked to them they were the most generous of all the soldiers; if you asked for a cigarette they gave you a whole packet.'

'That was then,' Khamees said, grinning at me. 'Now things have changed.'

'Do you see what my children are like?' his father said to me. 'They won't even get me a sweater from Damanhour so I can think of the winter without fear.'

At that Khamees rose abruptly to his feet and walked out of the room. His father watched him go with an unblinking stare.

'What am I to do with my children?' he muttered, under his breath. 'Look at them; look at Busaina, trying to rear her two sons on her own; look at Khamees, you can't talk to him any more, can't say a thing, neither me, nor his brothers, nor his wife. And every year he gets worse.'

He pulled his blanket over his ears, shivering spasmodically. 'Perhaps I'm the one who's to blame,' he said. 'I married him off early and I told him we wanted to see his children before we died. But that didn't work, so he married again. Now the one thought in his head is children—that's all he thinks about, nothing else.'

A few months later, in the spring, after nearly a year had passed and the time for my departure from Egypt was not far distant, I was walking back from the fields with Khamees and 'Eid one evening, when we spotted Imam Ibrahim sitting on the steps of the mosque.

Khamees stopped short, and with an uncharacteristic urgency in his voice he said: 'Listen, you know Imam Ibrahim, don't you? I've seen you greeting him.'

I made a noncommittal answer, although the truth was that ever after that ill-fated meal at Yasir's house the Imam had scarcely deigned to acknowledge my greetings when we passed each other in the village's narrow lanes.

'My wife's ill,' said Khamees. 'I want the Imam to come to my house and give her an injection.'

His answer surprised me, and I quickly repeated what Nabeel and his friends had said about the Imam's blunt needles, and told him that if his wife needed an injection there were many other people in the village who could do the job much better. But Khamees was insistent: it was not just the injection, he said—he had heard that Imam Ibrahim knew a lot about remedies and medicines and things like that, and people had told him that maybe he would be able to do something for him and his wife.

I understood then what sort of medicine he was hoping the Imam would give him.

'Khamees, he can't help in matters like that,' I said, 'and anyway he's stopped doing remedies now. He only does those injections.'

But Khamees had grown impatient by this time. 'Go and ask him,' he said, 'he won't come if I ask; he doesn't like us.'

'He doesn't like me either,' I said.

'That doesn't matter,' said Khamees. 'He'll come if you ask him—he knows you're a foreigner. He'll listen to you.'

It was clear that he had made up his mind, so I left him waiting at the edge of the square, and went across, towards the mosque. I could tell that the Imam had seen me—and Khamees—from a long way off, but he betrayed no sign of recognition and carefully kept his eyes from straying in my direction. Instead, he pretended to be deep in conversation with a man who was sitting beside him, an elderly shopkeeper with whom I had a slight acquaintance.

I was still a few steps away from them when I said 'good evening' to the Imam, pointedly, so he could no longer ignore me. He paused to acknowledge the greeting, but his response was short and curt, and he turned back at once to resume his conversation.

The old shopkeeper was taken aback at the Imam's manner; he was a pleasant man, and had often exchanged cordial salutes with me in the lanes of the village.

'Please sit down,' he said to me, in embarrassment. 'Do sit. Shall we get you a chair?'

Without waiting for an answer, he glanced at the Imam, frowning in puzzlement. 'You know the Indian doktór, don't you?' he said. 'He's come all the way from India to be a student at the University of Alexandria.'

'I know him,' said the Imam. 'He came around to ask me questions. But as for this student business, I don't know. What's he going to study? He doesn't even write in Arabic.'

'That's true,' said the shopkeeper judiciously, 'but after all, he writes his own languages and he knows English.'

'Oh those,' said the Imam scornfully. 'What's the use of those languages? They're the easiest languages in the world. Anyone can write those.'

He turned to face me now, and I saw that his mouth was twitching with anger and his eyes were shining with a startling brightness.

'Tell me,' he said, 'why do you worship cows?'

Taken by surprise I began to stammer, and he cut me short by turning his shoulder on me.

'That's what they do in his country,' he said to the old shopkeeper. 'Did you know? They worship cows.'

He shot me a glance from the corner of his eyes. 'And shall I tell you what else they do?' he said. He let the question hang in the air for a moment, and then announced, in a dramatic hiss: 'They burn their dead.'

The shopkeeper recoiled as though he had been slapped, and his hands flew to his mouth. 'Ya Allah!' he muttered.

'That's what they do,' said the Imam. 'They burn their dead.'

Then suddenly he spun around to face me and cried: 'Why do you allow it? Can't you see that it's a primitive and backward custom? Are you savages that you permit something like that? Look at you: you've had some education; you should know better. How will your country ever progress if you carry on doing these things? You've even been to Europe; you've seen how advanced they are. Now tell me: have you ever seen them burning their dead?'

A small crowd had gathered around us now, drawn by the Imam's voice, and under the pressure of their collective gaze, I found myself becoming increasingly tongue-tied.

'Yes, they do burn their dead in Europe,' I managed to say, my voice rising despite my efforts to control it. 'Yes, they have special electric furnaces meant just for that.'

The Imam turned away and laughed scornfully. 'He's lying,' he said to the crowd. 'They don't burn their dead in the West. They're not an ignorant people. They're advanced, they're educated, they have science, they have guns and tanks and bombs.'

Suddenly something seemed to boil over in my head, dilemmas and arguments I could no longer contain within myself.

'We have them too!' I shouted back at him. 'In my country we have all those things too; we have guns and tanks and bombs. And they're better than anything you've got in Egypt—

we're a long way ahead of you.'

'I tell you, he's lying,' cried the Imam, his voice rising in fury. 'Our guns and bombs are much better than theirs. Ours are second only to the West's.'

'It's you who's lying,' I said. 'You know nothing about this. Ours are much better. Why, in my country we've even had a nuclear explosion. You won't be able to match that even in a hundred years.'

It was about then, I think, that Khamees appeared at my side and led me away, or else we would probably have stood there a good while longer, the Imam and I: delegates from two superseded civilizations, vying with each other to establish a prior claim to the technology of modern violence.

At that moment, despite the vast gap that lay between us, we understood each other perfectly. We were both travelling, he and I: we were travelling in the West. The only difference was that I had actually been there, in person: I could have told him a great deal about it, seen at first hand, its libraries, its museums, its theatres, but it wouldn't have mattered. We would have known, both of us, that all that was mere fluff: in the end, for millions and millions of people on the landmasses around us, the West meant only this—science and tanks and guns and bombs.

I was crushed, as I walked away; it seemed to me that the Imam and I had participated in our own final defeat, in the dissolution of the centuries of dialogue that had linked us: we had demonstrated the irreversible triumph of the language that has usurped all the others in which people once discussed their differences. We had acknowledged that it was no longer possible to speak, as Ben Yiju or his Slave, or any one of the thousands of travellers who had crossed the Indian Ocean in the Middle

Ages might have done: of things that were right, or good, or willed by God; it would have been merely absurd for either of us to use those words, for they belonged to a dismantled rung on the ascending ladder of Development. Instead, to make ourselves understood, we had both resorted, I, a student of the 'humane' sciences, and he, an old-fashioned village Imam, to the very terms that world leaders and statesmen use at great, global conferences, the universal, irresistible metaphysic of modern meaning; he had said to me, in effect: 'You ought not to do what you do, because otherwise you will not have guns and tanks and bombs.' It was the only language we had been able to discover in common.

For a while, after Khamees and 'Eid had led me back to their house, I could not bring myself to speak; I felt myself a conspirator in the betrayal of the history that had led me to Nashawy; a witness to the extermination of a world of accommodations that I had believed to be still alive, and, in some tiny measure, still retrievable.

But Khamees and his family did not let me long remain in silence. They took me back to their house, and after 'Eid had repeated the story of my encounter with Imam Ibrahim, Khamees turned to me, laughing, and said: 'Do not be upset, ya doktór. Forget about all those guns and things. I'll tell you what: I'll come to visit you in your country, even though I've never been anywhere. When you leave, I'll come with you; I'll come all the way to India.'

He began to scratch his head, thinking hard, and then he added: 'But if I die there you must remember to bury me.'

MANGALORE

1

SEEN FROM THE sea, on a clear day, Mangalore can take a newcomer's breath away. It sits upon the tip of a long finger of steeply rising land; a ridge of hills which extends out of a towering knuckle of peaks in the far distance. Two rivers meet around the elliptical curve of the fingertip to form a great palm-fringed lagoon, lying tranquil under a quicksilver sky. Between the lagoon and the sea, holding back the waves, are two thin elbows of sand. They strain towards each other, but stop just short of touching, and through the gap between them flows a narrow channel, joining the lagoon to the open sea.

The boats that pass through that channel today are mainly small fishing craft; the lagoon's ancient functions as a harbour have now been delegated to a modern, artificially-dredged port a little to the north of the city. But it was the lagoon that first granted Mangalore its charter as a port, and it is from there that Ben Yiju would have had his first glimpse of the city he was to live in for close on two decades.

The geographical location is all that remains of the Mangalore that Ben Yiju saw: the city was sacked several times in the sixteenth century and afterwards, and today almost no trace of its medieval incarnation remains. The area that is now known as 'the old port' lies forgotten below the city's bustling business centres and market-places, at the bottom of a steep slope. It still bears the Persian name Bandar, 'port', but today its few moments of life are provided by a ferry that connects it to the fishing-villages on the sand-spit across the lagoon. Otherwise its docks are largely untenanted and its wharfs empty, except for a handful of barges and river-boats.

When Ben Yiju arrived in Mangalore there was probably a stretch of sand where the docks stand now: the ships that plied the Indian Ocean appear to have been designed to be beached rather than docked—the better to profit from the fine sands that lined those waters. The merchants of the city, including the large community of expatriate Middle Easterners, would have had their offices and godowns close to the Bandar, probably on the hillside above, from where they could keep an eye on incoming ships.

The expatriate merchant community of Mangalore was a large one, by all accounts. The Moroccan traveller Ibn Battuta, who visited the city some two hundred years after Ben Yiju, reports that it was the practice of most merchants from the Yemen and Persia to disembark there; the Sumatrans, on the other hand, along with others from the eastern reaches of the Indian Ocean, seem to have preferred other cities, such as Calicut and 'Fandarîna', a little further to the south. At the time of Ibn Battuta's visit the Muslims of Mangalore (and by implication) the foreign merchants, together formed a community of about 4,000 people, 'living in a suburb alongside the town.'

The settlement of foreigners at Mangalore was by no means the largest or the most cosmopolitan on the coast: Calicut, a couple of hundred miles to the south, appears to have housed an even larger and more diverse merchant community. There were thirteen 'Chinese' vessels in the harbour when Ibn Battuta's ship docked there, and he reports that the city regularly had visitors from 'China, Sumatra, Ceylon, the Maldives, Yemen, and Fars [Iran]...' A Portuguese sailor, Duarte Barbosa, who visited the city early in the sixteenth century, noted that the city's merchants included 'Arabs, Persians, Guzarates, Khorasanys, and Decanys', who were known collectively as pardesis, or foreigners. The pardesi merchants were not all itinerant traders; many of them were expatriates who had settled in Malabar for considerable lengths of time. '[They] possess in this place wives and children,' noted Barbosa, 'and ships for sailing to all parts with all kinds of goods.'

The lifestyle of these merchants was so sumptuous that even sophisticated travellers and courtiers, accustomed to the refinements of great royal courts, were taken by surprise upon being admitted into their circle. The Persian ambassador 'Abd al-Razzaq al-Samarqandi, for instance, was greatly impressed by their style of living when he passed through Malabar in 1442AD. 'They dress themselves in magnificent apparel,' he wrote, 'after the manner of the Arabs, and manifest luxury in every particular...' Duarte Barbosa was to echo those observations a few decades later: 'They have large houses and many servants: they are very luxurious in eating, drinking and sleeping...'

There is nothing now anywhere within sight of the Bandar to lend credence to the great mansions and residences that Ibn Battuta and Duarte Barbosa spoke of. Now the roads and lanes around the wharfs fall quiet after sunset; shipping offices shut their doors, coffee-shops pull down their shutters, and only a few passengers waiting to cross to the sand-spit remain. The imagination baulks at the thought that the Bandar once drew merchants and mariners from distant corners of the world.

For many hundreds of years, however, large numbers of foreign visitors congregated in the cities of this region, and it was Middle Eastern travellers who gave this part of the coast the Arabic name 'Malabâr'. In their usage, the name was applied loosely to the southern third of the west coast, an area that shares many aspects of a common culture. But Malabar is also divided into several smaller sub-regions, among which the district around Mangalore is perhaps the most distinctive. Being the northernmost frontier of the Malabar region, it forms a kind of double-headed causeway, between the south and the north on the one hand, and between the seaboard and the interior on the other. With its southerly neighbours it shares certain distinctive cultural institutions, as well as legacies bequeathed by a parallel history—forms of personal law based on principles of matrilineal descent, for instance, are common to many groups throughout the area. But in other respects its affiliations lie with the adjoining districts of the north and the east, and with the state of Karnataka, of which it is a part. Its speech, for example, while forming a distinct language in its own right, is also closely akin to Kannada, the majority language of the state.

The language of Mangalore is called Tuḷu, and it is one of the five siblings of the Dravidian family of languages: it is rich in folk traditions and oral literature, but it does not possess a script of its own and is usually transcribed in Kannada. It is this language that has given the area around Mangalore its name, Tuḷunâḍ: like so many other parts of the the subcontinent, it forms a cultural area which is distinctive and singular, while being at the same time closely enmeshed with its neighbours in an intricate network of differences.

Tulunad is not large—it is contained today within a single district—yet it has had a distinct identity since antiquity. Writing in Alexandria in the second century AD, the Greek geographer Ptolemy referred to it as 'Olokhoira'—a term which is thought to have been derived from 'Aḷupa', the name of Tulunad's long-lived ruling dynasty. For several hundreds of years, until the beginning of the fifteenth century, Tulunad's Alupa rulers succeeded in preserving a measure of autonomy for their small kingdom by picking allies judiciously among the various dynasties that followed each other to power in the hinterlands. It was during their rule that Mangalore became one of the principal ports of the Indian Ocean, and it was in the reign of the king Kavi Aḷupendra that Ben Yiju came to the city.

Ben Yiju, like so many other Middle Eastern merchants, was drawn to Mangalore because of the economic opportunities it offered as one of the premier ports of an extremely wealthy hinterland: a region that was well endowed with industrial crafts, apart from being one of the richest spice-producing territories of the medieval world. Later the area's wealth was to attract the much less welcome attention of the European maritime and colonial powers and it was in the course of the struggles that ensued that Mangalore came to lose virtually every trace of its extraordinary past.

But appropriately, Mangalore does not treat its lost history as a matter of crippling melancholy: it has always been a busy, bustling kind of place, and today it is again a thriving, relatively prosperous city. Its ancient connections with the Arab world have bequeathed it a more useful legacy than a mere collection of artefacts: thousands of its residents are now employed in the Persian Gulf, and its suburbs are awash with evidence of the extravagant spending of its expatriates.

In this, as in many other intangible ways, Mangalore remains perfectly true to its medieval heritage.

THE MORNING AFTER I arrived in Mangalore, one day in the summer of 1990, I found myself sitting in a coffee-shop, waiting eagerly to make the acquaintance of a scholar whose name I had heard mentioned several times on the way to the coast. I had been told on excellent authority, that this, if anyone, was the person who might be able to help me with the riddle of the Slave of MS H.6: his name was Professor B. A. Viveka Rai and he was one of the world's foremost experts on Tulu folklore and philology. For me a great deal depended on this meeting, for my unravelling of the Slave's history had been blocked by an intractable etymological puzzle: the mystery of his name.

My introduction to the puzzle had come from Goitein's translation of the letter that Khalaf ibn Ishaq wrote to Ben Yiju in 1139: at the end of the letter Khalaf happened to mention the Slave's name while sending him 'plentiful greetings'. In the translated version of the letter, the name was spelt 'Bama' and it was accompanied by a footnote which explained that Goitein had been informed by a specialist on Indian history that 'Bama' was 'vernacular for Brahma'.

At the time, captivated as I was by the letter's contents, I had not given the name any further thought. Years later, when I began working directly with the Geniza material, I discovered that the name occurred in some half-dozen documents, written by various different people—Madmun, Khalaf, and of course Ben Yiju himself. The name was always spelt in exactly the same way, with three characters: B-M-H. But of these, the last, 'H', was actually not a consonant at all, but rather an open vowel that is known in Arabic as the 'teh marbûṭa'. The three characters of the Slave's name were therefore, properly speaking, B-M-A. Clearly there was another vowel between the first and second characters, but it was never specified in the documents, for in Judæo-Arabic, as in written Arabic and Hebrew, short vowels are not usually indicated in handwritten texts. The vowel could have been 'u', 'o' or any other—one guess was about as good as another. In spelling the name as 'Bama', Goitein had taken it to be 'a', on the plausible assumption, as his footnote explained, that the word was derived from 'Brahma'.

My first doubts about the exact nature of the relationship between the letters 'B-M-A' and the word 'Brahma' arose while reading some medieval accounts of India written by Arab travellers and geographers. The word 'Brahma' and its cognates occurred often in those texts and it soon became clear to me that it had been well-known amongst educated people in the Middle East and North Africa since long before Ben Yiju's time. Indeed, it seemed possible that there had been an accepted way of spelling the word in Arabic through much of the Middle Ages.

Against that background it began to seem increasingly improbable that Ben Yiju and his friends would spell the Slave's name as B-M-A if it were actually 'Brahma'. If other Arabic-speakers, many of whom had never even visited India, could spell the term accurately, then surely Ben Yiju, who lived so many years in Mangalore, would have been able to do just as well, or better.

Clearly then, the Slave's name was not 'Brahma'. But it might of course have been a diminutive or a shortened form of that word. Yet if that were so, I began to suspect, the word would probably have had a slightly different shape: as a diminutive 'Bama' did not have a very convincing sound to my ear. I could think offhand of several other forms, from various Indian

247

languages, which sounded a great deal more persuasive.

At this point I realized that finding an acceptable solution to the puzzle of the Slave's name was a crucial step in determining his identity—indeed, it was the one clue that could provide some indication of where he was born and what his background and social circumstances were. But the moment that door swung open, a fresh host of problems appeared. The first among them was that there was no indication anywhere about what language the Slave was named in: after all the B-M-A of the documents could have had its origins in any one of several different languages.

Such information as I was able to find about slavery in the region of the Indian Ocean during the Middle Ages only served to complicate the matter further. The slave trade in Ben Yiju's time was a wide-ranging transcontinental phenomenon, with substantial numbers of slaves being brought into the region from distant parts of the world: from as far away as Central Asia, the Russian steppes, the Transcaucasus and Europe. Mangalore, as a major port, would certainly have been a way station for many of the slave-traders, and it was entirely conceivable that the Slave of MS H.6 had been brought there from the Middle East. Indeed, an obscure reference in one of Ben Yiju's letters suggested that he himself may have had occasional dealings with certain slave-traders from the Yemeni town of Zabid.

At the same time, there were good reasons to believe that the Slave of MS H.6 was in fact from the region of Mangalore rather than the Middle East: the spelling of his name for one. The slaves who were traded in the markets of Egypt were usually given Arabic names of a distinctive kind—Lu'lu ('Pearl'), for instance, and Jawhar ('Jewel')—names that served to locate them on the margins of human society. But the Slave's name, whatever it was, did not bear any resemblance to the usual run of Middle-Eastern slave-names, and indeed it did not appear to be of Arabic, or even Semitic origin. While the evidence was not conclusive by any means, it was certainly strong enough to suggest that Goitein was right in assuming that the Slave's origins lay in India.

But that only served to bring me back to that mysterious acrostic: B-M-A. After puzzling over those three characters for a long time, one last possibility suggested itself to me. In Judæo-Arabic (as in Arabic) a doubled letter is often represented by a single character. It was possible then that the single 'M' in the name was actually doing duty for two of its kind. If that were so, it would mean that there were actually four letters in the name: 'B-M-M-A'. If I then filled in a short vowel after the first letter, the result was 'Bomma' or 'Bamma', names which I knew to be common in certain parts of India.

Proceeding on that premise I began to look through the names in medieval inscriptions from Tulunad and its surrounding regions. The results were immediately gratifying. I discovered, for instance, that a man called Mâsaleya Bamma, who had worked as a servant for a group of warriors, had been killed, not far from Tulunad, just a few years before Ben Yiju arrived in India. His masters had caused an inscription to be carved in his memory: it was dated 15 June 1126, and it was discovered in a village about two hundred miles north-east of Mangalore. Another inscription from the same region records the name of one Seṭṭi Bamma, a man from a merchant family, who married a pious wife. From those, as well as other sources, it was soon clear to me that 'Bamma' had been a common name in that region in the Middle Ages.

Slowly the indications mounted, and just before leaving for Mangalore I came to be convinced that the Slave's name was actually 'Bamma' or something of the sort. Exciting as the discovery was, it also brought me to a standstill: I did not know whether the name was derived from the Sanskrit word 'Brahma' or from some other source, and I had no idea at all whether it might reveal anything about the Slave's origins by linking him to any particular caste, religion or social group.

And so it was not without reason that I found myself balancing on the edge of my seat, as I waited for Professor Viveka Rai that morning in Mangalore: it was as though the identity of an elusive and mysterious acquaintance were soon to be revealed.

3

PROFESSOR RAI PROVED to be a soft-spoken, youngish man, tall and bespectacled, with an air of gentle abstraction that hid a precise and immensely erudite mind. He quickly became absorbed in my account of my unravelling of the Slave's name, and it was not till I reached the end of the story that he broke in to correct me.

I had come very close, he said, in fact I was only fractionally off the mark: the Slave's name was probably 'Bomma' rather than 'Bamma'.

The name Bomma had once had wide currency within Tulu culture, he explained, and even until a generation or so ago it was commonly encountered in and around Mangalore. Over the last few decades it had passed out of general use as a personal name, but it was still preserved in the titles of various groups and clans in Tulunad. As for the derivation of the word, he said, it was a matter of critical importance to the story of the Slave, but the trail that led to its source was a circuitous one, traversing a wide swathe of Tulu culture and history.

The people of Tulunad were divided, by tradition, into several castes, ranging over a broad expanse of the social hierarchy—from immensely rich and powerful landlords, to poor peasants and Untouchables. But divided as they were by rank and occupation, the Tuluva still shared certain aspects of a common culture: they all spoke Tulu, for one, and they also followed matrilineal rules of inheritance for certain kinds of property. Equally, they shared in the worship of certain spirit-deities known as Bhûtas.

By tradition, each of the Tuluva castes and communities played a designated role in the Bhuta-cult, one providing financial support, for instance, one tending the shrines, others performing the ritual dances and so on. The cult was closely tied to the land, and those who did not own or work on the land—Brahmins, for example—were generally excluded from its rituals and celebrations. These rites were not just occasional events; they followed closely upon each other, even weekly in some seasons, and so the people who participated in them were thrust together at frequent and regular intervals. As a result they stood apart, in some ways, from the other people in the region: their rites, their language, and their matrilineal institutions gave them a distinct identity within the diverse population that had drifted into Tulunad over the centuries.

The Brahmins, on the other hand, played an important role in an altogether different aspect of the religious life of the region;

they were the standard-bearers of the Pan-Indian Hindu tradition which formed the complementary other half of the folk-religion of Tulunad. As in much of India, the religious fabric of Tulunad was woven from an equal mixture of local forms of worship (the Bhuta-cult, in this case) and the high Sanskritic tradition. Along with its innumerable Bhuta shrines, Tulunad had its fair share and more of temples dedicated to the gods of the Sanskritic pantheon, and most of the Tuluva people participated enthusiastically in the worship of both sets of deities. There was no contradiction in this, of course, for to them Bhutas and Sanskritic deities represented aspects of divine and supernatural power that shaded gently and imperceptibly into each other. Indeed, under the benign cover of that shade, there was a good deal of trafficking between the two pantheons: some Bhuta deities would occasionally appear within the mists of high Sanskritism, while others fell from favour and vanished into the netherworld.

It is somewhere in those dark and shaded regions that the pedigree of the name Bomma takes a sudden and unexpected turn and leads away from the Brahma of classical Hindu mythology towards a deity of an altogether different character.

And, by an extraordinary coincidence, said Professor Rai, I could, if I wanted, have a glimpse of that deity, a darshan, that very night.

'How?' I asked, imagining a night-time vigil at a lonely shrine in a deserted and wind-tossed palm-grove. 'Is there going to be a secret exorcism?'

Professor Rai cast me a quizzical glance. 'On television,' came the laconic answer. 'In a film that's going to be broadcast this evening.'

The film was in black and white; it had been made some ten or fifteen years earlier by some friends of Professor Rai's, and besides serving as an advisor for it, he had also written some of the songs. It was one of a small number of films made in the Tulu language, and it was based upon the most celebrated folk-epic of Tulunad, a legend that recounted the deeds of two heroic brothers, Koti and Chennaya.

When the heroes appeared on the screen, I noticed they were carrying small sickles around their waists. The sickles were symbols of their caste, Professor Rai explained, for the brothers were Billavas, whose traditional occupation was that of brewing and extracting palm-wine or toddy.

Through no fault of their own, Koti and Chennaya eventually ran afoul of the ruler of their area—a man of the Bant caste, which was traditionally the landowning community of Tulunad. Soon their enmity became very bitter, and the brothers were sentenced to exile and sent away from their native region. Before setting out on their travels, however, they managed to go to the shrine of their personal deity to seek his succour and protection.

'Now watch this scene,' said Professor Viveka Rai with a smile, as the two heroes went up to the shrine and began to sing a devotional song, their hands joined in prayer.

Listening carefully, I soon recognized a name that was repeated over and over again; it was the only word I could understand, for the song was, of course, in Tulu. This particular word, however, was instantly familiar: it was none other than 'Brahma'.

Having recognized the name of the deity, I thought I knew exactly what I would see when the camera turned towards the shrine's interior: a four-headed, four-armed image, accompanied by a goose—the traditional representation of the god Brahma according to the rules of classical iconography. But instead, to my great surprise, the camera revealed an elongated wooden figure, with curling moustaches, holding a sword in one hand. It was an image of a warrior-deity, wholly unrelated to the Brahma of the Sanskritic pantheon.

I knew now why Professor Rai had smiled so enigmatically: the deity of the Tulu myth was evidently not the same as the Brahma of classical Sanskritic mythology.

Later, he explained that the god depicted in the film had originally had a wholly different name: he was Berme or Bermeru, the principal figure in the pantheon of Tuluva Bhuta-deities. Over time, with the growth of Brahminical influence, the Tulu deity Berme had slowly become assimilated to the Sanskritic deity 'Brahma'.

So the pedigree of the name Bomma in the Tulu language probably stretched back to a time before the deities of Tulunad had begun to assume Sanskritic incarnations: in all likelihood it was a diminutive of 'Berme', the figure who stood at the pinnacle of the Tuluva pantheon of Bhuta-spirits.

It took me a long time afterwards to check the steps in the argument and to work out the consequences that this derivation would have for the history of the Slave. Speculative though it was, the argument seemed to lead to the conclusion that the Slave of MS H.6 had been born into one of the several matrilineal communities which played a part in the Bhuta-cult of Tulunad.

It was thus that Bomma finally came of age and was ready at last to become a protagonist in his own story.

4

THERE IS ONLY one incident in Bomma's life of which we have direct knowledge. By yet another odd coincidence this story also happens to be the one with which Bomma entered the annals of the Geniza: the letter which recounts it is the earliest known document in which his name is mentioned.

The principal reason why the story has been preserved is that it was set in Aden, and thus earned a mention in a letter written by Madmun. The letter in question is one of the most important that Madmun ever wrote, for he included in it a description of an unusual and dramatic event: a piratical raid on Aden by the ruler of a small kingdom in the Persian Gulf. Yet in the letter, Bomma's doings actually took precedence over the raid and from the pattern of Madmun's narrative it seems possible that Bomma was actually present, on his very first appearance in the Geniza, at the enactment of a full-blooded historical event, more than a thousand miles from his home in Mangalore.

The events which Madmun described in his letter are known to have occurred in 1135, so the letter must have been written soon afterwards. Bomma happened to be in Aden at the time because Ben Yiju had sent him there on an expedition that appears to have been partly a business trip and partly a shopping jaunt. When he returned to Mangalore, he brought back a large consignment of goods, including a whole array of clothes, household utensils and presents for Ben Yiju and his family. Altogether, the purchases that Bomma made in Aden added up to about ninety-three dinars. It is worth adding— since it is only human to be curious about other people's shopping expenses—that this sum of money could have paid the wages of a mason or builder for more than two and a half years, or it could have bought somewhere in the region of 2,000 kilograms of meat or 3,000 kilograms of olive oil. Alternatively, with the addition of a mere seven dinars it would even have served to ransom the lives of three adult Spaniards at the going rates.

Ben Yiju gave Bomma a fairly generous monthly allowance while he was in Aden—two dinars a month, or about the wage of any artisan—but the figure was a paltry one compared to the sums of money that Bomma was handling in Aden. Madmun's accounts show that the consignment of goods that Bomma took with him to Aden fetched about 685 dinars on the market: a sum that would have been large enough to buy Ben Yiju a splendid mansion in Fustat. But of course, Bomma for his part must have been accustomed to dealing with sums of that kind, for it is worth remembering that this small fortune represents the value of just a single consignment of goods sent from Mangalore to Aden—probably no more than a season's earnings, and that, too, for a newly established merchant with a business of relatively modest size.

The volume of goods and money that flowed through Aden was evidently huge and it was the prospect of those rich pickings that made the city the object of a raid in the year of Bomma's visit.

The expedition was not perhaps an event that properly deserves to be called 'historic', yet it did make a deep enough impression to earn a mention in a chronicle written by the historian Ibn Mujawwir a century and a half later. As for Ben Yiju's friends in Aden, at least two of them were moved to describe it at length in their correspondence: Madmun, when he wrote to Ben Yiju, and Khalaf ibn Ishaq, in a letter to their common friend, the traveller Abu Saʻid Halfon.

The villains of the piece, by common agreement, were the rulers of Kish (or, properly speaking, Qaiṣ), an island at the mouth of the Straits of Hormuz, which by virtue of its location commanded the sea routes to the Persian Gulf. The Amirs of that tiny kingdom were amongst the most ambitious representatives of a breed that proliferated in the Indian Ocean: pirates, who made their living by preying on the rich merchant vessels that plied the trade-routes.

Pirate attacks were fairly frequent occurrences throughout the Indian Ocean, and there are several references to them in the Geniza documents. The Amirs of Kish, for example, had sent raiding expeditions up and down the coasts of Africa and India, and even so distant a port as Cambay in Gujarat had to take special precautions to guard against their depredations. But an attack such as the raid on Aden was unusual, for generally the pirates tried not to invite the attention of the stronger rulers of the region. Even at their worst, they were a nuisance rather than a serious threat to commerce, and neither they nor any of the powers of the Indian Ocean, no matter how large or well-armed, ever tried to gain control of the seas or to take over the trade routes by force.

But clearly, on this occasion the pirates of Kish decided that they would try to expand their horizons. First, at the beginning of the seafaring season, the Amir's son sent an expedition to Aden demanding a part of the city in payment for protection against a raid. When the demand was refused he sent a fleet of fifteen ships which forced their way into the city's harbour and took up positions there. The raiding party did not attempt a landing; their intention was to capture a merchant vessel on its way back from India.

As it turned out, their plan failed. Aden's soldiers gave the pirates no respite in the time they spent waiting in the harbour; they were constantly attacked and harried, many were killed in skirmishes, while others died of hunger and thirst. At length, when a prize of the kind they had been waiting for finally did appear on the horizon, it happened to be a convoy of two ships that belonged to one of the most powerful merchants in the Indian Ocean—a trader called Abû'l Qâsim Râmisht, who was based in the Persian Gulf port of Sirâf.

Ramisht of Siraf was rich beyond computation: a contemporary writer relates that one of his clerks alone was worth half a million dinars, while the silver plate his family ate out of weighed approximately one ton. Ramisht's trading empire stretched as far as China, and the traders of Aden and Mangalore, including Ben Yiju and his friends, frequently used his ships for transporting their merchandise.

The pirates from Kish attacked Ramisht's ships as soon as they appeared in the harbour. But the city sent troops to their rescue and eventually the pirates were driven back to the open sea where they quickly dispersed. 'Thus God did not give them victory,' wrote Madmun in his letter, 'and they made off in the most ignominious way, after having suffered great losses and humiliation...'

But despite his obvious delight in the pirates' defeat, it was not the raid that was uppermost in Madmun's mind when he wrote the letter: that honour was kept for Bomma. It appears that Bomma, determined to enjoy his trip to the full, had spent his wages on an extended drinking bout during which he had presented himself several times in Madmun's office, demanding money.

This is how Madmun put it:

And after that he [Bomma] started on other things. He said: Give me more money, [what I have] is not enough. He took 4 months money from me, eight dînârs. Often he would come here, very drunk, and would not listen to a word I said.'

We cannot be sure of course, but it is not impossible that the Adenese soldiers were cheered into battle by a drunken Bomma, standing on the shore and waving a flask.

5

THE GENIZA DOCUMENTS provide no indication at all about how Bomma's path came to cross Ben Yiju's. From certain references in Ben Yiju's papers it seems likely that he took Bomma into his service as a business agent and helper soon after he had established himself as a trader in Mangalore.

Whatever the circumstances of their meeting, the terms under which Bomma entered Ben Yiju's service were probably entirely different from those suggested by the word 'slavery' today: their arrangement was probably more that of patron and client than master and slave, as that relationship is now understood. If this seems curious, it is largely because the medieval idea of slavery tends to confound contemporary conceptions, both of servitude and of its mirrored counter-image, individual freedom.

In the Middle Ages institutions of servitude took many forms, and they all differed from 'slavery' as it came to be practised after the European colonial expansion of the sixteenth century. In the lifetimes of Bomma and Ben Yiju, servitude was a part of a very flexible set of hierarchies and it often followed a logic completely contrary to that which modern expectations suggest. In the Middle East and northern India, for instance, slavery was the principal means of recruitment into some of the most privileged sectors of the army and the bureaucracy. For those who made their way up through that route, 'slavery' was thus often a kind of career opening, a way of gaining entry into the highest levels of government.

At a more modest level, merchants and traders often used slavery as a means of finding apprentices and agents; the 'slaves' who entered employment in this way often took a share of their firm's profits and could generally be sure of obtaining manumission, and even of attaining the rank of partner or shareholder.

In the medieval world, slavery was also often used as a means of creating fictive ties of kinship between people who were otherwise unrelated. Amongst the Jewish merchants of medieval Cairo, for instance, as with many tribes in Africa, slaves were sometimes gradually incorporated into their masters' households and came to be counted as members of their families. Equally, in some vocations, the lines of demarcation between apprentice, disciple and bondsman were so thin as to be invisible: to be initiated into certain crafts, aspirants had to voluntarily surrender a part of their freedom to their teachers.

Perhaps the most elusive aspect of medieval slavery is its role as spiritual metaphor, as an instrument of the religious imagination. In south India, amongst the pietist and fiercely egalitarian Vachanakara saint-poets of Bomma's own lifetime, for example, slavery was often used as an image to represent the devotee's quest for God: through the transforming power of metaphor the poets became their Lord's servants and lovers, androgynous in their longing; slaves, searching for their master with a passion that dissolved selfhood, wealth, caste and gender, indeed, difference itself. In their poetry it was slavery that was the paradoxical embodiment of perfect freedom; the image that represented the very notion of relationship, of human bonds, as well the possibility of their transcendence.

This imagery would not have been unfamiliar to Ben Yiju. He and his friends were all orthodox, observant Jews, strongly aware of their distinctive religious identity. But they were also part of the Arabic-speaking world, and the everyday language of their religious life was one they shared with the Muslims of that region: when they invoked the name of God in their writings it was usually as Allah, and more often than not their invocations were in Arabic forms, such as inshâ'allâh and al-ḥamdul-illâh. Distinct though their faith was, it was still a part of the religious world of the Middle East—and that world was being turned upside down by the Sûfis, the mystics of Islam.

Judaism too soon felt the impact of Sufism. Shortly before Ben Yiju's lifetime the Jewish mystic Baḥya Ibn Paqûda composed The Duties of the Heart, a treatise culled largely from Sufi sources, which was to have a powerful impact on the world of Mediterranean Judaism, infusing generations of readers with Sufi ideas. Egypt, in particular, was a fertile ground for mystical beliefs and over the centuries, many members of the congregation of the Synagogue of Ben Ezra in Fustat were to be greatly influenced by Sufism. Abraham Maimonides (1186–1237), a son of the great Talmudist Moses Maimonides, even composed a Sufi text of his own, and he is known to have remarked once that the Sufis were 'worthier disciples of the Prophets of Israel than were the Jews of his time.'

261

Most Sufis would have regarded the Vachanakara saint-poets as pantheistic and blasphemous in their desire to merge themselves in their Lord. Their own conceptions of extinction (fanâ) and subsistence (baqâ) always assumed an utterly transcendent God. Yet they would probably have acknowledged a commonality in the nature of their quest, and they would certainly have perceived a similarity in their use of poetic imagery.

For the Sufis as for the Vachanakaras, the notion of being held by bonds was one of the central metaphors of religious life. They too drew some of their most powerful images from the institution of slavery: metaphors of perfect devotion and love strung together in an intensely charged, often erotic, spiritual imagery. Thus, in Sufi tradition, Sultan Mahmud of Ghazni, the eleventh-century soldier who built an immense empire in Central Asia, was not the fearsome and bloodthirsty conqueror that he is often depicted to be, but rather a symbol of mystical longing, because of the ties that bound him to his soldier-slave, Ayaz. A Sufi parable relates that once when the mythical bird, Huma, the touch of whose shadow was said to confer kingdoms, appeared in the skies above Mahmud's army, the emperor found himself suddenly alone, abandoned by his most faithful courtiers—all except one, Ayaz. While the others went chasing after Homa's shadow, Ayaz stepped instead into the shadow of Mahmud, so that his master might know that for him the world contained no better kingdom. In the telling of the Sufis, that perfect act of love works a miraculous spiritual transformation and the world-conquering Mahmud becomes 'the slave of his slave'.

The imagery of the Vachanakaras and the Sufis would seem to be far distant from Bomma and Ben Yiju, and the workaday relations of a trader and his business agent. But even the most mundane institutions have their life-giving myths and against the setting of that distant backdrop of legend and metaphor, the elements of slavery in the ties that bound an apprentice to a master craftsman, an accountant to a merchant, would have appeared, perhaps, not as demeaning bonds, but rather as links that were in some small way ennobling—human connections, pledges of commitment, in relationships that could just as well have been a matter of a mere exchange of coinage.

Bomma may never have known of the saint-poets of his time and their teachings, but he would certainly have been intimately acquainted with some of that great range of popular traditions and folk beliefs which upturn and invert the categories of Sanskritic Hinduism. Ben Yiju, for his part, as a man of wide education, would probably have read something of the Sufis, and he may well have shared in some of the beliefs and practices that have always formed the hidden and subversive counter-image of the orthodox religions of the Middle East: the exorcism cults, the magical rites, the customs of visiting saints' graves and suchlike. Amongst the members of his community in Cairo, those ideas and practices formed almost as important a part of daily observance as the orthodox aspects of their religion: a very large number of the documents in the Geniza, for example, consist of magical formulae, and treatises related to esoteric rites.

It was probably those inarticulate counter-beliefs, rather than the formal conversion that Bomma probably had to undergo while in Ben Yiju's service, that eventually became a small patch of level ground between them: the matrilineally-descended Tulu and the patriarchal Jew who would otherwise seem to stand on different sides of an unbridgeable chasm.

6

WHILE MAKING MY way around Mangalore, I often had Bhuta-shrines pointed out to me: there seemed to be dozens of them dotted around the city and its outskirts, small, modest structures, perched on columns, gazing serenely over gardens and palmgroves. They were always brightly-painted and well-tended, and often there were flowers and offerings lying upon their thresholds.

As the days passed I became increasingly curious about the religious practices that were enshrined in those structures. But when I began to look for material I discovered that as far as most of the standard authorities were concerned the Bhuta-cult did not count as 'religion' at all: it fell far beneath the Himalayan gaze of canonical Hindu practice. Such detailed studies as there were, I found, were mainly carried out by anthropologists and folklorists; it was otherwise often dismissed as mere 'devil worship' and superstition.

Then, one day, quite unexpectedly, I was presented with an opportunity to visit a shrine when a taxi I was travelling in stopped beside one, on the outskirts of the city. The driver apologized for the delay and said it would only be a matter of minutes: it was just that he always made it a point to stop there, when he was passing by, to say a quick prayer and make an offering. The shrine was a very famous one, he explained, and visitors were always welcome.

The shrine stood on top of a mound, a small tiled enclosure surrounded by ricefields, with the sand-dunes of the coastline visible in the near distance. The image inside was a very simple one, a white, circular mask with an emblematic face depicted on it in bold black lines: a pair of curling moustaches were its most striking features. On either side of the mask was a sword, propped upright against the wall.

The spot was tended by a Pujari, a large, friendly man with gold rings in his ears, who touched our foreheads with sandalwood and gave us handfuls of prasad. He explained, through the taxi-driver, who translated into Hindi for my benefit, that once every year the Bhuta who dwelt in the shrine emerged to take possession of him. A great festival was held then, and after a long cycle of dances and rituals the spirit was ceremonially restored to its proper place within the shrine.

It was an extraordinary experience, the Pujari said, to feel the Bhuta within him, for the spirit of that shrine was greatly renowned for his powers. Many stories surrounded the shrine, he said, and one of them had become famous throughout the region. Years ago, when Mangalore's new port was completed, the government's engineers had started building a road to connect it with the city, some fifteen miles to the south. But soon, to general consternation, it was discovered that if the work were to go ahead as planned, the road would cut straight through the shrine. The people of the area had protested mightily, but the government had ignored them and sent out notices of eviction to all the farmers who owned land in the area. Sure enough, one day, the engineers arrived with their machines to begin the work of demolition. But then there was a miracle: their bulldozers were immobilized soon after they had begun to move; they were frozen to the ground before they could touch the shrine's walls. Completely confounded, the engineers called in high-ranking government officers, and technicians with yard-long degrees. But there was nothing anyone could do and eventually, admitting defeat, they agreed to divert the road so that it skirted around the shrine.

This was a story everyone knew, said the Pujari, and every year at the time of the festival, people would tell it over and over again.

Later, when we got back into the car, the driver asked me to look through the rear window. I watched the road carefully as we drove away, and from the angle of its curve it did indeed look as though it had made a loop to spare the shrine.

Smiling, the driver said: 'Have you ever heard of anything like that?'

A recollection suddenly stirred in my mind.

'Yes,' I said, 'I heard a very similar story once. In Egypt.'

He nodded politely, but disbelief was written all over his face.

7

BOMMA WAS NOT to remain long in Aden: he came back carrying the very letter in which Madmun described his drunken revelries to Ben Yiju. Madmun's complaints, however, do not appear to have excited an excess of wrath in Ben Yiju, and nor did Madmun himself bear a grudge for long—in his later letters he was always careful to include a word of friendly greeting for Bomma. Over the years, as Bomma's role as business agent grew in importance, Ben Yiju's friends in Aden came to regard him with increasing respect, and in time Khalaf ibn Ishaq even began to prefix his name with the title of 'Shaikh'.

Ben Yiju, for his part, seems to have reposed a great deal of trust in Bomma from the very beginning of their association.

When Bomma went to Aden in 1135, for example, he was responsible not only for delivering a quantity of merchandise, but also for bringing back a large shipment of goods for Ben Yiju and his household. Among the items he brought back were four ḥaṣîra-s or mats from Berbera (in modern Somaliland), a leather table cloth of a special kind on which chess and other games could be played, an iron frying-pan, a sieve, a large quantity of soap, two Egyptian gowns, and several presents from Madmun, such as sugar, raisins, 'a quire of white paper', as well as a piece of coral for Ben Yiju's son, Surur.

The two 'gowns' that Bomma brought back with him were almost certainly intended for Ben Yiju himself, because it is clear from other references in his correspondence that he, like his fellow expatriates, continued to wear the customary garments of the Middle East—robes, turbans and the like—all the while that he was in India. The people of Malabar, on the other hand, generally left the upper parts of their bodies bare, men and women alike—their preferred markers of class distinction being ornaments and jewellery rather than articles of clothing. 'They wear only bandages around the middle,' wrote 'Abd al-Razzaq al-Samarqandi, '[garments] called lankoutah, which descend from the navel to above the knee.'

To Middle Eastern merchants like Ben Yiju, on the other hand, being properly dressed meant wearing a double layer of clothing, first a loose undergarment and over that a robe, a garment that covered the covering, so to speak, of the body's nakedness and rendered it fit to be seen in public: anything less they would have considered immodest.

Ben Yiju, for one, was clearly fastidious about his clothing. Several of his letters and accounts mention imported Egyptian robes and fine Alexandrian cloaks, while others refer to lengths of cloth and kerchiefs that may have served as turbans. He clearly had a reputation as a careful dresser amongst his friends; Madmun, for instance, when sending him a shawl once, thought it prudent to extol its qualities: 'I have also for my own part, sent for you…a fine new Dîbîqî shawl, with nicely worked borders—an appropriate garment for men of eminence.'

The most important of his imports, as far as Ben Yiju was concerned, was paper. In the Malabar, as in most parts of India, the material most commonly used for writing at that time was the palm-leaf—paper appears to have been rare and difficult to obtain. In the Middle East, on the other hand, paper was being produced on a large scale by the eleventh century, and like most of his contemporaries Ben Yiju must have grown accustomed to it in his youth. Once he moved to India his friends went to great pains to keep him well-supplied and packages of paper were included in virtually every shipment sent to him from Aden.

Ben Yiju's friends evidently knew of the great importance that writing played in his life, and they often showed a touching concern for the quality of the paper they bought on his behalf. Madmun, for example, once assured him that the Egyptian Ṭalḥî paper he had acquired for him was 'the best available', and on another occasion he proudly assured him that his two large quires of Sulṭânî paper were so fine that 'no one has its like'. Madmun was not exaggerating: the paper he and his friends sent to Ben Yiju was of so matchless a quality that even today, eight hundred years later, a surprising number of those sheets are still marvellously well-preserved, despite the heat and humidity they have endured in the course of their travels between Egypt and India.

That Ben Yiju was a man with a taste for good living is also evident in many of his household purchases. Much of his kitchenware for instance, was imported from Aden—even such things as frying-pans and sieves—and he also regularly had crockery, soap, goblets and glasses sent out from the Middle East. For his mats he looked to the Horn of Africa, and he is known to have purchased at least one velvet-like carpet, made in Gujarat.

Ben Yiju also seems to have had something of a sweet tooth. His friends often sent him raisins and other delicacies such as nougat and dates. The various kinds of palm-sugar that were in use in Malabar were clearly not to his taste, and his friends seem to have had standing instructions to dispatch Middle Eastern cane-sugar with every consignment of goods.

If it seems curious today that somebody should import sugar into sweet-besotted India, it would not have appeared so in Ben Yiju's time. In the Middle Ages, it was Egypt that pioneered the large-scale production of cane-sugar and its exports of that commodity were such that in many parts of Asia to this day some sugar products bear names that link them to an Egyptian source. No matter that the Arabic word sukkar (hence the English 'sugar') is itself ultimately derived from a Sanskrit source: today, throughout north India, crystallized sugar is still known as misri in commemoration of traders like Ben Yiju and the tastes they imported from Masr.

8

I HAD NOT been in Mangalore long when Bomma provided me with an insight into the uses of History.

Among the many castes and religious communities of the Malabar coast few have a past as interesting as that of a small group of fisher-folk, known variously by the name of 'Magavîra' or 'Mogêra'. The sixteenth-century Portuguese traveller, Duarte Barbosa, left a brief description of them in his account of his travels on the Malabar coast. He referred to them as 'another sect of people still lower [than the others]...which they call moguer...These people for the most part get their living at sea, they are mariners and fishermen.' But although the Magavira were traditionally linked with fishing, Barbosa notes that many amongst the group had also prospered in trade: 'They are some of them very rich men who have got ships with which they navigate, for they gain much money with the Moors.'

According to tradition, the Magaviras have always been closely linked with the foreign merchants and mariners who came to trade in Malabar. As fishermen they would perhaps have been the natural associates of Middle Eastern sailors and seafarers, partly because of their expertise in sailing, and partly because of their position on the margins of the caste-structure of Hindu society which would have rendered them free of the restrictions that might have hampered other groups in trade and travel. Some amongst them were clearly successful traders and ship-owners in their own right, but there must also have been a great many others who entered the maritime trade in different ways—by becoming seamen on trading vessels, for example, or by apprenticing themselves or their children to foreign merchants and traders.

Soon after I reached Mangalore, I discovered that the Magavira's links with the foreign merchants were commemorated in the traditional symbol of their distinctive identity—a deity known as the Bobbariya-bhuta, deemed by legend to be the spirit of a Muslim mariner and trader who died at sea. No Magavira settlement, I learnt, was without its Bobbariya-shrine: usually a simple pillar and platform of stone, with a wooden mace propped up beside it.

On hearing of this I was immediately seized with curiosity, and I soon succeeded in prevailing upon a friend, Father D'Souza—a Jesuit priest and a specialist in the religious traditions of Tulunad—to take me to visit a Bobbariya-shrine. Being from the region himself, it was a relatively easy matter for my friend to arrange a visit, particularly because, as a teacher in one of Mangalore's best-known colleges, he had many Magavira students. The nearest Bobbariya-shrine, he told me, was in the fishing-village on the sand-spit that lay directly across the lagoon from Mangalore's old port. A few days later, after he had told his students to expect us, we boarded the ferry together and crossed the lagoon.

Two of my friend's students were waiting for us when the ferry docked at the jetty. They received us with a shy, schoolboy deference, clearly overcome with both delight and apprehension at the prospect of a visit from a teacher. The village lay behind them, tranquil in the shade of a thick awning of coconut palms, its pathways cool and sandy, the open sea visible on the far side of the sand-spit.

I soon discovered that this village was quite unlike the fishing-villages I had seen in other parts of the country: there were no shanties, no palm-leaf huts—everything around us, the well-tended gardens and the pastel-coloured bungalows with their thickets of TV aerials, spoke of quietly prosperous, suburban lives. The walls of the houses around us were painted prominently with the letter 'Om' and other symbols of Hindu piety, and it was hard to tell that this had once been a fishing-village whose inhabitants had been relegated to the bottom edge of orthodox caste society. It was clear that this was a community whose fortunes had soared in recent years.

After walking through the village, we were led to one of the students' houses: a large new bungalow, with an 'Om' painted prominently on its walls. Chairs had been set out in the garden in expectation of our arrival, and we were greeted at the gate by a group of our host's female relatives. The family was a large one, our host explained—his mother was the senior member of her matrilineal clan, so several of her sisters and aunts shared their house. His mother was a small, capable-looking woman, with an air of quiet command: within a few minutes of our arrival she had orchestrated the presentation of several trayloads of snacks and coconut water.

Towards the end of our visit, I prompted my Jesuit friend to ask her a question, in Tulu: had she ever encountered the name Bomma amongst people of the Magavira caste?

She was taken by surprise at the question. No, she said, shaking her head vigorously, you would never hear a name like that in the village nowadays; all the boys here had names like Ramesh and Vivek now, proper names, like you heard on the radio and TV.

But then, casting her mind back, she smiled and said, well, yes, in the old days, sometimes, you would hear names like that. But not now, never: everybody had good Sanskritic names nowadays—names like 'Bomma' belonged to a time when very few people in the community had been educated and fishermen had ranked at the bottom of the social ladder.

She broke off to say a few words to her son, and he ran into the house and fetched an illustrated pamphlet. She opened it reverently, to the first page, her face lit by a smile of intense pride: it was a short history of the village, financed and published by community subscription.

Towards sunset we bid the family goodbye and set out to visit the Bobbariya-shrine. It was almost dark now and silver television-shadows flickered across the lanes as we walked past. With glares of disapproval, our guides led us quickly past a small but boisterous crowd that had gathered at a corner toddy-shop: there had been a lot of drinking in the community once, they explained, but now the younger people were trying to put an end to the sale of alcohol in their village.

When we were still a fair distance away, one of the students pointed towards the lights of the shrine. It looked nothing like any of the simple Bhuta-temples that dotted the countryside around Mangalore: it was a large, modern building, modelled after a classical Hindu temple. When we approached it, I noticed that its walls bore the posters of a fundamentalist Hindu political organization, an upper-caste group notorious for its anti-Muslim rhetoric: it was a clear indication that this community, so long relegated to the peripheries of the Hindu order, had now resolved to use a political short-cut to break into the Sanskritic fold. Having transformed its social and economic position it was now laying claim to the future, in the best tradition of liberalism, by discovering a History to replace the past.

Leading us into the shrine, the students told us how the old structure had been torn down and the new one built, at great expense, by community subscription. It was not really a Bhuta-shrine any more, they explained proudly: it had become a real

Hindu temple, and the main place in it was now reserved for Vishnu, the most Brahminical of gods.

Once we went inside, however, it turned out that one small aspect of the past had ingeniously escaped re-invention: the spirit of the Bobbariya-bhuta still remained in the temple although in a wholly altered guise. The students pointed him out to us; he stood beside the image of Vishnu, but at a slightly lower level. The old symbols, the mace and the pillar, had been dispensed with: he was now represented by an image, like a Hindu god.

I had to struggle with myself to keep from applauding the ironies enshrined in that temple. The past had revenged itself on the present: it had slipped the spirit of an Arab Muslim trader past the watchful eyes of Hindu zealots and installed it within the Sanskritic pantheon.

As we walked away, I was glad to think that in Bomma's lifetime the inhabitants of that sand-spit would have had no need of a temple to lay claim to the future: they would in fact have been witnesses to a great revival in an entirely different aspect of Hinduism—the tradition of personal devotion which, time and time again, has confronted the hierarchical ideology of caste with a critique of millenarian power.

In Bomma's own lifetime, no more than a few hundred miles from his home town, one of the most remarkable of those egalitarian devotional movements was being sung into existence by the Vachanakara saint-poets, who had set about creating fraternal communities of artisans and working people, defying the rules of caste and kinship.

Had Bomma passed his childhood on that sand-spit, as he may well have done, he might have heard one of the Vachanakara's songs being sung where today that brand-new temple projects its shadow into the future and the past:

> With a whole temple
> in this body
> where's the need
> for another?
>
> No one asked
> for two.

9

BEN YIJU'S LIFE in Mangalore was extraordinarily rich in relationships: his connection with Ashu, for one, brought an entire constellation of relatives with it. Dealing with this newly-acquired family was not always easy for Ben Yiju: indeed, on the one occasion on which he is known to have called down God's curses it was on someone who was probably connected to him through Ashu's family.

The person in question was a kârdâr, an agent or middleman who helped traders in the buying of spices and other commodities. But the story of this particular kardar, as it develops in Ben Yiju's papers, is a good deal more complex than an account of the dealings between an exporter and his agent.

The plot begins with a set of accounts (reckoned in coins called mithqâls and units of weight called bahârs). 'The kâ(r)dâr, may God curse him,' Ben Yiju scribbled, 'owed...14 mithqâls, for two bahârs of cardamom. He did not deliver the cardamom, so I bought...two bahârs from Fandarîna as a substitute, for 17 mithqâls.'

What had happened, evidently, is that the kardar had offered to procure a consignment of cardamom at unusually low rates, and Ben Yiju, in the hope of making a quick killing, had given him an advance to make the purchase. But when the time came to send the consignment on to Aden, the kardar defaulted, and Ben Yiju was caught in the classic bind of a futures speculator: he had gambled on a commodity that hadn't turned up in time.

In fact, Ben Yiju had committed not just his own but some of his partners' money too, and they took a dim view of the matter when they found out. Yusuf ibn Abraham wrote to say: 'You, my master, mentioned that you approached the kârdâl gently in order to get something for us back for him. Perhaps you should threaten him that here in Aden we [disgrace] anyone that owes us something and does not fulfil his commitments...If he does not pay, we shall issue an official letter of [censure] and send it to him, so that he will become aware of his crime.'

Even Khalaf ibn Ishaq, the closest of Ben Yiju's friends, reacted sharply on this occasion. 'As for the delay [in the delivery of the kârdâr's cardamom],' he wrote to Ben Yiju, 'may God curse him. I have spoken to some people about the matter, and they said to me that the cardamom was yours, and we had no share in it. It is a matter between you and the kârdâr: deal with this thing individually with him, separately from us.' Clearly Khalaf had a suspicion that there was something in Ben Yiju's relationship with the kardar that did not quite meet the eye, and he was evidently resentful of the way Ben Yiju had involved him in a set of private arrangements. He and Yusuf continued to press Ben Yiju for several years, but to no avail: there is no indication that they ever recouped their losses in this affair.

The clue that gives away the nature of Ben Yiju's connection with the kardar lies in a throwaway line on a tiny scrap of paper: it suggests that the kardar was a close relative of Ashu's brother, the man whom Ben Yiju referred to as 'Nair'.

Nair is mentioned only twice in all of Ben Yiju's papers, and in both cases the references consist of little more than the name and a couple of brief words. Yet, if there was anyone who was located at the precise juncture where Ben Yiju's instilled responses could be expected to run into conflict with Ashu's, it was none other than her brother, Nair. By the matrilineal reckoning of the Nairs the bond between brother and sister was far more important than the tie between husband and wife; in their practice it was a woman's brother and not her husband who was entitled to the guardianship of her children. Thus, by the customs of Ashu's community it would have been Nair who held the reins of authority over her progeny; it would have been he—not Ben Yiju—who played Laius to their Oedipus.

It was not without reason therefore that Khalaf suspected that the relationship between Ben Yiju and the kardar extended beyond their business dealings: it could well be that Ben Yiju had given him the advance principally because Ashu or Nair had asked him to make a loan to their relative. It is even possible that the reason why the money was never returned was that her family saw it as their compensation for forgoing their rights over her children. But of course the simplest of solutions is also the most likely: that the kardar had effected a clever swindle by exploiting a family connection.

Fortunately for Ben Yiju, his social and professional life in Mangalore extended far beyond his family. The names that are sprinkled through his papers speak of a startlingly diverse network of associations: entered into a file, the list would yield nothing to the Rolodex of an international businessman today.

Some of Ben Yiju's closest business connections, for instance, lay with a group of merchants whom he and his friends in Aden referred to as the 'Bâniyân of Mangalore'—Hindu Gujaratis of the 'Vania' or trading caste. Long active in the Indian Ocean trade, Gujarati merchants had plied the trade routes for centuries, all the way from Aden to Malacca, and they exerted a powerful influence on the flow of certain goods and commodities. They evidently played a significant role in the economy of Malabar in Ben Yiju's time, and were probably instrumental in the management of its international trade. Madmun, for one, was on cordial terms with several members of the Gujarati trading community of Mangalore, whom he kept informed of trends in the markets of the Middle East. He, in turn, appears to have handed on those connections to Ben Yiju when he set up his business in Mangalore. Over the years, Ben Yiju often served as a courier for Madmun, delivering letters as well as messages and greetings to the 'Bâniyân of Manjalûr', and on occasion he even brokered joint entrepreneurial ventures between them and Madmun.

In matters of business, Ben Yiju's networks appear to have been wholly indifferent to many of those boundaries that are today thought to mark social, religious and geographical divisions. Madmun, for instance, is known once to have proposed a joint venture between himself and three traders in Mangalore, each of different social or geographical origins—one a Muslim, one a Gujarati Vania, and the third a member of the landowning caste of Tulunad. Equally, the ships that Ben Yiju and his friends used for transporting their goods were owned by a wide variety of people. Among the many nâkhudas or ship-owners who are mentioned in Ben Yiju's papers, there is one Pattani-Swami, probably the head of a merchant guild or caste, a man called Nambiar, evidently from Kerala, and many others, including of course 'Abd al-Qasim Ramisht of Siraf. The ties forged by trade were so close that Madmun's kinsman, the nakhuda Mahruz (in a letter written for him by Ben Yiju), once remarked of a ship-owner called 'Tinbu', probably of Tamil extraction, that, 'between him and me there are bonds of inseparable friendship and brotherhood.'

Ben Yiju's closest affiliations in Mangalore would of course have lain with the community with which he shared his spoken language and his taste in food and clothing: the expatriate Muslim Arabs who were resident in the city—indeed, for most purposes he would have counted himself as one of them. Muslim traders figure frequently in his papers, as do the names of the Arab sailors and ships' captains who carried his letters and brought him news from other parts of the world.

Ben Yiju's business interests also brought him into contact with a large number of agents and retailers, and those relationships seem to have often overlapped with the kinship networks of his household. In addition, Ben Yiju was also closely connected with a group of metalworkers specializing in certain bronze objects and utensils which were much in demand in Aden. The names of these craftsmen, who appear to have been Brahmins from Tamilnad, often figure in Ben Yiju's household accounts, and it is possible that their workshop was attached to his warehouse.

The vast network of relationships that Ben Yiju fitted himself into in Mangalore was clearly not a set of random associations: on the contrary, it appears to have had a life of its own, the links being transmitted between generations of merchants, just as they were from Madmun to Ben Yiju. Membership in the network evidently involved binding understandings of a kind that permitted individuals to commit large sums of money to joint undertakings, even in circumstances where there was no legal redress—understandings that clearly presuppose free and direct communications between the participants, despite their cultural, religious and linguistic differences.

But here lies a mystery into which Ben Yiju's papers offer no insight at all: the question of what language the merchants used in their dealings with each other. Madmun's letters, for instance, leave no doubt that he wrote regularly to his friends amongst the 'Bâniyân' of Mangalore. But what neither Madmun nor Ben Yiju ever reveal is what language they used in communicating with their Indian associates.

As far as their letters are concerned, the most likely solution is that they conducted their correspondence largely in Arabic, making liberal use of scribes and translators. But that still leaves a host of other questions unanswered: what language did Ben Yiju speak with Ashu, for instance? Or for that matter, how did he communicate with Bomma, or with the merchants from various regions in India and beyond, with whom, given the nature of his occupation, he must have had to do business? On the evidence of his papers there is no reason to suppose that he ever acquired fluency in Tulu or any other south Indian language: such Indian words that found their way into his writings were all of northern derivation. Indeed, learning any one language would not have solved Ben Yiju's problems of communication, for the Indians he dealt with evidently came from several different linguistic regions.

Common sense suggests that in an area as large and as diverse as the Indian Ocean, business could not possibly have been conducted in Tulu, Arabic, Gujarati or indeed any tongue that was native to a single group of traders; to function at all the language of everyday business would have had to be both simpler and much more widely dispersed than any ordinary language. Given what we know about the practices of Arab traders in other multilingual areas (the Mediterranean for example) it seems likely that the problem was resolved by using a trading argot, or an elaborated pidgin language. The Arab geographer Mas'ûdî refers, in fact, to a language called 'Lâriyya', which he describes as being spoken along much of the length of the Malabar Coast. Since no language corresponding to that name is known to exist, it is possible that he was referring to a pidgin, one that was possibly compounded largely of Perso-Arabic and north Indian elements, and was in use amongst merchants and traders all along the coast.

It is easy enough to imagine that Ben Yiju used a specialized trade language to communicate with his fellow merchants in Mangalore: the difficulties lie in imagining how he and Ashu adapted that argot to the demands of a marital bedroom.

10

IN ALL THE eighteen years or more that Ben Yiju spent in India he appears never to have ventured away from the Malabar coast; it would seem that he had no interest at all in the peninsular mainland, on the other side of the mountains. Yet Ben Yiju and his circle did not conceive of Malabar as a region separate from the mainland; as far as they were concerned Mangalore fell squarely within a loosely defined entity that covered most of the subcontinent, a territory which they referred to in their letters, as al-Hind, or bilâd al-Hind, 'the country of India.' Thus to speak of Ben Yiju living in 'India', or to refer to Bomma as an 'Indian' is not to anticipate the borders and the political vocabulary of the twentieth century: those words are merely direct translations of the terms used by Ben Yiju and his friends.

Ben Yiju's usage, in this regard, was entirely in keeping with the academic geography of the Arabic-speaking world, in which the Indian subcontinent, beginning at the eastern border of Sind and extending as far as Assam and even beyond, was generally referred to as one unit, al-Hind, just as China was al-Ṣîn. There is of course, an intriguing asymmetry in this coupling, for China was recognizably a single state, an empire whose provinces were merely constituent parts of a larger political unity. India, on the other hand, as the Arab geographers well knew, was divided into several kingdoms, large and small, and in their descriptions they were always careful to demarcate the various regions and principalities of the subcontinent. Yet, at the same time, Arab travellers and geographers appear to have believed that al-Hind had a centre, recognized by all its kings and its various different regions. For several centuries they seem to have been more or less in agreement on this subject: al-Hind, as they knew it, was centred in the domain of a king called the Ballahrâ, whose capital lay in the city of 'Mankîr'.

The names are puzzling, for they do not correspond to any known political entity, and they occur even in periods when there were frequent shifts in the centres of power in the subcontinent. An eminent scholar of Arabic, Doctor S. M. H. Nainar, has suggested that 'Mankîr' corresponded to the town of Malkhed, now in Andhra Pradesh, and that 'Ballahrâ' was an Arabic representation of 'Vallabharaja' (Supreme King), a title assumed successively by the rulers of several dynasties in the region of south-west India. But if those were indeed the original referents of those terms, in time they seem to have drifted away from their roots until they eventually became metaphors which represented, in a fashion easily comprehensible within Arab culture, India's idiosyncratic ways of giving shape to its luxuriant diversity.

In any event, there can be no doubt that in the Middle Ages, for much of the outside world, the geographical centre of India lay somewhere in the southern peninsula; to Ben Yiju in Mangalore, the northern reaches of the subcontinent may have seemed much like a distant and unruly frontier, on the outer edge of the country. For his own part he appears to have been perfectly content to stay within the Malabar coast, an area that was itself divided into a number of small kingdoms and principalities. It was within the interlinked principalities of the coast that Ben Yiju conducted his business: scattered references in his papers link him with a handful of towns, all in the Malabar—places with names such as 'Fandarîna', 'Dahfattan' and 'Jurbattan', all within easy reach of Mangalore.

Today the names of those towns carry not the faintest resonance, but in the Middle Ages they were well-known all along the trade routes of the Indian Ocean and even beyond, to scholars, geographers and travellers throughout the Arabic-speaking world. They have long since vanished from the map, at least in their earlier incarnations, but unlike many other medieval ports of the Indian Ocean 'Fandarîna', 'Jurbattan' and 'Dahfattan' did not quite disappear: they still exist, not as spectacular ruins, but in the most unexpected avatar of all; as small towns and villages which have prospered, once again, because of their connections with the far side of the Indian Ocean—in this instance the oil-producing countries of the Arab world. They lie hidden in quiet anonymity within the hills and palm-shaded lagoons of the coast, amongst some of the most beautiful landscapes in the Indian subcontinent.

The place that was known as 'Jurbattan' in medieval Arabic texts has been identified as Srikandapuram, a small town in the foothills of the Western Ghats, about a hundred miles south of Mangalore. The hills around it fall amongst the richest pepper- and spice-producing areas in Malabar, and in the Middle Ages the town probably served as a major market where traders could buy directly from producers. The hills possess other attractions as well: a cool, fresh climate and streams and valleys of a kind which even then, long before romanticism made nature an object to marvel at, could not have failed to capture the attention of those who saw them for the first time.

'Jurbattan's' combination of blessings was clearly an attractive one, and Ben Yiju appears to have visited it regularly—partly to buy spices and partly, no doubt, for pleasure. For Ashu the town may have held an added allurement: being a Nair, it is more than likely that she had relatives in the area and it may have been at her insistence that those visits were undertaken.

For Ashu, Ben Yiju, and their children, the journey would have begun with a voyage down the coast from Mangalore, for a distance of a hundred miles or so. After about two days at sea, their boat would have entered a harbour whose Arabic name, 'Budfattan', was probably a garbled rendition of Baliapatam.

Today a quiet palm-fringed road leads north towards Baliapatam from the nearby city of Cannanore, past large houses, some new, with sharp geometric lines and bright pastel colours that speak eloquently of their owners' affiliations with the Persian Gulf. Dotted between them are a few older and gentler dwellings, with carved wooden doorposts and tall red-tiled roofs that sweep high above the palm-tops. The road comes to a halt beside what appears to be a small duck-pond, with two diesel-pumps perched inexplicably on its edge. A wharf lies hidden under weeds on the bank, and on the far side there is a channel that connects it to a wide expanse of water: a great river-mouth that was once the harbour of 'Budfattan'.

From there Ashu and her family would probably have travelled upstream on river-boats as far as the current permitted, before beginning the overland journey into the hills, along the pathway to 'Jurbattan'. For much of the distance they would have used palanquins carried by porters—then the preferred mode of travel amongst those who could afford it.

Today the road that leads to Srikandapuram runs through vast plantations of cashew and rubber, with low-slung motels and lavish residences dotted along its curves and bends. In the valleys, crops seem to grow in two layers, thriving on the exuberant fertility of the land, with coconut and areca palms soaring above long rows of velvety green pepper-vines. Srikandapuram, when it arrives, proves to be a thriving little town: the houses on the outskirts are bright and new, with sleek shops and sparkling clinics dotted between them. The bazaar at the centre, however, seems to belong to another time; the shops are crammed with sacks of spices, and their owners sit cross-legged behind low counters, bargaining at leisure with their customers.

A narrow road leads south from Srikandapuram, at a precipitous angle, and, after a rapid descent to the coast, it passes through several places that would have been well-known to Ben Yiju, long before he came to India. The 'Dahfattan' of his correspondence lies at the junction of two rivers, a small cluster of Gulf-gilded houses known to the world today as Dharmadam. A little further down the coast is Pantalayini Kollam, the 'Fandarîna' of the Arabs, and the 'Pandarene' of the Portuguese, a quiet town on the

285

sea, a little to the north of Calicut.

The journey ends on a beach between 'Fandarîna' and Calicut, at a small fishing-village, hidden behind the shelter of a sand-dune. It is a quiet spot: a few catamarans and fishing-boats lie on a great crescent of sand, a vast beach that is usually empty, except when the fishing-boats come in. The village is called Kappkadavu and on one side of it beside the road is a worn white marker which tells the passer-by that this was where Vasco da Gama landed, on his first voyage to India, on 17 May 1498—some three hundred and fifty years after Ben Yiju left Mangalore.

Within a few years of that day the knell had been struck for the world that had brought Bomma, Ben Yiju and Ashu together, and another age had begun in which the crossing of their paths would seem so unlikely that its very possibility would all but disappear from human memory.

A bare two years after Vasco da Gama's voyage a Portuguese fleet led by Pedro Alvarez Cabral arrived on the Malabar coast. Cabral delivered a letter from the king of Portugal to the Samudri (Samudra-raja or Sea-king), the Hindu ruler of the city-state of Calicut, demanding that he expel all Muslims from his kingdom as they were enemies of the 'Holy Faith'. He met with a blank refusal; then as afterwards the Samudri steadfastly maintained that Calicut had always been open to everyone who wished to trade there—the Portuguese were welcome to as much pepper as they liked, so long as they bought it at cost price. The Portuguese fleet sailed away, but not before Calicut had been subjected to a two-day bombardment. A year or so later Vasco da Gama returned with another, much more powerful Portuguese fleet and demanded once again that all Muslim traders be expelled from Calicut.

During those early years the peoples who had traditionally

participated in the Indian Ocean trade were taken completely by surprise. In all the centuries in which it had flourished and grown, no state or king or ruling power had ever before tried to gain control of the Indian Ocean trade by force of arms. The territorial and dynastic ambitions that were pursued with such determination on land were generally not allowed to spill over into the sea.

Within the Western historiographical record the unarmed character of the Indian Ocean trade is often represented as a lack, or failure, one that invited the intervention of Europe, with its increasing proficiency in war. When a defeat is as complete as was that of the trading cultures of the Indian Ocean, it is hard to allow the vanquished the dignity of nuances of choice and preference. Yet it is worth allowing for the possibility that the peaceful traditions of the oceanic trade may have been, in a quiet and inarticulate way, the product of a rare cultural choice—one that may have owed a great deal to the pacifist customs and beliefs of the Gujarati Jains and Vanias who played such an important part in it. At the time, at least one European was moved to bewilderment by the unfamiliar mores of the region; a response more honest perhaps than the trust in historical inevitability that has supplanted it since. 'The heathen [of Gujarat]', wrote Tomé Pires, early in the sixteenth century, 'held that they must never kill anyone, nor must they have armed men in their company. If they were captured and [their captors] wanted to kill them all, they did not resist. This is the Gujarat law among the heathen.'

It was because of those singular traditions, perhaps, that the rulers of the Indian Ocean ports were utterly confounded by the demands and actions of the Portuguese. Having long been accustomed to the tradesman's rules of bargaining and compromise they tried time and time again to reach an understanding with the Europeans—only to discover, as one historian has put it, that the choice was 'between resistance and submission; co-operation was not offered.' Unable to compete in the Indian Ocean trade by purely commercial means, the Europeans were bent on taking control of it by aggression, pure and distilled, by unleashing violence on a scale unprecedented on those shores. As far as the Portuguese were concerned, they had declared a proprietorial right over the Indian Ocean: since none of the peoples who lived around it had thought to claim ownership of it before their arrival, they could not expect the right of free passage in it now.

By the time the trading nations of the Indian Ocean began to realize that their old understandings had been rendered defunct by the Europeans it was already too late. In 1509AD the fate of that ancient trading culture was sealed in a naval engagement that was sadly, perhaps pathetically, evocative of its ethos: a trans-continental fleet, hastily put together by the Muslim potentate of Gujarat, the Hindu ruler of Calicut, and the Sultan of Egypt was attacked and defeated by a Portuguese force off the shores of Diu, in Gujarat. As always, the determination of a small, united band of soldiers triumphed easily over the rich confusions that accompany a culture of accommodation and compromise.

The battle proved decisive; the Indian and Egyptian ships were put to flight and the Portuguese never again had to face a serious naval challenge in the Indian Ocean until the arrival of the Dutch. Soon, the remains of the civilization that had brought Ben Yiju to Mangalore were devoured by that unquenchable, demonic thirst that has raged ever since, for almost five hundred years, over the Indian Ocean, the Arabian Sea and the Persian Gulf.

GOING BACK

GOING BACK

1

LOOKING BACK, IT seems to me now that until I returned in 1988, Shaikh Musa had not realized himself quite how dramatically things had changed in Lataifa since my departure, seven years ago. As we sat talking on that rainy evening when I arrived at his door, I had the impression that he was looking back with new eyes, as though the sharp edges of my memories had served to strip away a dense layer of accretions that had gathered upon his surroundings, like bark.

But it was not long before he entered gleefully into the spirit of my wonderment, and soon enough he even began to manufacture little surprises of his own for our mutual delectation. The morning after I arrived, for example, he sent his grandson scampering out of the room on a secret errand while we were eating our breakfast. When the boy returned he had a tray in his hands, and sitting in the middle of it, like a crown on a cushion, was a richly-beaded glass of iced water.

Shaikh Musa paused to listen to the tinkling of the ice as he handed me the glass. 'You see,' he said, 'even my brother's house is full of wonders now.'

It was a couple of years since his brother's refrigerator had arrived: it had been bought for him by Mabrouk, his eldest son, who was away working in Iraq. He had come home at the end of Ramadan and one afternoon he and some other boys had hired a truck and gone off to Damanhour without telling anyone. When they returned in the evening, the truck was carrying a refrigerator, hidden under a sheet of tarpaulin.

That was two years ago, of course, when refrigerators were still a novelty. Now, every other house in Lataifa had one: many people had iced water sent out to them in the fields while they were working, and some families froze the meat they sacrificed at 'Eid so that it lasted for weeks on end.

Shaikh Musa's was one of the few houses that had neither a refrigerator nor a television set. Being deprived of something that other people took for granted was a novel and unaccustomed experience for Shaikh Musa's family: they had never really felt the lack of anything before since they owned more land than most. But of course, you couldn't buy things like refrigerators with earnings that came solely from the land: for money of that kind you had to go away, to Iraq, or Libya, or the Gulf.

Once, on his way to the market in Damanhour, Shaikh Musa had stopped to look at the showroom where his nephew Mabrouk had bought his refrigerator. It was near the centre of the city, a huge place, with glass windows, and salesmen dressed in suits and ties. He looked in through the window, but he hadn't felt like walking in, dressed in his fellah's jallabeyya and cap. It had come as a shock to think that boys like Mabrouk thought nothing of going into places like that, no matter what they were wearing: they went straight in and sent those effendis running around, in their suits and ties, obeying their orders.

Shaikh Musa laughed when I reminded him how Mabrouk had once come running up to my room to take me to see the

'Indian machine' his father had just bought; how everyone had been taken by surprise because Mabrouk was thought to be one of the shyest boys in the hamlet.

'You wouldn't know him now,' said Shaikh Musa. 'He's so smart, he can paint the air with his talk.'

Most of the young men of Mabrouk's generation were gone now, all but a handful of the eager schoolboys who had never tired of asking me questions; those who had stayed back had done so only because they hadn't been able to find a job 'outside', or because their families needed them on the land. There had always been a fair number of people from the area working 'outside' of course, but now it was different; it was as though half the working population had taken leave of the land and surged into Iraq.

The flow had started in the early 1980s, a couple of years after the beginning of the war between Iraq and Iran; by then Iraq's own men were all tied up on one front or another, in Iran or Kurdistan, and it was desperately in need of labour to sustain its economy. For several years around that time it had been very easy for an Egyptian to find a job there; recruiters and contractors had gone from village to village looking for young men who were willing to work 'outside'. People had left in truckloads: it was said at one time that there were maybe two or three million Egyptian workers in Iraq, as much as a sixth of that country's population. It was as if the two nations had dissolved into each other.

But after the war with Iran ended the Iraqis had immediately changed their policies; their demobilized soldiers had wanted jobs and in order to encourage the migrant workers to go home the government had made new rules and regulations, restricting the flow of currency and suchlike. Over the last couple of years it had become hard to find jobs 'outside' and some of the young men who had left had begun to trickle back to their villages.

Ahmed, Shaikh Musa's son, had often talked of going to work in Iraq: he'd wanted to give his wife and children some of those things that other people had in their houses—a television set, a fridge, perhaps a washing-machine. But Shaikh Musa had refused to hear of it—he had told him to put the idea out of his head, at least so long as he was alive. The reports he had heard about Iraq had made him anxious: the boys who went there often came back with frightening stories—about how they had been mistreated by their employers and sometimes even attacked on the streets by complete strangers for no apparent reason. The Iraqis resented immigrants, he had been told, because they took their jobs away while they were fighting on the front: their 'souls had sickened', as the saying went, through their long years of war, and they often vented their rage on foreigners.

After hearing those stories Shaikh Musa had resolved not to let Ahmed go. What if something were to happen to him while he was away, far from home? He had already lost one son; he couldn't bear to think of another picture hanging on his guest-room wall, next to Hasan's. He would not let Ahmed go, no matter how many things other people had in their houses; it would have been good to have those things, but it was better to live in peace and fear God.

Of my younger friends in Lataifa, only one still remained in Egypt—Jabir. Shaikh Musa had sent word to his family early that morning, knowing that I would want to see him, but Jabir had gone to Damanhour and wouldn't be back till later.

'Why hasn't Jabir "gone outside"?' I asked. 'Didn't he ever want to leave?'

'Oh yes,' said Shaikh Musa. 'He went once for a few months

while he was in college and he's wanted to go back again, ever since. All his friends are outside; even Mohammad, his younger brother, has gone away to Jordan. Jabir has been trying to go for a long time, but it just hasn't worked out, that's all. But I heard recently that he's found something and might be on his way soon; they say he's even cut his beard in preparation.'

'His beard!' I said in surprise. 'Did Jabir have a beard?'

Shaikh Musa laughed perfunctorily.

Yes, he said, Jabir had sported a beard for a while; he had grown it while he was away in college, in the city of Tanta. Everybody was amazed when he came back for the holidays one summer, wearing a beard cut in a distinctively Muslim style. It wasn't surprising of course, for Jabir was always a bright boy, and all the brightest young men had beards now, and many wore white robes as well. Jabir sometimes delivered the Friday sermon in the mosque nowadays, and he too wore white robes for those occasions. He surprised everyone the first time, including his uncle Ustaz Mustafa: he had looked very impressive in his flowing robes and beard, and he had spoken very well too, in beautiful language, with many quotations and polished phrases. Ustaz Mustafa, who had studied in Alexandria himself, said later that Jabir had spoken well even by the standards of the best orators in colleges and universities.

There was a touch of awe in Shaikh Musa's voice now, as though he could barely imagine the courage and daring it would cost a fellah boy, from a tiny hamlet like Lataifa, to throw himself into the flamboyantly public world of religious debate in cities and universities. Even though he was as devout and strictly observant a Muslim as any, he would not have dreamed of entering that milieu: he considered himself far too ignorant to enter into learned arguments on matters of religion.

After breakfast we set off to visit Abu-'Ali: Shaikh Musa had decided that since he was the person who had first introduced me to Lataifa, it was only fitting that I go to see him before visiting any other house in the hamlet. The prospect of meeting Abu-'Ali was not one that I had looked forward to, yet once we set out for his house I was suddenly curious, eager to know how he and his family had fared.

From what I knew of Abu-'Ali, I was fairly sure that his fortunes had more than kept pace with his neighbours', but I was still taken by surprise when I entered his compound. A large soaring new carapace had sprouted upon the dilapidated, low-slung house of my memories: the room on the roof, where I had gone to live, years ago, was now a part of a brightly-painted, three-storeyed mansion. The spindly old moped that had so miraculously borne Abu-'Ali to and from Damanhour had vanished, and in its place was a gleaming new Toyota pick-up truck.

But Abu-'Ali himself was exactly where he had always been, stationed at a vantage point overlooking the road. The moment we stepped into his compound, he thrust his head out of a window, sidewise, like the MGM lion. 'Come in, come in,' he roared. 'Where have you been all these years, my son? Come in, come in and bring blessings upon my house.'

At the sound of his voice his wife rushed out to the veranda to greet us, followed closely by several new additions to her family. Smiling warmly, sweet-natured as ever, she welcomed me into the house, and after we had gone through a long list of salutations, she introduced me to three recently-recruited daughters-in-law, pointing out each of their children, one by one.

I had half-expected, from the unforeseen vigour of Abu-'Ali's roar of welcome, that he too would come hurrying out to the veranda to greet us; in my imagination I had already pictured our meeting, quailing at the thought of exchanging hugs and kisses across the billowing expanse of his stomach. But although Abu-'Ali's roars continued unabated, he failed to materialize in person. I discovered why when his wife led us to him. He had grown even fatter than I remembered; the image of an engorged python that I had carried away with me seemed pitifully inadequate for the sight I was now confronted with: his stomach now soared above him like a dirigible in flight as he lay on his back, intermittently flapping his hands and feet as though to propel himself through the air.

His voice had not been diminished by his body's spectacular enlargement however, and as soon as we were seated he began to chronicle the growth of his family's fortunes in an earth-shaking roar. Much as I had expected, he had been one of the first people in the area to become aware of the opportunities that were opening up in Iraq, during the war with Iran. He had sent his eldest son there soon after I left, and the others had followed, one by one. He had taken care, however, to make sure that they were never all away at the same time; he needed at least one of them at home, to help with the running of his business in Lataifa. There was a lot to take care of, for he was no longer just a shopkeeper now—with the money his sons had sent back from Iraq, he had bought two pick-up trucks and gone into transportation. So successful had the venture been that he was now thinking of setting up yet another business, a flour-mill, or maybe even a modern poultry-farm.

While telling us the story, Abu-'Ali broke off from time to time to order his daughters-in-law and grandchildren to fetch some of the things his sons had brought back from Iraq.

Following his instructions, they filed obediently through the guest-room, carrying by turns a TV set, a food processor, a handful of calculators, a transistor radio, a couple of cassette-players, a pen that was also a flashlight, a watch that could play tunes, a key-ring that answered to a handclap and several other such objects. Shaikh Musa and I stared awestruck as these possessions floated past us like helots gazing at the spoils of Pharaoh.

When the parade was complete, at Abu-'Ali's instructions his wife led us upstairs to show us their newly built apartments. Following her up the staircase I was assaulted by a sudden sensation of dislocation, as though I had vaulted between different epochs. The dirt and chaos of the ground floor, where Abu-'Ali and his wife lived, the flies, the grime, and the scattered goats' droppings, stopped abruptly halfway up the staircase: above that point the floors were meticulously clean, covered in mosaic tiles. Where my room, the old chicken-coop, had once stood, there was now a large kitchen, adjoining an opulently furnished bedroom. It had been incorporated into a complex of four apartments, one for each of Abu-'Ali's sons. The three who were married had already moved in, but the youngest, a bachelor, still lived downstairs whenever he came home on visits from Iraq.

We visited the apartments of her three married sons in turn. They were very alike, each with a drawing-room appointed with ornate furnishings of a kind often seen in the windows of shops in Cairo and Alexandria. It was evident that the drawing-rooms were rarely used, and even Abu-'Ali's wife seemed hesitant to step past their curtained doorways. Neither Shaikh Musa nor I could bring ourselves to go in, despite her repeated urgings: it was clear that Abu-'Ali had now risen to an estate where neither

his family nor his neighbours were fit to use his furniture.
Such were his gleanings from that distant war.

2

IT WAS PROBABLY in the mid-1140s or so that Ben Yiju began to
think seriously of returning to the Middle East. At about that
time, after many years of silence, he finally received news about
a member of his family—his younger brother Mubashshir, who
as far as he knew was still living in their homeland, Ifriqiya.

The news probably arrived in the wake of a long series of
distressing reports from Ifriqiya: travelling merchants and
friends had probably kept Ben Yiju informed of how the region
had been laid waste by Sicilian armies over the last several years,
and of how its people had been stricken by famine and disease.
Thus Ben Yiju was probably already in a state of severe anxiety
when his friend Khalaf wrote to him from Aden, relaying a brief
message from his brother.

'Shaikh Abû Isḥâq ibn Yûsuf arrived here this year,' wrote
Khalaf. 'He reports that your brother Mubashshir has arrived in
Egypt. He has asked for passage to join you: you should know
this.'

Ben Yiju's papers provide only indirect signs of the impact
this message had on him. His immediate response was probably
to write to his friends to beg for more news, and to ask them to
make arrangements for the payment of his brother's onward
passage to India. As it turned out, however, his efforts were to
no avail: his brother proved more elusive than he had expected

and his inquiries met with nothing more than comforting generalities. 'Concerning the news of your brother Mubashshir,' Khalaf wrote back, 'he is well, but he has not arrived here [in Aden] yet.'

But Ben Yiju must have continued to write to his friends at regular intervals, asking them to persist in their inquiries, and to do what they could to send Mubashshir on to Mangalore. For their part, they appear to have exerted themselves on both counts, but despite their efforts Mubashshir continued to absent himself from Aden. Eventually, despairing of success, Yusuf ibn Abraham wrote back to say: 'My master [Ben Yijû] mentioned Mubashshir, his brother [in his letter]: he has not arrived here in all this time, and nor have I seen a letter for my master from Egypt. If such a letter for my master appears his servant will send it to him.' Later in the same letter he added the ominous comment: 'As for the news of Egypt, my master will hear it from the traders...'

Such news as Ben Yiju received from the Middle East could only have given him further cause for anxiety. From 1143 onwards, for several successive years, his homeland, Ifriqiya, had been the target of attacks launched by King Roger II of Sicily. Disease and famine had followed upon these raids and large numbers of people fled the region. Along with a substantial section of the Jewish population of Ifriqiya, the Ben Yiju family was swept away from Mahdia at about this time and deposited in Sicily—unbeknownst to their brother Abraham, living in quiet, untroubled prosperity in distant Mangalore.

At the same time other, still more sombre, portents were taking shape on the two mirrored rims of the Mediterranean. In western Europe the sermons of Bernard of Clairvaux had aroused a frenzy of religious fervour, and preparations for a new

Crusade were under way amidst widespread massacres of Jews. In Germany things had come to such a pass that the despairing Jews of Cologne had begun to lament: 'Behold the days of reckoning have come, the end has arrived, the plague has begun, our days are completed, for our end is here.' At about the same time, in the far west of North Africa the al-Muwaḥḥid (Almohad) dynasty was gaining in strength, and its armies were advancing steadily through the Maghreb, towards Ifriqiya. Between 1145 and 1146 they took the cities of Oran, Tlemcen and the oasis of Sijilmasa, on the north-western border of the Sahara. For seven months they tried peaceably to convert Sijilmasa's large Jewish population to Islam. When their efforts went unrewarded they put a hundred and fifty Jews to the sword. The rest, led by their judge, quickly converted. They were relatively lucky: at about the same time a hundred thousand Christians and Jews were massacred by the Almohads in Fez, and a hundred and twenty thousand in Marrakesh.

Far away though he was, Ben Yiju was probably not unaware of the bloodshed and turmoil that had stricken his homeland: it so happens that the Geniza has yielded a letter addressed to Ben Yiju's friend, the indefatigable traveller Abu Zikri ha-Kohen Sijilmasi, which contains a detailed account of the events in North Africa. The letter was written by Abu Zikri's son, in Cairo, and sent to him in Aden, in 1148. Not long before, in about 1145, Abu Zikri Sijilmasi had been stranded in Gujarat after being captured by pirates. On that occasion Ben Yiju had penned a letter to him, on behalf of his brother-in-law, the 'nakhoda' Mahruz, from Mangalore. Now, three years later, upon learning of the events in North Africa, Abu Zikri would certainly have made an effort to pass the news on to Ben Yiju in Mangalore.

As luck would have it, there was more bad news in store for

Ben Yiju: his friend Khalaf had come to know that Mubashshir was now thinking of travelling to Syria, rather than India, and in 1148 he wrote to Ben Yiju to let him know that his hopes for a reunion with his brother were unlikely to be soon fulfilled.

'I asked [some people] about your brother Mubashshir,' Khalaf wrote. 'They said that he is in good health and that everything is well with him. I asked them about his departure for Syria and they said they knew nothing of it, but that all is well with him. Should he happen to come to Aden your servant will do his best for him, without my master's asking because he esteems him [my master] greatly.'

It may have been this piece of news, following hard upon other events, that finally made up Ben Yiju's mind. He had probably already written to Madmun to sort out whatever tangle it was that had kept him so long absent from Aden. From his friends' letters it would seem that he had written to others as well, mentioning thoughts of return. 'Every year you speak of coming to Aden,' wrote Khalaf in his letter of 1148, 'but you never do it.'

This time Ben Yiju did do it: a year later, in 1149, he was back in Aden, with all his worldly goods and his two adolescent children.

On 11 September 1149, Ben Yiju wrote his brothers a long letter from Aden. His return had stirred many long-settled memories, and he was now overcome with a desire to reclaim his family and the remembered landscapes of his childhood: 'I do not know what to write,' the letter begins, 'so strong is my longing and so ardent my yearning.'

The thought uppermost in Ben Yiju's mind at the time of writing was of providing reassurance and succour to his family. He had heard, he wrote, that their circumstances were now so dire that they had been reduced 'to a single loaf of bread' and he had tried to send them some goods to tide them over the worst, but the shipment had gone astray because of the uncertainty of their present location. He was writing now to offer them whatever else he could; to let them know that he had returned from India and arrived safely in Aden, 'with my belongings, life, and children well preserved', and money 'enough to live on for all of us'. '[Therefore], I ask you, my brother[s],' he urged, 'come to me under any circumstances and without delay...I have a son and a daughter, take them and take with them all the money and riches—*may God fulfil my wishes and yours for the good.* Come quickly and take possession of this money; this is better than strangers taking it.'

But he had another reason too for urging his brothers to join him in Aden 'under any circumstances and without delay': with his departure from India his yearning for his family had grown so powerful that he now longed to reaffirm his bonds with them through a familial union of another kind. 'Also, find out,' he directed them, 'who is the best of the sons of my brother [Yûsuf] or the sons of your sister Berâkhâ, so that I may marry him off to my daughter.'

But it was not until he penned the last lines of the letter that Ben Yiju gave expression to the anxiety that the recent events in North Africa had caused him: 'I heard of what happened on the coast of Ifriqiya, in Tripoli, Jerba, Kerkenna, Sfax, al-Mahdia and Sousse. But I have had no letter to tell me who lives and who is dead. For God's sake, write to me about it and send the letter in the hands of trustworthy people so that I may have some peace of mind. Shalom.'

The address that Ben Yiju wrote on the back was every bit as expressive of the uncertainties of the time as the letter itself. It

303

was sent to al-Mahdia, 'if God will, or anywhere else in Ifriqiya.'

In the event, the letter did not fulfil the destiny Ben Yiju had intended for it. As luck would have it, it fell into the hands of his brother Mubashshir, in the port of Messina, in northern Sicily. His other brother, the pious and unworldly Yusuf, was then living at the far end of the island, in Mazzara, along with his wife and his three sons, Surûr, Moshe and Shamwâl. Disobeying his brother's instructions, Mubashshir chose not to inform Yusuf's family about the letter: as Ben Yiju was to learn to his cost, Mubashshir was a man who had few scruples where money was concerned.

Ultimately rumour proved more conscientious than kinship, and somehow Yusuf did eventually learn that a letter from his brother Abraham had made its way to Sicily. Yusuf's sons were all well-educated and dutiful young men, and none more so than the eldest, Surur. Having heard rumours of the letter, and possibly also of the proposal of marriage contained in it, Surur appears to have taken the task of locating his uncle on his own shoulders. A letter that he wrote at that time to a family acquaintance in Mahdia bears witness to the painstaking thoroughness with which he conducted his inquiries.

'I wished to ask,' Surur wrote, 'whether [my master] has any news of my father's brother, Abraham, known as Ben Yijû, for we have not heard from him [for some time]...Last year...a letter of his reached Messina, where it fell into the hands of my uncle Mubashshir, who took it with him. We have not seen it, and do not know what was in it. So our minds are in suspense, as we wait to hear news of how he is. May I request my Master, to kindly write us a brief note, to let us know whether he has heard any news of him and where he is...'

But the times were hard: the entire region was in turmoil, devastated by war. It would be a long time before Surur and his family next heard news of their uncle 'Abraham, known as Ben Yiju.'

3

WITHIN MINUTES OF leaving Abu-'Ali's house, I was brought to a halt by the sound of a familiar voice calling out my name. A moment later Jabir was beside me, and we were pounding each other on the back, exchanging handshakes, slapping our hands together, sending echoes down the lanes.

Jabir was greatly changed and looked much older than his twenty-five years: his face had grown considerably rounder and heavier; the hair at the top of his head had receded and at his temples there were two very prominent patches of grey (mere spots, as he was quick to point out, compared to mine). Once the greetings were over, we quickly agreed that we had a great deal to talk about, so we took leave of Shaikh Musa and headed towards his house. He had a room to himself now, Jabir said, and we could sit there in peace and talk as long as we liked.

On reaching the house, he led me quickly down a corridor, past his cousins and aunts, to a small room furnished with a desk and a bed. After ushering me in, he slammed the door and turned the key, locking out the troop of children who were following close behind us.

I was astonished: in all the time I had spent in Lataifa and Nashawy, I had never seen anyone shut a door upon people in their own house. But when I remarked on this it was Jabir's turn to be surprised.

'You used to shut your door,' he said. 'Have you forgotten or what? We had to bang on it if we wanted to come in.'

Gesturing to me to seat myself on the bed, he cocked his head at the door. 'There's too much noise outside,' he said. 'Too many people: I was away in college for such a long time that now it's become very hard for me here, with so many people in the house.'

He had first left Lataifa in 1982, he said, the year after my departure from Egypt. He had gone to Tanta, a large town about sixty miles from Cairo, to do a degree in commerce at the university there.

'It was wonderful,' he said wistfully. 'I lived on the campus, sharing a room with other students, and we all became close friends. We spent most of our time together, in class and afterwards.'

'Did you find it hard?' I asked. 'Being away from your cousins, your family?'

He threw me a look of surprise. 'No,' he said. 'Not at all, and anyway I saw them from time to time. I was very busy, I was learning so many things, seeing new places, it was so exciting to be there…'

Cutting himself short, he reached under his bed and pulled out a green plastic suitcase. A few shirts and trousers were neatly packed away inside, along with some books and several small packets, carefully wrapped in paper. Picking out one of those packages, he handed it to me and watched, smiling, as I undid the string.

'It's the wallet you gave me before you left Lataifa and went to Nashawy,' he said. 'You brought it back from Cairo—do you remember? I always use it when I go to the city, and if people ask me about it, I tell them about the Indian who gave it to me, and how he once mistook the moon for Ahmed Musa's torch.'

Laughing, he reached into his suitcase again, thumbed through a wad of photographs and handed me one. It was a picture I had taken myself, years ago, of Jabir, in a field near Lataifa; I had sent it to him later, from India, with one of my letters. I was proud of the picture, for I had succeeded in catching him at an unguarded moment, looking towards the camera in the way that came most naturally to him, with an expression that was at once challenging and quizzical, something between a smile and scowl. Seeing that picture again, after so many years, I realized that it was neither Jabir's grey hair nor the shape of his face that was responsible for the difference in his appearance: the real change lay somewhere else, in some other, more essential quality. In the Jabir who was sitting in front of me I could no longer see the sly, sharp-tongued ferocity my camera had captured so well that day—its place had been taken by a kind of quiet hopelessness, an attitude of resignation.

Jabir explained the other photographs in the pile as he handed them to me, one by one: they had been taken later, mainly in the gardens and buildings of his university. In the earlier photographs he was always with the same group of friends, classmates with whom he had shared a room for a couple of years. Most of them were working 'outside' now, so they had lost touch with each other. But they had been inseparable for the first couple of years; they had studied together and gone on holidays together, to Cairo, Aswan and the Sinai. It was clear from the tone of Jabir's voice that the memories of those friendships meant a great deal to him, yet I couldn't help noticing that in many of the pictures he looked like the odd man out, standing straight and looking fixedly into the camera, while the others around him threw themselves into attitudes of exuberant student horseplay. It was easy to see that they were all city boys, from middle-class families: they wore different clothes in each picture, pastel-coloured running-shoes, jeans and T-shirts. Jabir's clothes, on the other hand, looked as though they had been bought in the bazaar at Damanhour, and the same few shirts and trousers recurred in several pictures in succession, as though to prove that he had stayed true to his frugal village upbringing.

The beard that Shaikh Musa had mentioned appeared about three-quarters of the way through the pile of photographs. At first it had the look of cotton fluff, but later it took on a quite impressive appearance, reaching down to the line of his collar.

'It took me a long time to grow that beard,' he said. 'I looked much better when I had it—more respectable. I never had to bargain when I went to the market—no one would try to cheat me.'

I made no comment and, after turning over a few more pictures, he added that it was in college that he had begun to learn the real meaning of Islam, from talking to some of his teachers and fellow-students. They had read the Quran together every day and held long discussions that lasted late into the night.

'I was not involved in politics or anything,' he said, 'and I didn't join any groups or societies. But I learnt to recognize what is wrong and what is true. I don't know how to explain these things to you: you don't understand matters like these.'

'Why did you shave your beard off?' I asked.

His fingers slid over his freshly shaven chin in a slow, exploratory movement. 'My family wanted me to,' he said.

'Especially my mother.'

'Why?'

'They were afraid,' he said. 'There's been trouble between the government and certain Islamic groups, and they were worried that something might happen to me—even though I don't belong to any group or party.'

He shook his head and let out an ironic snort of laughter. 'This is a Muslim country,' he said. 'And it isn't safe to look like a Muslim.'

Then, abruptly, he dropped the subject and began asking me why I had not written for so long and what I had been doing since I left Egypt. My recital was a long one, and towards the end of it he grew pensive and began to ask detailed questions—about how much I had paid to fly to Egypt and the current exchange rates of the Indian rupee, the American dollar and the Egyptian pound.

'I may have to buy an air-ticket soon,' he said, at length. 'I've been trying to get a job outside. I worked in Iraq while I was in college, and if God wills I shall go there again.'

The first time he went, he said, was after his second year in college. One of his cousins, who was a foreman on a construction site in Baghdad, had taken him there so he could earn some money during his summer vacation. He had had to get a special kind of passport, because as a rule the Egyptian government did not allow its citizens to go abroad until they had completed their time in the army. Getting the passport hadn't been easy, but it had proved to be well worth it, in the end. He had earned so much money that his father was able to add a new room to their house.

He showed me a few photographs taken in Iraq, and I immediately recognized several other faces, besides his—friends and cousins of his, whom I'd known in Lataifa or Nashawy. The pictures were mostly taken in markets and parks in Baghdad, on holidays—I could almost see them myself, setting off in their best clothes, their faces alight with the pleasurable apprehension of being on their own in a faraway city, with their pockets full of money, well out of the reach of their parents and elders.

'What was it like there?' I asked.

'I was young then,' Jabir said, 'and I was sometimes a little scared.'

The Iraqis were very rough in their ways, he explained. He and his cousins and friends wouldn't usually go out at nights; they would stay in their rooms, all of them together, and cook and watch television. But despite all that, Iraq was better than some other places; from what he had heard, the Gulf Emirates were much worse. At least in Iraq everyone got paid properly. As far as he was concerned, he didn't care how the Iraqis behaved —all he wanted was to go back, after finishing with college and the army.

For a while it had looked as though things would go exactly as he had planned. His time in the army had passed quickly and without hardship, for his college degree had earned him a comfortable bookkeeping job in his unit.

'I was near Alexandria and it was nice,' he said. 'The officers treated me differently, not like the other soldiers, because I'd been to college and everything. They treated me almost like I was one of them.'

He had applied for a passport as soon as he got out of the army, and wasted no time in writing letters to his friends and cousins in Iraq, asking them to look out for job openings. He had expected that he'd be able to find a job without difficulty, just as he had the last time. But soon he discovered that things had changed. Iraqi soldiers and reservists had begun to go back to work and there were fewer and fewer jobs for foreigners. Worse still, the Iraqi government had established strict new laws which made it hard for Egyptian workers to send money home. But dozens of his friends and relatives were still there, of course, and they were managing well enough—anything was better than sitting idly at home, after all. So he had written to them again and again, asking them to let him know as soon as they heard of a job—he didn't care what it was, he just wanted a job, somewhere 'outside', in Iraq or wherever.

In the meantime, he had come back to Lataifa to wait until he was notified about the government job to which he was entitled by virtue of his college degree. It was not much to look forward to, for the salary was a pittance, a fraction of what a construction worker could earn in Iraq. But still, it was something. He had waited for months to hear about the job, and when the notification still hadn't arrived, he had begun to work with a bricklayer, as an apprentice: there were many houses being built now, in Lataifa and Nashawy, with the money that people were receiving from 'outside'.

'It's just for the time being,' Jabir said quickly. 'Until I find a job outside. I'll leave as soon as I hear of something, insha'allah.'

Piling the photographs together, he put them away again, rearranging his suitcase in the process. I could tell from the way he did it that packing his suitcase had become a habit with him.

'I made a mistake,' he said at last, shutting the suitcase. 'I thought a degree would help me, so I went to college. It was an exciting time and I learnt so much, but at the end of it, look, what am I doing? I'm a construction worker. I wasted time by going to college; I missed the best opportunities.'

And as a measure of his folly, there was the example of his brother Mohammad, who had planned his future better.

Mohammad was a year younger than Jabir, but he looked older, being taller and more heavily built. Unlike Jabir, he had never taken an interest in his studies and had barely managed to get through school; the thought of going to college had never entered his mind. Instead, he did his National Service as soon as possible, and then apprenticed himself to a carpenter in a nearby village. After spending a few months in acquiring the rudiments of the trade, he got himself a job in Jordan—that was at a time when jobs were still easy to get. He'd been in Jordan ever since, making good money. Recently he had written to say that he was coming home for a while—there was a chance that he might be able to get a job in Italy soon and he wanted to make arrangements for his future.

Jabir broke off there, his lips tightly pursed. He wouldn't say any more but the rest was clear enough: Mohammad wanted to get married before going off again. He had probably saved enough money to buy a house or an apartment—in Damanhour perhaps, or somewhere else—so he was now in a position to make a good marriage and set up house. In all likelihood, the only reason he had waited so long was because Jabir was older, and therefore entitled, by custom, to marry first. But, of course, Jabir had no savings and no means of buying an apartment of his own. And without one he wouldn't be able to marry someone compatible, a girl with a college education—instead he would have to marry a cousin from Lataifa, and live with his family, with no place to call his own. That was why it was imperative for him to find a job as soon as possible; time was running out— Mohammad had waited long enough, and no one would blame him now if he went ahead and got married. He had more than done his duty by custom.

In some part of his mind, Jabir was probably entirely in

sympathy with his brother's predicament, yet if Mohammad were to be the first to marry, it would be a public announcement of his own failure. I had only to look at Jabir's face to know that if that happened he would be utterly crushed, destroyed.

Turning his back on me, Jabir busied himself with his suitcase, repacking it yet again, as though to satisfy a craving. 'I'll be going back to Iraq soon,' he said, in a voice that was barely audible.

I couldn't see his face but I knew he was near tears.

4

THE RETURN TO Aden, undertaken with such gladness of spirit, was to bring nothing but tragedy to Ben Yiju. Such were the misfortunes that befell him there that within three years or so he uprooted himself once again. It was to Egypt that he now moved, and shortly after his arrival there, he tried once more to establish direct communication with his brother Yusuf, in Sicily.

The letter he wrote on this occasion was a long one, like the last, but his mood and his circumstances were greatly changed and the nostalgic exuberance that had seized him upon his return to Aden had now yielded to a resigned and broken-hearted melancholy. Writing to his brother now, he felt compelled to provide him with an account of some of the events that had befallen him since he last wrote, in 1149.

'I wrote a letter to you a while ago,' Ben Yiju told Yusuf. 'It reached Mubashshir, but he did not care to deliver it to you: [instead] he arrived in Aden [himself].'

But Mubashshir's visit, so long awaited, had not turned out as
Ben Yiju had expected: 'I did all that was in my power for him
and more, but he dealt me a ruinous blow. The events would
take too long to explain, O my brother...' A couple of lines
scribbled in the margin provides a hint of what had passed
between them. In the course of his stay in Aden, Mubashshir
had defrauded his brother of a huge sum of money: 'As for
Mubashshir, he is nothing but a lazy man; malevolent in spirit.
I gave him whatever he asked for, and in return he dealt me a
ruinous blow. The price of my deeds was a thousand dînârs...'

Yet, painful as it was, the discovery of his brother's dishonesty
was a small matter compared to the weight of Ben Yiju's other
misfortunes: in the meantime he had also suffered the loss of his
first child, the son born of his union with Ashu, to whom he
had given the joyful name Surur.

The surviving copy of the letter still contains a part of the
passage in which Ben Yiju tells Yusuf of his son's death. He had
once had, he writes, 'two children like sprigs of sweet basil...'—
but here the sentence breaks off, for the letter has been badly
damaged over the centuries. The little that remains of the
passage is punctuated with a bizarrely expressive succession of
silences, as though time had somehow contrived to provide the
perfect parentheses for Ben Yiju's grief by changing the scansion
of his prose. It reads:

And the elder [of the two children] died in Aden...
I do not know what to describe of it...
I have left a daughter, his sister...

It was partly because of this daughter, Sitt al-Dâr, that Ben
Yiju was now writing to his brother; he had been separated
from her for prolonged periods over the last several years, and

her future was now his most pressing concern.

Soon after moving to Aden, Ben Yiju had transferred his base out of that city and into the highlands of the interior, to a city called Dhû Jibla, which served as one of the principal seats of the ruling Zuray'id dynasty. For about three years afterwards he had lived mostly in the Yemeni mountains while his daughter remained in Aden, in the custody of his old and faithful friend Khalaf ibn Ishaq, living in his house as a member of his family.

The reasons for Ben Yiju's move are not entirely clear, but the loss of his son must have played a part in inducing him to leave Aden. In any event, he was already living in the mountains when he received news of yet another loss, just a couple of years after his arrival in Aden.

In 1151 Ben Yiju's old friend and one-time mentor, Madmun ibn Bundar, died in Aden. Ben Yiju was to read of his death in a letter from a correspondent: 'The news reached your exalted honour's slave, of the death of the lord and owner Madmûn…the stalwart pillar, Nagîd of the land of Yemen, Prince of the communities, Crown of the Choirs…' To Ben Yiju the news of Madmun's death must have come as a terrible blow: among his few surviving pieces of verse is a Hebrew poem, composed in memory of his friend.

In some ways, however, Ben Yiju evidently found a good deal of fulfilment in his new home in the Yemeni highlands. Such documentation as there is on this period of his life suggests that he enjoyed a position of some prominence within the Jewish communities of the interior, and he may even have been appointed to serve as a judge. Yet there must also have been many anxieties attendant on living in that relatively inaccessible region: his correspondence shows that he was greatly concerned about the safety of the roadways, for instance, which is hardly surprising considering that he was separated from his only surviving child by a wide stretch of difficult terrain, in a divided and war-torn land.

An extraordinary dilemma was to result from Ben Yiju's long separation from his daughter. His friend Khalaf, whose house she was living in, eventually approached him with a proposal of marriage for her, on behalf of one of his sons. The documents provide no indication of what her wishes in the matter were, but it is more than likely of course that Khalaf was acting with her consent; it is even possible that it was the young couple themselves who had prevailed upon him to speak to Ben Yiju about a betrothal, expecting that the request could hardly be refused when it came from a friend of such long standing.

But close though Ben Yiju was to his friends in Aden, he stood apart from them in one respect: their family origins, unlike his own, lay in the region of Iraq. The matter need not have made a difference had Ben Yiju chosen to ignore it, for such marriages were commonplace within their circle. But in the event Ben Yiju chose to disregard his long-standing association with Khalaf and his family: almost as though he were seeking to disown a part of his own past, he now decided that he could not let his daughter marry a 'foreigner'. Instead, he began to dream again of reaffirming his bonds with his family in the accepted fashion of the Middle East, by marrying her to her cousin, his brother Yusuf's eldest son, Surur.

In his letter to his brother he explained the matter thus:

Shaikh Khalaf [ibn Ishaq] ibn Bundâr, in Aden, [asked her hand] for his son. She had lived 3 years in their house. But I refused him when I heard of your son Surûr. I said: the brother's son comes before foreign people. Then, when I came with her to Egypt, many people sought her hand of me. I write to you to tell you of this: to say less than this would have been enough.

But in a culture where marital negotiations can cast the whole weight of a family's honour upon the scales of public judgement, the refusal of a proposal from an old friend, of distinguished lineage, cannot have been a simple matter. It is probably not a coincidence therefore that the Geniza contains no record of any further communication between Ben Yiju and his friends in Aden. His rejection of Khalaf's offer may well have led to an irreversible break with him and his kinsmen, including Yusuf ibn Abraham: indeed, it may even have been the immediate cause of his departure.

Thus it was on a note of real urgency that Ben Yiju wrote to his brother upon arriving in Egypt. He had been told, he said, that Yusuf had a son, Surur, 'who is learned in the Torah', and if he were to send him now to Egypt, to marry his daughter, he would have all his goods—'and we will rejoice in her and in him, and we will wed them...' For Ben Yiju everything now hung on a quick response from his brother. 'Address your letters to me in Egypt, insha'allâh,' he exhorted Yusuf, 'let there be a letter in the hands of your son, Surûr.'

Indeed, beset by grief, disillusionment and misfortune, Ben Yiju now had no recourse other than his brother and his nephews. To the two couriers who were to carry his letter to Sicily he entrusted a confession of quiet despair.

'Sulîmân and Abraham will tell you of the state I am in,' Ben Yiju wrote. 'I am sick at heart.'

5

I COULD HAVE found Nabeel's house myself of course, but in the end I was grateful to the children who insisted on leading me there: on my own I would have been reluctant to knock on the doors of the structure that stood there now. The mud-walled rooms I so well remembered were gone and in their place stood the unfinished shell of a large new bungalow.

The door was opened by Nabeel's sister-in-law, Fawzia. She clapped her hands to her head, laughing, when she saw me outside. The first thing she said was: 'Nabeel's not here—he's not in the village, he's gone to Iraq.'

Then, collecting herself, she ushered me in and after putting a tea-kettle on the stove, she sat me down and told me the story of how Nabeel had left for Iraq. His father, old Idris the watchman, had died the year after I left, and his wife had not long outlived him. Nabeel had been away from the village on both occasions. He was in the army then, and he hadn't been able to return in time to see them before they died. On her deathbed his mother had called out for him, over and over again—he had always been her favourite and she had long dreamed of dancing at his wedding. On both occasions Nabeel had come down for a quick visit, to attend the ceremonies; he did not say much, either time, but it was easy to see that he had been profoundly affected.

His best friend, Fawzia's brother Isma'il, had long been urging him to apply for a passport so he could work in Iraq after finishing his National Service. Nabeel was not particularly receptive to the idea at first: he had always wanted a job in a government office, a respectable clerical job, and he knew that in Iraq he would probably end up doing manual labour of some kind. But the death of his parents changed his mind. He put in an application for a passport, and in 1986, soon after finishing his time in the army, he left for Iraq with Isma'il.

Things had turned out well for him in Iraq; within a few months he had found a job as an assistant in a photographer's shop in Baghdad. It didn't pay as much as Isma'il's job, in construction, but it was a fortune compared to what he would have earned in Egypt.

Besides it was exactly the kind of job that Nabeel wanted. 'You know him,' Fawzia said, laughing. 'He always wanted a job where he wouldn't have to get his hands dirty.'

There was a telephone where he worked, she said, and the man who owned the shop didn't mind him receiving calls every now and again. 'We'll give you the number,' she told me. "Ali's got it written down somewhere; he'll find it for you when he gets back.'

Once every couple of months or so the whole family—she, her husband 'Ali and his younger brothers—made the trip to Damanhour to telephone Nabeel in Baghdad. When it was Nabeel's turn to get in touch with them he simply spoke into a cassette-recorder and sent them the tape. In the beginning he had written letters, but everyone had agreed that it was nicer to hear his voice. He'd even sent money for a cassette-recorder, so they wouldn't have to take the tapes to their neighbours.

Later Nabeel had sent money for a television set and a washing-machine and then, one day, on one of his tapes he had talked about building a new house. Those tumbledown old rooms they'd always lived in wouldn't last much longer, he'd said. He would be glad to have a new house ready, when he came back to Egypt. He would be able to get married, and move in soon afterwards. His brothers were overjoyed at the suggestion: they called back immediately and within a month he had sent them the money to begin the construction.

'He sent a new tape a few days ago,' Fawzia said. 'We'll listen to it again, as soon as 'Ali gets back.'

After we had finished our tea Fawzia showed me proudly around the house: three or four rooms had already been completed on the ground floor, including a kitchen, a bathroom and a veranda. The wiring was not complete and the walls were still unpainted, but otherwise the house was perfectly habitable.

When the ground floor had received its finishing touches, Fawzia said, the builders would start on a second floor. After his marriage, Nabeel and his wife would live upstairs, they would have the whole floor to themselves. Their other brothers could build on top of that, if they wanted to, later; it all depended on whether they went away as Nabeel had, and earned money 'outside'.

'How different it is,' I said, when Fawzia took me into the new guest-room and showed me their television set and cassette-recorder. 'The first time I came here was at the time of your wedding, when you and 'Ali were sitting outside, with your chairs up against the mud wall.'

Fawzia smiled at the recollection. 'The saddest thing,' she said, 'is that their mother and father didn't live to see how things have changed for us.'

Her voice was soft and dreamlike, as though she were speaking of some immemorially distant epoch. I was not surprised; I knew that if my own memories had not been preserved in such artefacts as notes and diaries, the past would have had no purchase in my mind either. Even with those reminders, it was hard, looking around now, to believe how things had once stood for Nabeel and his family—indeed for all of Nashawy. It was not just that the lanes looked different; that so many of the old adobe houses had been torn down and replaced with red-brick bungalows—something more important had changed as well, the relations between different kinds of people in the village had been upturned and rearranged. Families who at that time had counted amongst the poorest in the community—Khamees's, 'Amm Taha's, Nabeel's—were now the very people who had new houses, bank accounts, gadgetry. I could not have begun to imagine a change on this scale when I left Nashawy in 1981; revisiting it now, a little less than eight years later, it looked as though the village had been drawn on to the fringes of a revolution—except that this one had happened in another country, far away.

Earlier that day, I had talked at length with Ustaz Sabry about the changes in Nashawy, the war between Iran and Iraq, and the men who'd left to go 'outside' (he was leaving himself soon, to take up a good job in a school in the Gulf).

'It's we who've been the real gainers in the war,' he told me. The rich Arab countries were paying the Iraqis to break the back of the Islamic Revolution in Iran. For them it was a matter of survival, of keeping themselves in power. And in the meantime, while others were taking advantage of the war to make money, it was the Iraqis who were dying on the front.

'But it won't last,' he had said, 'it's tainted, "forbidden" money, and its price will be paid later, some day.'

It had occurred to me then that Jabir, in his exclusion, was already paying a price of one kind; now looking around the house Nabeel had built, I began to wonder whether he was paying another, living in Iraq.

'What are things like in Iraq?' I asked Fawzia. 'Does Nabeel like it there?'

321

She nodded cheerfully. He was very happy, she said; in his tapes he always said he was doing well and that everything was fine.

'You can hear him yourself when 'Ali comes home,' she said. 'We'll listen to his tape on the recorder.'

There was a shock in store for me when 'Ali returned: he had one of his younger brothers with him, Hussein, who I remembered as a shy, reticent youngster, no more than twelve or thirteen years old. But now Hussein was studying in college, and he had grown to resemble Nabeel so closely in manner and bearing that I all but greeted him by that name. Later, noticing how often Nabeel's name featured in his conversation, I realized that the resemblance was not accidental: he clearly worshipped his elder brother and had modelled himself upon him.

We listened to the tape after dinner: at first Nabeel's voice sounded very stiff and solemn and, to my astonishment, he spoke like a townsman, as though he had forgotten the village dialect. But Fawzia was quick to come to his defence when I remarked on this. It was only on the tapes that he spoke like that, she said. On the telephone he still sounded exactly the same.

Nabeel said very little about himself and his life in Iraq; just that he was well and that his salary had recently been increased. He listed in detail the names of all the people he wanted his brothers to convey his greetings to, and he told them about various friends from Nashawy who were also in Iraq—that so and so was well, that someone had moved to another city, that someone else was about to come home and so on. Then he went through a set of instructions for his brothers, on how they were to use the money he was sending them, the additions they were to make to the house and exactly how much they were to spend. Everyone in the room listened to him rapt, all the way to the final farewells, though they had clearly heard the tape through several times before.

Later, Fawzia got Hussein to write down Nabeel's address, and the telephone number of his shop, on a slip of paper. 'The owner will probably answer the phone,' she said, handing it to me. 'You have to tell him that you want to talk to Nabeel Idris Badawy, the Egyptian. It costs a lot, but you can hear him like he was in the next room.'

Hussein took hold of my elbow and gave it a shake. 'You must telephone him,' he said emphatically. 'He'll be so pleased. Do you know, he's kept all your letters, wrapped in a plastic bag? He still talks of you a lot. Tell me, didn't you once say to him...'

And then, almost word for word, he recounted a conversation I had once had with Nabeel. It was about a trivial matter, something to do with my university in Delhi, but for some reason I had written it down in my diary at the end of the day, and so I knew that Hussein had repeated it, or at least a part of it, almost verbatim. I was left dumbfounded when he finished; it seemed to me that I had witnessed an impossible, deeply moving, defiance of time and the laws of hearsay.

'You can be sure that I will telephone him,' I said to Hussein. I explained that I was travelling to America soon, in connection with the research for the book I was writing, and I promised to call Nabeel as soon as I arrived.

'You must tell him that we are well,' said Hussein, 'and that he should send another cassette.'

'He'll be really surprised!' said Fawzia. 'He'll think someone's playing a joke on him.'

'We'll write and tell him,' said 'Ali. 'We'll write tomorrow so he won't be surprised. We'll tell him that you're going to phone him from America.'

For a while we talked of other things, of the state of politics in India and the Middle East and what it was like to watch the World Cup on television. It was only when it was time for me to leave that I got to ask 'Ali whether Nabeel liked living in Iraq.

'Ali shrugged. As far as he knew, he said, Nabeel was well enough. That was what he always said at any rate. The fact was, he didn't know; he had never been there himself.

'God knows,' he added, 'people say life is hard out there.'

It was dark outside now and I couldn't stay any longer. After we had said our goodbyes, Hussein insisted that he would see me to the main road. On the way, we stopped at his cousins' house and took one of Isma'il's younger brothers along with us. It turned out that they, like Nabeel and Isma'il before them, were best friends, and were studying at the same college as their brothers had.

It was eerie crossing the village with the two of them beside me. It was as though a moment in time had somehow escaped the hurricane of change that had swept Nabeel and Isma'il away to Iraq: the two cousins so much resembled their brothers that I could have been walking with ghosts.

6

BEN YIJU'S SECOND letter, unlike his first, did eventually reach his brother Yusuf and his family. They were then resident in a small town called Mazara (Mazara del Vallo), near the western

tip of Sicily, not far from Palermo. Mazara had once been a busy
port, serving ships from North Africa and the Levant, but the
current hostilities between Sicily and Ifriqiya had affected its
traffic badly and sent it into a sharp decline. In terms of
material sustenance it had little to offer Yusuf and his family,
who were reduced to extremely straitened circumstances while
living there. But it had other compensations: through its long
trade contacts with Ifriqiya, it had imbibed something of the
cultural and educational ambience of that region, and Yusuf and
his sons probably felt more at home there than they would have
in other, more rudely prosperous parts of the island. Still, there
can be no doubt that they felt themselves to be suffering the
privations of exile in their new home: looking across the sea
from the shores of that provincial town, the material and
scholarly riches of Egypt must have shone like a beacon in the
far distance.

It is easy to imagine, then, the great tumult of hope and
enthusiasm that was provoked in this dispossessed and
disheartened family by the arrival of Ben Yiju's letter. The young
Surur for one clearly received his uncle's proposal of marriage
with the greatest warmth: his immediate response was to set off
for Egypt to claim his bride.

The preparations for Surur's voyage threw his whole family
into convulsions of excitement. The elderly Yusuf and his wife
launched upon a severe regimen of fasting and prayer to ensure
his safe arrival, and Surur's brother Moshe went along to
accompany him on the first leg of the journey.

To arrange Surur's passage to Egypt, the two brothers had first
to proceed to a major port, since Mazara itself no longer served
large eastbound ships. In the event they decided to go to
Messina on the other end of the island rather than to nearby

Palermo—probably because they knew that that was where they would find the courier of their uncle's letter, Sulîmân ibn Ṣaṭrûn. They boarded a boat on a Friday night, having agreed upon a fare of three-eighths of a gold dinar, in exchange for being taken to a lighthouse adjoining Messina.

Arriving in Messina nine days later, they sought out their wayward uncle, Mubashshir, who was then living in that city. In this instance, Surur reported in a letter to his father, his uncle 'did not fall short [of his family duties],' and invited him and his brother to stay in his house. Later, the brothers sought out two friends of Ben Yiju's, one of whom was the courier Suliman ibn Satrun. Their efforts were immediately rewarded: 'I shall take care of your fare,' said Ibn Saṭrun to Surur, 'and you will go up [i.e. to Egypt] with me, if God wills.'

But now, seized by a yearning for travel, young Moshe too began to insist that he wanted to go on to Egypt with Surur. Ibn Satrun and their uncle Mubashshir both counselled against it—'they said: "There is nothing to be gained by it. He had better go back to his father"'—but Moshe was determined not to go back to Mazara 'empty-handed'. The matter was now for their father to decide, Surur wrote, and in the meanwhile they would stay in Messina to await his instructions.

Upon receiving the letter, Yusuf must have decided against allowing Moshe to go any further, for when Surur next wrote to his parents he was already in Egypt and his brother was back in Mazara. The letter he wrote on this occasion was a short one. 'I have sent you these few lines to tell you that I am well and at peace,' he wrote, and then went on to convey his greetings in turn to various friends at home as well as to his parents and his brothers, Moshe and Shamwal. But Surur had yet another reason for writing home at this time: he wanted a certain legal document from his father and in the course of his letter he asked him to send it on to Palermo, possibly with Moshe, so that it could be forwarded to him in Egypt.

As it happened, the letter rekindled Moshe's yearning for travel and prompted him to set out for Egypt himself. But the times were not propitious and the store of good fortune that had carried Surur safely to his destination ran out on his brother: Moshe's ship was attacked on the way and he was imprisoned in the Crusader-controlled city of Tyre.

Their parents, already prostrate with anxiety, were to learn of these developments in a letter from Surur. 'We were seized with grief when we read your letter,' Shamwal wrote back from Sicily, 'and we wept copiously. As for [our] father and mother *they could not speak.*' But their tears were soon stemmed: later in the same letter, they discovered that matters had already taken a happier turn. Moshe had since written to Surur from Tyre to let him know that he was now 'well and in good cheer.'

At home in Sicily meanwhile, things had got steadily worse. Food was short, the price of wheat had risen and the family had already spent most of its money. 'If you saw [our] father,' wrote Shamwal, 'you would not know him, for he weeps all day and night…As for [our] mother, if you saw her, you would not recognize her [so changed is she] by her longing for you, and by her grief. God knows what our state has been after you left…Know that all we have is emptiness since God emptied [our house]. Do not forget us, oh my brothers; to visit us and to write to us. You must know that those of your letters that reached us conjured up your two noble faces [for us]. Send us letters telling us your news, the least important and the most; do not scorn to tell us the smallest thing, till we know everything.'

But gradually things improved. The brothers were reunited in

Egypt, and Surur must have announced his wedding to his cousin shortly afterwards. His father, overwhelmed, wrote back to say: 'Come quickly home to us, you and your uncle's daughter…and [we shall] prepare a couple of rooms for her, and we shall celebrate [the wedding]…'

The marriage did indeed take place: a list recording Sitt al-Dar's wedding trousseau, now preserved in St. Petersburg, is proof that this child of a Nair woman from the Malabar was wedded in 1156 to her Sicilian cousin, in Fustat.

Both Surur and Moshe went on to become judges in rabbinical courts in Egypt, where they were probably later joined by their parents and Shamwal.

As for Ashu, neither Ben Yiju nor his nephews mention her in their letters. In all likelihood she never left India but remained in Mangalore after Ben Yiju's departure.

Ben Yiju himself disappears from the records after his daughter's marriage. His son-in-law and his other nephews do not mention him in their later correspondence, and nor, as far as I know, is his death referred to in any other document in the Cairo Geniza. There are many conceivable endings to Ben Yiju's story and if the most pleasing amongst them is one which has him returning to Ashu, in the Malabar, the most likely, on the other hand, is a version in which he dies in Egypt, soon after his daughter's wedding, and is buried somewhere in the vicinity of Fustat.

As for Bomma, there is no mention of him either, in Ben Yiju's correspondence with his brothers. But his story is not ended yet: one last journey remains.

7

MY RETURN TO Nashawy and Lataifa culminated in an unforeseen ending.

It so happened that my visit coincided with one of the region's annual events, a mowlid dedicated to the memory of a saintly figure known as Sidi Abu-Hasira, whose tomb lies on the outskirts of Damanhour.

As with all mowlids, a buzz of anticipation preceded the start of this one, and over a period of a few days I had the story of Sidi Abu-Hasira repeated to me over and over again. Except for a few unexpected twists, it was very similar to the legends that surrounded other local holy men such as those of Nashawy and Nakhlatain: like those other legends, it was set in a distant past, and it recounted the miracles wrought by a man of exemplary piety and goodness. The Sidi had been born into a Jewish family in the Maghreb, it was said, but he had transported himself to Egypt through a miracle that later found commemoration in his name: he had crossed the Mediterranean on a rush mat, which was why he was called 'Sîdî Abû-Ḥaṣîra', 'the Saint of the Mat'.

After arriving in Egypt, the story went, he had converted to Islam and had soon come to be recognized as a 'good man', endowed with the blessed and miraculous gift of 'baraka'. Eventually the Sidi had settled in Damanhour, where a large group of disciples and followers had gathered around him. Upon his death, they had built a tomb for him, on the outskirts of Damanhour, and it was there that his mowlid was now celebrated. Because of his Jewish origins, I was told, the Sidi still had many followers in Israel and ever since the opening of the borders they came to Damanhour in large numbers every year.

Indeed so many tourists came to attend the mowlid nowadays, and recently a large new memorial had been built on the site of Sidi Abu-Hasira's tomb.

I had missed the mowlid while living in Nashawy, because I had happened to be away in Cairo over the week when it was celebrated; now it seemed as though everyone I knew was determined to prevent my missing it again. The mowlid was a wonderful spectacle, I was told; there would be lights everywhere, stalls with pistols and airguns, swings and carousels; the streets would be lined with kebab-shops and vendors' carts and thronged with crowds of sightseers. The tourists alone were a good reason to go, they said, it was not often that one got to see foreigners in a place like Damanhour.

I was persuaded easily enough, but I had so much to catch up with in Lataifa and Nashawy after my long absence that I didn't have time to think of much else. The mowlid began towards the end of my visit, and my time seemed so pitifully short that I let it pass with no particular sense of regret. A couple of days before my departure I was told that the mowlid was over: that would have been the end of the story had it not been for Mohsin the taxi-driver.

Mohsin was from a hamlet near Nashawy, a corpulent youth in his mid-twenties or so. He had a little bristling moustache, and he always wore freshly laundered white jallabeyyas—great, dazzling garments that billowed around him like parachutes. Mohsin was a good talker, full of self-confidence, and amazingly knowledgeable about such things as the exchange rates of various kinds of dinars and the prices of Nikons and Seikos. He had acquired this stock of information while living in the Gulf where he had spent a couple of years working in construction. He hadn't cared much for his work however; climbing scaffolding didn't suit him. Eventually he had succeeded in persuading two of his brothers, who had jobs in Iraq, to join him in investing in a second-hand van, and for the last several months he had been ferrying passengers back and forth between the towns and villages of the district.

The day before my departure Mohsin drove me to the railway station in Damanhour to buy a ticket for Cairo, ánd on the way he explained that he was growing tired of spending his days on those dusty rural roads. Lately, seeing so many tourists coming into Damanhour for the mowlid, he had begun to think along a different track. It had occurred to him that it would be nice to have a permit that would let him take tourists back and forth from Alexandria and Cairo and places like that.

That was how the idea of our paying a visit to the tomb of Sidi Abu-Hasira came to be mooted. He had never been there himself, said Mohsin, but he had always wanted to go, and he would be glad to take me there next morning, on the way to the station. It was no matter that the mowlid was already over—the stalls and lights would probably be there still, and we would be able to get a good whiff of the atmosphere. And so it was agreed that we would stop by at the tomb when he picked me up at Lataifa next morning, to take me to the station.

I spent the rest of the day making a last round of Nashawy, saying good-bye to my friends and their families: to Khamees, now a prosperous landowner with two healthy children; to Busaina, who had recently bought a house with her own earnings, in the centre of the village; to their brother 'Eid, newly-returned from Saudi Arabia, and soon to be married to the girl to whom he had lost his heart, years ago; to Zaghloul, miraculously unaffected by the storm of change that was whirling through the village; to 'Amm Taha, whose business in eggs had now expanded into a minor industry and made him a man of considerable wealth; even, inadvertently, to Imam Ibrahim, who greeted me civilly enough, when we ran into each other in the village square. Finally I said goodbye to Fawzia, 'Ali and Hussein, who made me promise, once again, that I would soon telephone Nabeel in Iraq.

When Mohsin arrived in Lataifa next morning, I was taking my leave of Shaikh Musa, Jabir, and several others who had gathered in his guest-room. The leavetaking proved even harder than I had imagined and in one way or another my farewells lasted a great deal longer than I had expected.

In the meanwhile Mohsin had busied himself in preparing an appropriate accompaniment for the moment of my departure: a cassette of Umm Kolthum's had been cued and held ready, and the moment I climbed into the van a piercing lament filled the lanes of Lataifa. We began to roll forward in time with the tune, and after a final round of handshakes, Mohsin sounded a majestic blast on his horn. The younger boys ran along while the van picked up speed, and then suddenly Lataifa vanished behind us into a cloud of dust.

We stopped to ask directions on the borders of Damanhour, and then turned on to a narrow road that skirted around a crowded, working-class area. Nutshells and scraps of coloured papers lay scattered everywhere now, and it was easy to tell that the road had recently been teeming with festive crowds. Mohsin had never been to this part of the city before but he was confident that we were headed in the right direction. When next we stopped to ask for the tomb of Sidi Abu-Hasira, we were immediately pointed to a large structure half-hidden behind a row of date palms, a little further down the road.

I was taken by surprise at my first glimpse of the building; it looked nothing like the saints' tombs I had seen before. It was a sleek, concrete structure of a kind that one might expect to see in the newer and more expensive parts of Alexandria and Cairo: in that poor quarter of Damanhour, it was not merely incongruous—its presence seemed almost an act of defiance.

A long, narrow driveway led from the entrance of the compound to a covered porch adjoining the tomb. The grounds seemed deserted when we turned in at the gate, and it was not till we were halfway down the drive that we noticed a handful of men lounging around a desk, in the shade of the porch. One of them was dressed in a blue jallabeyya; the rest were armed and in uniform.

At the sight of those uniforms Mohsin suddenly became tense and apprehensive. Like me, he had expected to see a domed tomb, with some candles burning outside perhaps, and a few people gathered around a grave: the uniforms instantly aroused that deep mistrust of officialdom that had been bred into him by generations of fellah forefathers. I could tell that his every instinct was crying out to him to turn the van around and speed away. But it was already too late: the men were on their feet now, watching us, and some of them were fingering their guns.

The van was surrounded the moment we drew up under the porch. Reaching in through my window, a hand undid the lock and jerked the door open. I stepped out to find myself face to face with a ruddy, pink-cheeked man, dressed in a blue jallabeyya. He was holding the door open for me, and with a deep bow and a smile he gestured towards a police officer seated at the desk under the porch.

The officer was a young man, probably a recent graduate from training school. He watched with a puzzled and slightly annoyed expression as I walked over to his desk.

'What are you doing here?' he snapped at me, in the kind of tone he might have used towards a slow-witted subordinate.

'I came to look at the tomb,' I said. 'I heard there was a mowlid here recently.'

On hearing me speak he realized I was a foreigner and there was an instant change in his tone and manner. He looked me over, smiling, and a gleam of recognition came into his eyes.

'Israïli?' he said.

When I told him I was Indian, his smile vanished and was quickly replaced by a look of utter astonishment. Confirming what I had said with a glance at my passport, he turned to me in blank incomprehension. What was my business there, he wanted to know; what was I doing at that tomb?

My Arabic was becoming tangled now, but as best I could I explained that I had heard about the mowlid of Sidi Abu-Hasira and decided to pay the tomb a visit on my way to the station.

From his deepening frown, I knew that my answer had not been satisfactory. The mowlid was over, he said, the tourists were gone, and the tomb was closed. The time for sightseeing was now well past.

Opening my passport, he thumbed through it again, from back to front, coming to a stop at the page with my photograph.

'Are you Jewish?' he said.

'No.'

'Muslim?'

'No.'

'Christian?'

When I said no yet again he gave a snort of annoyance and slammed my passport on the desk. Turning to the others, he threw up his hands. Could they understand it? he asked. Neither Jewish, nor Muslim, nor Christian—there had to be something odd afoot.

I started to explain once more, but he had lost interest in me now. Rising to his feet, he turned towards Mohsin, who was waiting near the van. The man in the blue jallabeyya was standing beside him, and when the officer beckoned, he pushed Mohsin forward.

Mohsin was terrified now, and he would not look at me. His habitual confidence and good humour had ebbed away; he was cringing, his vast rotund form shaking with fear. Before the officer could speak, he began to blurt out an explanation. 'It's nothing to do with me, Your Excellency,' he cried, his voice rising in panic. 'I don't know who the foreigner is and I don't know what he's doing here. He was staying in a village next to ours, and he wanted to visit this tomb on the way to the station. I don't know anything more; I have nothing to do with him.'

The officer spun around to look at me. 'What were you doing in a village?' he snapped. 'What took you there? How long have you been travelling around the countryside without informing the proper authorities?'

I started to explain how I had first arrived in Lataifa as a student, years ago, but the officer was in no mood to listen: his mind could now barely keep pace with his racing suspicions. Without a pause he rattled off a series of questions, one after another.

Who had I been meeting in the villages? he asked. Were they from any particular organization? What had I talked about? Were there any other foreigners working with me?

My protests and explanations were brushed aside with an impatient gesture; the officer was now far too excited to listen. I would soon have an opportunity to explain to someone senior, he told me—this was too serious a matter for someone in his position to deal with.

Seating himself at his desk he quickly wrote out a note and handed it to the ruddy-faced man in the jallabeyya, along with my passport and Mohsin's papers.

'Go with him,' he told me. 'He will take you where you have to go.'

Mohsin and I found ourselves back on the van within moments, with the man in the jallabeyya sitting between us. He was holding Mohsin's papers and my passport firmly in his hands.

'Everything will soon be clear, sir,' he said, when I asked him where he was taking us. He was heavily-built, with a moustache that was almost blonde, and a clear-cut, angular profile that hinted at Macedonian or Albanian forbears somewhere in his ancestry.

He raised our papers reverentially to his forehead and bowed. 'I'm under your orders and at your command, taht amrak wa iznak...'

I noticed then that his speech, except for its elaborate unctuousness, was exactly that of a fellah, with only the faintest trace of a city accent. Dressed as he was, in his fellah's cap and jallabeyya, he would have been perfectly at home in the lanes of Nashawy and Lataifa.

Mohsin interrupted him, with a sudden show of anger, demanding to know what crime he had committed. He had regained his composure a little now that he was back in his van.

In reply the man began to thumb through Mohsin's licence and registration papers. Then, in a voice that was silky with feigned deference, he pointed out that the permit did not allow him to carry passengers.'

Instantly Mohsin's shoulders sagged and his self-possession

evaporated: the man had taken his measure with practised accuracy. The papers had probably taken Mohsin months to acquire, maybe cost him a substantial sum of money, as well as innumerable hours spent standing at the desks of various government officials. The thought of losing them terrified him.

When Mohsin next spoke his voice was hoarse and charged with an almost hysterical urgency. 'You sound as though you're from the countryside around here, sir,' he said. 'Is your village in this area?'

The man in the jallabeyya nodded, smiling affably, and named a village not far from Damanhour. The name seemed to electrify Mohsin. 'Alhamdu'lillah!' he cried. 'God be praised! I know that village. I know it well. Why I've been there many times, many times.'

For the rest of the drive, in a desperate effort to invoke the protective bonds of neighbourhood and kinship, to tame the abstract, impersonal terror the situation had inspired in him, Mohsin mined every last vein of his memory for a name that would be familiar to his captor. The man humoured him, smiling, and deflected his questions with answers that were polite but offhand. Skilled in his craft, he knew perfectly well that there was no more effective way of striking terror into a village boy like Mohsin than by using his own dialect to decline his accustomed terms of communication—those immemorial courtesies of village life, by which people strove to discover mutual acquaintances and connections.

By the time we reached our destination, a high-walled, heavily-guarded building on a busy road, Mohsin was completely unnerved, drenched in sweat. He protested feebly as we were herded in past an armed sentry, but no one paid him any attention. He was marched quickly off towards a distant wing of the building while I, in turn, was led to a room at the end of a corridor and told to go in and wait.

The room was a pleasant one, in an old-fashioned way, large, airy and flooded with light from windows that looked directly out into a garden. From what I could see of it, the building seemed very much in the style of colonial offices in India with high ceilings and arched windows: it took no great prescience to tell that it had probably been initiated into its current uses during the British occupation of Egypt.

In a while the curtain at the door was pushed aside and a tall man in gold-rimmed aviator sunglasses stepped into the room. He was casually dressed, in a lightweight jacket and trousers, and there was a look of distinction about him, in the manner of a gracefully ageing sportsman.

Taking off his sunglasses, he seated himself behind the desk; he had a lean gunmetal face, with curly hair that was grizzled at the temples. He placed my passport and the note from the officer in front of him, and after he had looked them through he sat back in his chair, his eyes hard and unsmiling.

'What is the meaning of this?' he said.

I knew I had to choose my words with care, so speaking slowly, I told him that I had heard many people talking about the mowlid of Sidi Abu-Hasira over the last several days. They had said that many tourists came to Damanhour to visit the mowlid, so I had decided to do some sightseeing too, before catching the train to Cairo, later in the day.

He listened with close attention, and when I had finished, he said: 'How did you learn Arabic? And what were you doing travelling in the countryside?'

'I'd been here years ago,' I said, and I explained how, after learning Arabic in Tunisia, I had come to Egypt as a doctoral student and been brought to that district by Professor Aly Issa, one of the most eminent anthropologists in Egypt. Fortunately I had taken the precaution of carrying a copy of the permit I had been given when I first went to live in Lataifa and I handed it to him now as proof.

My interrogator examined the document and then, giving it back to me, he said: 'But this does not explain what you were doing at the tomb. What took you there?'

I had gone there out of mere curiosity, I told him. I had heard people talking about the mowlid of Sidi Abu-Hasira, just as they talked about other such events, and I had thought I would stop by to take a look, on the way to the station. I had had no idea that it would become a matter of such gravity, and I was at a loss to understand what had happened.

A gesture of dismissal indicated that my interrogator had no intention of offering me an explanation. 'What was it that interested you about that place?' he asked again. 'What exactly took you there?'

'I was just interested,' I said. 'That's all.'

'But you're not Jewish or Israeli,' he said. 'You're Indian—what connection could you have with the tomb of a Jewish holy man, here in Egypt?'

He was not trying to intimidate me; I could tell he was genuinely puzzled. He seemed so reasonable and intelligent, that for an instant I even thought of telling him the story of Bomma and Ben Yiju. But then it struck me, suddenly, that there was nothing I could point to within his world that might give credence to my story—the remains of those small, indistinguishable, intertwined histories, Indian and Egyptian, Muslim and Jewish, Hindu and Muslim, had been partitioned long ago. Nothing remained in Egypt now to effectively challenge

his disbelief: not a single one, for instance, of the documents of
the Geniza. It was then that I began to realize how much
success the partitioning of the past had achieved; that I was
sitting at that desk now because the mowlid of Sidi Abu-Hasira
was an anomaly within the categories of knowledge represented
by those divisions. I had been caught straddling a border,
unaware that the writing of History had predicated its own self-
fulfilment.

'I didn't know Sidi Abu-Hasira was a Jewish saint,' I said at
last. 'In the countryside I heard that everyone went to visit the
tomb.'

'You shouldn't have believed it,' he said. 'In the villages, as
you must know, there is a lot of ignorance and superstition; the
fellaheen talk about miracles for no reason at all. You're an
educated man, you should know better than to believe the
fellaheen on questions of religion.'

'But the fellaheen are very religious,' I said. 'Many amongst
them are very strict in religious matters.'

'Is it religion to believe in saints and miracles?' he said
scornfully. 'These beliefs have nothing to do with true religion.
They are mere superstitions, contrary to Islam, and they will
disappear with development and progress.'

He looked down at his papers, indicating that the subject was
closed. After a moment's silence he scribbled a couple of
sentences on a slip of paper and rose slowly to his feet.

'We have to be careful, you understand,' he said in a polite,
but distant voice. 'We want to do everything we can to protect
the tomb.'

He stood up, gave my hand a perfunctory shake and handed
me my passport. 'I am going to instruct the man who brought
you here to take you straight to the station,' he said. 'You

should catch the first train to Cairo. It is better that you leave Damanhour at once.'

Leaving me sitting at his desk, he turned and left the room. I had to wait a while, and then a policeman came in and escorted me back to the van.

Mohsin was sitting inside, next to the man in the blue jallabeyya; he looked unharmed, but he was subdued and nervous, and would not look me in the eyes. The railway station was only a few minutes away, and we drove there in silence. When we got there, I went around to Mohsin's window, and after paying him the fare, I tried to apologise for the trouble the trip had caused. He took the money and put it away without a word, looking fixedly ahead all the while.

But the man in the jallabeyya had been listening with interest, and he now leant over and flashed me a smile. 'What about me, sir?' he said. 'Are you going to forget me and everything I did to look after you? Isn't there going to be anything for me?'

At the sight of his outstretched hand I lost control of myself. 'You son of a bitch,' I shouted. 'You son of a bitch—haven't you got any shame?'

I was cut short by a nudge from Mohsin's elbow. Suddenly I remembered that the man was still holding his papers in his hands. To keep myself from doing anything that might make matters worse for Mohsin, I went quickly into the station. When I looked back, they were still there; the man in the jallabeyya was waving Mohsin's papers in his face, haggling over their price.

I went down to the platform to wait for my train.

Over the next few months, in America, I learnt a new respect for the man who had interrogated me that morning in Damanhour: I discovered that his understanding of the map of

341

modern knowledge was much more thorough than mine. Looking through libraries, in search of material on Sidi Abu-Hasira, I wasted a great deal of time in looking under subject headings such as 'religion' and 'Judaism'—but of course that tomb, and others like it, had long ago been wished away from those shelves, in the process of shaping them to suit the patterns of the Western academy. Then, recollecting what my interrogator had said about the difference between religion and superstition, it occurred to me to turn to the shelves marked 'anthropology' and 'folklore'. Sure enough, it was in those regions that my efforts met with their first rewards.

I discovered that the name Abu-Hasira, or Abou-Hadzeira, as it is spelt when transcribed from Hebrew, belongs to a famous line of zeddikim—the Jewish counterparts of Islamic marabouts and Sufi saints, many of whom had once been equally venerated by Jews and Muslims alike. Ya'akov Abou-Hadzeira of Damanhour, I discovered, was one of the most renowned of his line, a cabbalist and mystic, who had gained great fame for his miracles in his lifetime, and still had a large following among Jews of North African and Egyptian origin. 'The tomb of Rabbi Abû-Ḥaṣîra of Morocco [in Damanhour] attracted large numbers of pilgrims,' I learnt, 'both Jewish and non-Jewish, and the festivities marking the pilgrimage closely resembled the birthday of Muslim saints…'

It seemed uncanny that I had never known all those years that in defiance of the enforcers of History, a small remnant of Bomma's world had survived, not far from where I had been living.

EPILOGUE

Soon after I arrived in New York I tried to call Nabeel in Baghdad. It wasn't easy getting through. The directory listed a code for Iraq, but after days of trying all I got was a recorded message telling me that the number I had dialled didn't exist.

In the end I had to book a call with the operator. She took a while to put it through, but then the phone began to ring and a short while later I heard a voice at the other end, speaking in the blunt, rounded Arabic of Iraq.

'Ai-wah?' he said, stretching out the syllables. 'Yes? Who is it?'

I knew at once I was speaking to Nabeel's boss. I imagined him to be a big, paunchy man, sitting at the end of a counter, behind a cash-box, with the telephone beside him and a Kodacolor poster of a snow-clad mountain on the wall above. He was wearing a jallabeyya and a white lace cap; he had a pair of sunglasses in his breast pocket and a carefully trimmed moustache. The telephone beside him was of the old-fashioned kind, black and heavy, and it had a brass lock fastened in its dial. The boss kept the key, and Nabeel and the other assistants had to ask for it when they wanted to make a call.

It was late at night in New York so it had to be morning in

Baghdad. The shop must have just opened; they probably had no customers yet.

'Is Nabeel there?' I asked.

'Who?' said the voice.

'Nabeel Idris Badawy,' I said. 'The Egyptian.'

He grunted. 'And who're you?' he said. 'Wa mîn inta?'

'I'm a friend of his,' I said. 'Tell him it's his friend from India. He'll know.'

'What's that?' he said. 'From where?'

'From India, ya raiyis,' I said. 'Could you tell him? And quickly if you please, for I'm calling from America.'

'From America?' he shouted down the line. 'But you said you were Indian?'

'Yes, I am—I'm just in America on a visit. Nabeel quickly, if you please, ya raiyis…'

I heard him shout across the room: 'Ya Nabeel, somebody wants to talk to you, some Indian or something.'

I could tell from Nabeel's first words that my call had taken him completely by surprise. He was incredulous in the beginning, unwilling to believe that it was really me at the other end of the line, speaking from America. I was almost as amazed as he was: it would never have occurred to me, when I first knew him, that we would one day be able to speak to each other on the phone, thousands of miles apart.

I explained how I had recently been to Egypt and visited Nashawy, and how his family had given me his telephone number and told me to call him, in Baghdad. Suddenly, he gave a shout of recognition.

'Ya Amitab,' he cried. 'How are you? Zayyak? Where were you? Where have you been all these years?'

I gave him a quick report on how I had spent the last several years, and then it was my turn to ask: 'What about you? Zayyak inta?'

'Kullu 'âl,' he said, mouthing a customary response. Everything was well; he and his cousin Isma'il were managing fine, sharing rooms with friends from back home. Then he asked me about India, about each member of my family, my job, my books. When I had finished giving him my news, I told him about his own family in Nashawy, and about my visit to their new house. He was eager to hear about them, asking question after question, but in a voice that seemed to grow progressively more quiet.

'What about you, ya Nabeel?' I said at last. 'How do you like Iraq? What is the country like?'

'Kullu 'âl,' he said—everything was fine.

I wanted him to talk about Iraq, but of course he would not have been able to say much within earshot of his boss. Then I heard a noise down the line; it sounded as though someone was calling to him from across the room. He broke off to say, 'Coming, just one minute,' and I added hurriedly, 'I'm going back to India soon—I'll try to stop by and visit you on the way, in Baghdad.'

'We'll be expecting you,' he said. 'You must come.'

'I'll do my best,' I said.

'I'll tell Isma'il you're coming,' he said hurriedly. 'We'll wait for you.'

I heard his boss's voice again, shouting in the background. 'I'll come,' I promised. 'I'll certainly come.'

But as it turned out I was not able to keep my word: for a variety of reasons it proved impossible to stop in Baghdad on the way back to India. My breaking of that promise made me all the more determined to keep another: I resolved that I would do everything I could to return to Egypt in 1990, the following year. I had given my word to Shaikh Musa that I would.

I was certain that by then Nabeel would be back in Nashawy.

BOMMA'S STORY ENDS in Philadelphia.

At the corner of 4th and Walnut, in the heart of downtown Philadelphia, stands a sleek modern building, an imposing structure that could easily be mistaken for the headquarters of a great multinational corporation. In fact, it is the Annenberg Research Institute, a centre for social and historical research: it owes its creation to the vast fortune generated by the first and most popular of America's television magazines, 'TV Guide'.

Housed within the Institute's resplendent premises is a remarkable collection of Judaica, including manuscripts of many different kinds. Among them is a set of Geniza documents that was once in the possession of Philadelphia's Dropsie College.

The documents are kept in the Institute's rare book room, a great vault in the bowels of the building, steel-sealed and laser-beamed, equipped with alarms that need no more than seconds to mobilize whole fleets of helicopters and police cars. Within the sealed interior of this vault are two cabinets that rise out of the floor like catafalques. The documents lie inside them, encased in sheets of clear plastic, within exquisitely crafted covers.

Between the leaves of one of those volumes lies a torn sheet of paper covered with Ben Yiju's distinctive handwriting. The folio is a large one, much larger than any of Ben Yiju's other papers, but it is badly damaged and almost a quarter of the sheet is missing. The handwriting on the remaining parts of the fragment is unmistakably Ben Yiju's, but the characters are tiny and faint, as though formed by an unsteady and ageing hand.

The document is one of Ben Yiju's many sets of accounts, but the names of the people and the commodities that are mentioned in it are very different from those that figure in his earlier papers: they suggest that these accounts belong to the years he spent in Fustat, towards the end of his life.

The document mentions several people to whom Ben Yiju owed money for household purchases such as loaves of bread of various different kinds. Much of the document is indecipherable, but amongst the sentences that are clearly legible there is at least one that mentions a sum of money owed to Bomma.

It provides proof that Bomma was with Ben Yiju when he went back to settle in Egypt in the last years of his life.

In Philadelphia then, cared for by the spin-offs of 'Dallas' and 'Dynasty' and protected by the awful might of the American police, lies entombed the last testament to the life of Bomma, the toddy-loving fisherman from Tulunad.

Bomma, I cannot help feeling, would have been hugely amused.

AN ENTRY IN my passport records that I left Calcutta for Cairo on 20 August 1990, exactly three weeks after the Iraqi invasion of Kuwait. Newspapers were already talking of plans for the mobilization of hundreds of thousands of American and European troops: the greatest army ever assembled.

My most vivid memories of the journey are of reading about the vast flood of Egyptian workers that was now pouring out of Iraq, and of looking for Nabeel and Isma'il in the packed lounges of the airport at Amman, while changing planes.

In Egypt, everyone I talked to seemed to be in a state of confused apprehension: in the taxi from Cairo to Damanhour, the other passengers talked randomly of disaster, killing and vengeance. In the countryside the confusion was even worse than in the cities; Lataifa alone had five boys away in Iraq, and none of them had been heard from since the day of the invasion. Jabir, I discovered, was not amongst that five. He was still at home, in Lataifa, although he had been trying to leave for Iraq virtually until the day of the invasion. Shaikh Musa was well, but desperately worried: his nephew Mabrouk was one of the five who were away in Iraq.

Walking to Nashawy to inquire about Nabeel and Isma'il, my mind kept returning to that day, almost exactly a decade ago now, when Mabrouk had come running up to my room, and dragged me to his house to pronounce judgement on the 'Indian machine' his father had bought. And now, that very Mabrouk was in the immediate vicinity of chemical and nuclear weapons, within a few minutes' striking distance of the world's most advanced machinery; it would be he who paid the final price of those guns and tanks and bombs.

Fawzia was standing at the door of their family house; she saw me as I turned the corner. 'Nabeel's not back yet, ya Amitab,' she said the moment she saw me. 'He's still over there, in Iraq, and here we are, sitting and waiting.'

'Have you had any news from him? A letter?'

'No, nothing,' she said, leading me into their house. 'Nothing at all. The last time we had news of him was when Isma'il came back two months ago.'

'Isma'il's back?'

'Praise be to God,' she smiled. 'He's back in good health and everything.'

'Where is he?' I said, looking around. 'Can you send for him?'

'Of course,' she said. 'He's just around the corner, sitting at home. He hasn't found a job yet—does odd jobs here and there, but most of the time he has nothing to do. I'll send for him right now.'

Looking around me, I noticed that something seemed to have interrupted the work on their house. When I'd seen it last I had had the impression that it would be completed in a matter of months. But now, a year and a half later, the floor was still just a platform of packed earth and gravel. The tiles had not been laid yet, and nor had the walls been plastered or painted.

'Hamdu'lillah al-salâma.' Isma'il was at the door, laughing, his hand extended.

'Why didn't you come?' he said, once the greetings were over. 'You remember that day you called from America? Nabeel telephoned me soon after he'd spoken to you. He just picked up the phone and called me where I was working. He told me that you'd said that you were going to visit us. We expected you, for a long time. We made place in our room, and thought of all the places we'd show you. But you know, Nabeel's boss, the shop-owner? He got really upset—he didn't like it a bit that Nabeel had got a long-distance call from America.'

'Why didn't Nabeel come back with you? What news of him?'

'He wanted to come back. In fact he thought that he would. But then he decided to stay for a few more months, make a little more money, so that they could finish building this house. You see how it's still half-finished—all the money was used up. Prices have gone up this last year, everything costs more.'

'And besides,' said Fawzia, 'what would Nabeel do back here? Look at Isma'il—just sitting at home, no job, nothing to do…'

Isma'il shrugged. 'But still, he wanted to come back. He's been there three years. It's more than most, and it's aged him. You'd see what I mean if you saw him. He looks much older. Life's not easy out there.'

'What do you mean?'

'The Iraqis, you know,' he pulled a face. 'They're wild...they come back from the army for a few days at a time, and they go wild, fighting on the streets, drinking. Egyptians never go out on the streets there at night: if some drunken Iraqis came across you they would kill you, just like that, and nobody would even know, for they'd throw away your papers. It's happened, happens all the time. They blame us, you see, they say: "You've taken our jobs and our money and grown rich while we're fighting and dying."'

'What about Saddam Hussein?'

'Saddam Hussein!' he rolled his eyes. 'You have to be careful when you breathe that name out there—there are spies everywhere, at every corner, listening. One word about Saddam and you're gone, dead.'

Later Isma'il told me a story. Earlier in the year Egypt had played a football match with Algeria, to decide which team would play in the World Cup. Egypt had won and Egyptians everywhere had gone wild with joy. In Iraq the two or three million Egyptians who lived packed together, all of them young, all of them male, with no families, children, wives, nothing to do but stare at their newly bought television sets—they had exploded out of their rooms and into the streets in a delirium of joy. Their football team had restored to them that self-respect that their cassette-recorders and television sets had somehow failed to bring. To the Iraqis, who have never had anything like a normal political life, probably never seen crowds except at pilgrimages, the massed ranks of Egyptians must have seemed like the coming of Armageddon. They responded by attacking them on the streets, often with firearms—well-trained in war, they fell upon the jubilant, unarmed crowds of Egyptian workers.

'You can't imagine what it was like,' said Isma'il. He had tears in his eyes. 'It was then that I decided to leave. Nabeel decided to leave as well, but of course he always needed to think a long time about everything. But then at the last minute he thought he'd stay just a little bit longer...'

My mind went back to that evening when I first met Nabeel and Isma'il; how Nabeel had said: 'It must make you think of all the people you left at home when you put that kettle on the stove with just enough water for yourself.' It was hard to think of Nabeel alone, in a city headed for destruction.

A little later we went to Isma'il's house to watch the news on the colour TV he had brought back with him. It sat perched on its packing case, in the centre of the room, gleaming new, with chickens roosting on a nest of straw beside it. Soon the news started and we saw footage of the epic exodus: thousands and thousands of men, some in trousers, some in jallabeyyas, some carrying their TV sets on their backs, some crying out for a drink of water, stretching all the way from the horizon to the Red Sea, standing on the beach as though waiting for the water to part.

There were more than a dozen of us in the room now. We were crowded around the TV set, watching carefully, minutely, looking at every face we could see. There was nothing to be seen except crowds: Nabeel had vanished into the anonymity of History.

NOTES

Prologue

13. The slave's first appearance: E. Strauss (now Ashtor), 'Documents for the Economic and Social History of the Near East' (*Zion*, n.s. VII, Jerusalem, 1942).

13. Khalif ibn Iṣḥaq: The ṣ and the ḥ in the name Iṣḥaq are distinct consonants. The system of notation used here for transcriptions from Arabic is broadly similar to that of the *Encyclopaedia of Islam*. In general, I have tried to keep transcriptions to a minimum, usually indicating the spelling of a word or name only upon its first occurrence. As a rule I have included the symbol for the Arabic consonant 'ain (') wherever it occurs, except in place names, where I have kept to standard usage. Specialists ought to be forewarned that if, in these pages, they seek consistency in the matter of transcription, they shall find only confusion—a result in part of the many different registers of Arabic that are invoked here. On the whole where the alternative presented itself, I have favoured the dialectical usage over the literary or the classical, a preference which may seem misleading to some since the rural dialects of the Delta differ markedly in certain respects from the urban dialect that is generally taken to represent colloquial Egyptian Arabic.

14. A German army had arrived: Ibn al-Qalânisî, *The Damascus Chronicle of the Crusades*, pp. 280, (ed. and trans. H. A. R. Gibb, Luzac & Co. Ltd., London, 1967).

14. 'That year the German Franks': The historian was the famous Ibn al-Athîr (quoted by Amin Maalouf in *The Crusades through Arab Eyes*, tr. Jon Rothschild, Al Saqi Books, London, 1984).

14. Among the nobles: See Steven Runciman, *History of the Crusades*, Vol. II, pp. 279–80, (Cambridge University Press, Cambridge, 1952).

14. 'There was a divergence': Ibn al-Qalanisi, *Damascus Chronicle*, p. 282.

15. 'the German Franks returned': Ibn al-Athir, quoted by Amin Maalouf in *The Crusades through Arab Eyes*. Ibn al-Qalanisi wrote a vivid description of this engagement in *The Damascus Chronicle*, pp. 281–4. See also Steven Runciman, *History of the Crusades*, Vol II, pp. 281–4; and Virginia G. Berry, 'The Second Crusade', in *A History of the Crusades*, Vol. I, pp. 508–10 (ed. K. M. Setton, University of Wisconsin Press, Madison, 1969). Hans Eberhard Mayer discusses the Crusaders' decision to attack Damascus in *The Crusades*, p. 103, (tr. John Gillingham, Oxford

University Press, Oxford, 1988).

16. **They were…quick to relay news:** One of the services that merchants rendered each other in this period was the supplying of information (see Norman Stillman's article, 'The Eleventh Century Merchant House of Ibn 'Awkal (A Geniza Study)', p. 24 (in *Journal of the Economic and Social History of the Orient*, XVI, pt. 1, 1973). Not long after Khalaf ibn Ishaq's lifetime an Arab scholar was to tell Sultan Salâḥ al-Dîn's (Saladin's) son, al-Malik al-Ẓâhir, that merchants were 'the scouts of the world'. (Cf. S. D. Goitein, 'Changes in the Middle East (950–1150), as illustrated by the documents of the Cairo Geniza', p. 19, in *Islamic Civilisation*, ed. P. Richards, Cassirer, Oxford, 1973).

16. **'things which have no price':** My translation is based on Strauss's transcription in 'Documents for Economic and Social History of the Middle East'. The line quoted here is line 17.

16. **'two jars of sugar':** Ibid., line 18.

16. **'plentiful greetings':** Ibid., line 23.

17. **The Slave's second appearance:** S. D. Goitein, *Letters of Medieval Jewish Traders*, Princeton University Press, Princeton, 1973 (henceforth *Letters*). The quotations from Khalaf ibn Ishaq's letter in the next four paragraphs are all taken from Goitein's translation in this volume (pp. 187–92).

17. **This is another eventful year:** Cf. Steven Runciman, *History of the Crusades*, Vol. II, p. 226. See also, H. A. R. Gibb, 'Zengi and the Fall of Edessa', in *A History of the Crusades*, Vol. I.

19. **I had…won a scholarship:** The body in question is the Inlaks Foundation, of London, and I would like to take this opportunity to thank them. I am grateful, in particular, to the foundation's director Count Nicoló Sella di Monteluce for his encouragement and support.

19. **At that moment, I…expected to do research:** I would like to add a tribute here to the late Dr Peter Lienhardt of the Institute of Social Anthropology, who supervised my D.Phil. at Oxford. I consider myself singularly fortunate in having had him as my supervisor: he was endlessly generous with encouragement, fearsome in his debunking of pretension, and tireless in the orchestration of logistical support. Yet if I think of him today as the best of supervisors, it is not for all those virtues, inestimable as they are, but one yet more valuable still, being the rarest of all in academics: that he did everything he could to make sure that I was left to myself to follow my interests as I chose. My gratitude to him is inexpressible.

19. **Laṭaîfa:** Neither this nor the names of any of the settlements around it are their actual names; nor are the names of those of their inhabitants who are referred to in the following pages.

Laṭaîfa

29. **Being the kindest…of men:** I would like to acknowledge here my enormous debt to the late Professor Aly Issa of the Department of Anthropology, Faculty of Arts, Alexandria. Professor Issa cleared a path for me through all the official hurdles that surround the enterprise of 'fieldwork' and because of him I was able to move into Lataifa within a few weeks of arriving in Egypt. I remember him with the deepest respect and affection and it is a matter of profound regret to me that he is not alive today to see this book in print.

My thanks are due to many others in the Faculty of Arts, a place of which I have the warmest memories. Amongst others, Hisham Nofal, Mohammad Ghoneim, Moustafa Omar, Merwat al-Ashmawi Osman, Taysser Hassan Aly Gomaa and Moustafa Awad Ibrahim, who were research students in the Department of Anthropology at the time, did a great deal to make me feel welcome when I first arrived in Alexandria. I would like to thank them all for the hospitality and friendship which they showed me then, and with which they have enriched all my subsequent visits. I would also like to thank in particular Professor Ahmed Abu-Zeid of the Faculty of Arts.

32. **They are both…Maṣr:** The name is Miṣr, properly speaking.

32. **Like English, every major European language:** Albanian, which uses 'Misir' as well as 'Egjypt', is an exception—probably because of its large Muslim population.

34. **The fort has other names:** See Stanley Lane-Poole's *The Story of Cairo*, pp. 34–5 (J. M. Dent & Co., London, 1902); and Desmond Stewart's *Cairo, 5,500 years,* p. 28 (Thomas Y. Creswell & Co., New York, 1968). A. J. Butler also discusses the name of the fortress briefly in his monumental *Arab Conquest of Egypt* (Oxford University Press, Oxford, 1902), pp. 244–6.

34. **Babylon's principal embankment:** W. Kubiak points this out in his excellent monograph *Al-Fustat, Its Foundation and Early Urban*

Development, pp. 43–7 & 117–8 (American University in Cairo Press, Cairo, 1987). See also Oleg V. Volkoff's *Le Caire,* 969–1969, p. 7 (L'Institut Français d'Archéologie Orientale du Caire, 1971); and Janet L. Abu-Lughod's *Cairo, 1001 Years of the City Victorious,* pp. 4–5 (Princeton University Press, Princeton, 1971).

34. **In Ben Yiju's time:** See Nâṣir-e-Khosraw's *Safarnama* (Book of Travels), p. 55, (trans. W. M. Thackston Jr, Persian Heritage Series, ed. Ehsan Yarshater, No. 36, Persian Heritage Foundation, New York, 1986).

36. **'fossaton':** Cf. W. Kubiak, *Al-Fustat,* p. 11; Janet L. Abu-Lughod, *Cairo 1001 Years,* p. 13; and Desmond Stewart, *Cairo,* pp. 42–3.

36. **Their army routed the Egyptians:** Cf. Stanley Lane-Poole's *A History of Egypt in the Middle Ages,* p.102 (Frank Cass & Co. Ltd, London, new impression, 1968); and Oleg V. Volkoff's *Le Caire,* p. 44.

36. **In its original conception al-Qahira:** Volkoff, pointing out that it was not for nothing that the city was called al-Qâhira al-Maḥrûsa, 'the Guarded', compares it to Peking and Moscow (*Le Caire,* p. 49).

37. **Archæological excavations have shown:** The various different kinds of mud and earth that were used as building materials in medieval Fustat are discussed at length in Moshe Gil's article, 'Maintenance, Building Operations, and Repairs in the Houses of the Qodesh in Fusṭâṭ', p. 147–52 (*Journal of the Economic and Social History of the Orient,* XIV, part II, 1971). The terms used in Lataifa and Nashawy for the kinds of earth that serve as building materials are in many instances the same as those current in medieval Fustat (e.g. ṭîn aswad, ṭîn aṣfar, turâb).

37. **Possibly Fustat even had…look of an Egyptian village:** My speculations about the appearance of medieval Fustat are founded largely on Wladyslaw Kubiak's description of the archæological findings at the site (in his monograph *Al-Fustat*). I hasten to add that Kubiak does not himself suggest that the medieval city had a rustic appearance: however, the findings described in the monograph seem to me definitely to indicate that likelihood. See in particular the section on 'Streets', pp. 112–117. Some medieval travellers reported Fustat to be provincial in aspect but crowded and busy, while others spoke with admiration of large multi-storeyed buildings, suggesting that houses in some parts of Fustat were of imposing dimensions (Cf. Oleg V. Volkoff, *Le Caire,* p. 22; and S. D. Goitein, 'Urban Housing in Fatimid and Ayyubid Times', p. 14, *Studia Islamica,* 46–7, 1978). In all likelihood the township had a few

Notes

wealthy neighbourhoods which were built on a very different scale from the dwellings inhabited by the vast majority of the population. In many details the domestic architecture of medieval Fustat appears remarkably similar to that of rural (Lower) Egypt today. Indeed there was clearly a direct continuity between the living patterns of the surrounding countryside and those of the city of Fustat. Dwellings in medieval Fustat even made provision for cattle pens or zarîbas within the house (Cf. S. D. Goitein, 'A Mansion in Fustat: A twelfth-century Description of a Domestic compound in the Ancient Capital of Egypt', in *The Medieval City*, ed. H. A. Miskimin et. al., Yale University Press, New Haven, 1977). The word zarîba has of course passed into the English language as 'zareba'. A contemporary zarîba is soon to play a part in this narrative.

38. **The 'Palestinian' congregation:** The principal doctrinal division within the Jewish community of medieval Fustat lay between the Karaites and the other two groups, known collectively as the Rabbanites; the Karaites took the Bible as their sole sacred text while the others invested the Talmud and other later Rabbinical writings with the authority of Scripture as well, as do the majority of Jews today. Of the two Rabbanite groups, the 'Iraqis' consisted of Jews from the area of Mesopotamia, who followed the rites prescribed by the schools of that region, while the 'Palestinians' of course followed the rites of the school of Jerusalem. See S. D. Goitein's *A Mediterranean Society*, Vol. I, p. 18 (Univ. of California Press, Berkeley, 1967); and Norman Golb's article, 'Aspects of the Historical Background of Jewish Life in Medieval Egypt' (in *Jewish Medieval and Renaissance Studies*, ed. Alexander Altmann, Harvard University Press, Cambridge Mass., 1967).

39. **Incredible as it may seem, excavations:** See G. T. Scanlon's 'Egypt and China: Trade and Imitation', p. 88 (in *Islam and the Trade of Asia*, ed. D. S. Richards, Oxford and Philadelphia, 1971); and Ruth Barnes's article 'Indian Trade Cloth in Egypt: The Newberry Collection' (in the *Proceedings of the Textile Society of America*, 1990).

54. **For Ben Yiju the centre of Cairo:** It was once thought that the synagogue of Ben Ezra was originally a Coptic church, but that theory has long been discredited by S. D. Goitein, although it continues to be widely propagated. A church was indeed converted into a synagogue in Fustat, in the ninth century, but it probably belonged to a different congregation and stood upon another site. (Cf. *A Mediterranean Society*, Vol. I, p. 18; and Vol. II, p. 149, University of California Press, Berkeley, 1971).

Goitein has persuasively argued that the church which changed hands in the ninth century was bought by the 'Iraqi' congregation, which, being composed mainly of immigrants, probably needed a site for its synagogue. The site of the Synagogue of Ben Ezra on the other hand had probably belonged to the 'Palestinians' since antiquity.

54. It is known to have had two entrances: See S. D. Goitein's 'The Sexual Mores of the Common People', p. 47 (in *Society and the Sexes in Medieval Islam*, ed. A. L. al-Sayyid Marsot, Udena Publications, Malibu, 1979); and Vol. II of his *Mediterranean Society*, pp. 143–52.

55. For the Synagogue...the influx of migrants: Cf. S. D. Goitein, 'Changes in the Middle East (950–1150)', p. 25; and 'Mediterranean Trade in the Eleventh Century: Some Facts and Problems', p. 61, (in *Studies in the Economic History of the Middle East*, ed. M. A. Cook, Oxford University Press, London, 1970).

55. The North Africans...affinity for the flourishing trade: Jews and Muslims in North Africa and the Middle East may have turned increasingly to the India Trade after the tenth century because they had been squeezed out of the Mediterranean trade by the Christian states of the northern coast. (See, for example, S. D. Goitein's article 'Portrait of a Medieval India Trader; Three Letters from the Cairo Geniza', p. 449, *Bulletin of the School of Oriental and African Studies*, Vol. 50, part 3, 1987). After the twelfth century Jewish merchants appear to have been gradually pushed out of the eastern trade by the Muslim association of Kârimî merchants. (Cf. W. J. Fischel, 'The Spice Trade in Mamluk Egypt', pp. 166–7, *Journal of the Economic and Social History of the Orient*, Vol. I, part 2, E. J. Brill, London, 1958.)

56. The vast majority...were traders: See S. D. Goitein, *Studies in Islamic History and Institutions*, pp. 277–8 (Leiden, Brill, 1966). As Goitein points out elsewhere, the upper crust of the Jewish community in Fustat was formed largely by the members of the 'Iraqi' and Karaite congregations, not by the 'Palestinians': 'as a rule it was the middle and lower middle classes and not the economically and socially highest layer of Jewish society which have left us their day to day writings in the Geniza.' ('Changes in the Middle East [950–1150]' p. 18.) See also Goitein's article 'The Sexual Mores of the Common People', p. 50.

56. Their doctors...studied Hippocrates: Cf. S. D. Goitein, *A Mediterranean Society*, Vol. II, p. 249

56. The chambers...known by the term 'Geniza': Cf. S. D. Goitein, *A*

Mediterranean Society, Vol. I, p. 1.

57. **The Geniza...was added:** For the date of the construction of the Ben Ezra Geniza see S. D. Goitein, *A Mediterranean Society*, Vol. I, p. 18. On 31 December 1011, a Jewish funeral procession was attacked by Muslims, and twenty-three people were taken captive and threatened with death. They were saved at the last moment by the personal intervention of the Caliph. Goitein has suggested that this incident may have had a direct connection with the addition of the Geniza at the time of the synagogue's reconstruction in 1025. 'Recalling the terrifying events of December 1011, they must have mused: Corpses must be removed from the city notwithstanding the constant menace by the rabble. But why take the same risk with papers? Let's have a place in the synagogue roomy enough for storing discarded writings now and for ever. The idea was materialized and the result was the Cairo Geniza.' ('Urban Housing in Fatimid and Ayyubid Times', p. 6.) The Geniza does however contain several documents that predate the rebuilding of the Synagogue of Ben Ezra in the eleventh century. (See Simon Hopkins's article 'The Oldest Dated Document in the Geniza', in *Studies in Judaism and Islam*, ed. Shelomo Morag et al., Hebrew University, Jerusalem, 1981.)

57. **for some reason...was never cleared out:** The recent research of Mark R. Cohen and Yedida K. Stillman suggests that the practice of discarding manuscripts in a chamber within a synagogue and leaving them there permanently was common among Middle Eastern Jews well into this century. See their article 'The Cairo Geniza and the Custom of Geniza among Oriental Jewry: An Historical and Ethnographic Study', in the Hebrew journal *Pe'amin* (No. 24, 1985).

57. **The document...thought to be the last:** See S. D. Goitein, *A Mediterranean Society*, Vol. I, p. 9.

81. **From the late seventeenth century...Egyptomania:** See Erik Iversen's *The Myth of Egypt and its Hieroglyphs in European Tradition*, pp 88–123, (Geo Gad Publishers, Copenhagen, 1961).

81. **Concurrent with this...travellers undertook journeys:** Cf. Eric Iversen, *The Myth of Egypt*, pp 108–110.

81. **It was...the first report:** The Italian traveller, Obadiah of Be(a)artinoro had described the Synagogue of Ben Ezra in a letter to his father in 1488, but the Geniza does not figure in his account (Cf. Simon Hopkins, 'The Discovery of the Cairo Geniza', pp 144–6, *Bibliophilia Africana* IV, ed. C. Pama, Cape Town, 1981).

81. **The visit appears...unremarkable:** Cf. Norman Bentwich, *Solomon Schechter; A Biography*, p. 139, (Cambridge Univ. Press, Cambridge, 1938), and Simon Hopkins, 'The Discovery...', p. 147.

82. **In fact...Karl Leibniz:** See Erik Iversen's *The Myth of Egypt*, p. 125.

83. **'Can a man risk':** Simon Hopkins, 'The Discovery...', p. 149.

83. **'But who knows':** ibid., p. 150.

84. **The German scholar:** Paul Kahle, *The Cairo Geniza*, pp. 2–3, (Oxford University Press, London, 1947).

84. **He had obtained...documents:** Paul Kahle, for example, met Samaritan priests in Palestine who complained bitterly of how Firkowitch had swindled them of their manuscripts, paying them next to nothing (*The Cairo Geniza*, p. 4).

85. **'It is not often':** Elkan N. Adler, 'Notes of a Journey to the East', p. 6 (*Jewish Chronicle*, 7 December 1888).

85. **The Cattaouis:** See Gudrun Krämer's account of the history of the Cattaouis in *The Jews in Modern Egypt, 1914–1952*, pp. 88–98 (University of Washington Press, Seattle, 1989).

85. **By this time the indigenous Jews of Cairo:** Marion Woolfson, *Prophets in Babylon; Jews in the Arab World*, p. 102 (Faber and Faber, London 1980); and Gudrun Krämer and Alfred Morabia: 'Face à la Modernité: Les Juifs d'Egypte aux XIXe et XXe siècles', pp. 84–5, (in Jacques Hassoun ed. *Juifs du Nil*, Le Sycomore, Paris, 1981).

86. **Soon afterwards the British ambassador:** The Earl of Cromer, *Modern Egypt*, Vol. I, p. 336–41, (Macmillan, London, 1908).

86. **The Cattaouis...mansion:** Elkan N. Adler, 'Notes', p. 6 .

87. **The Bodleian Library...two members of its staff:** They were A. Cowley and A. Neubauer. Both Cowley and Neubauer were greatly excited by the newly discovered fragments and were desperately eager to lay their hands on more, but curiously enough, even as late as 1896 they do not appear to have had any idea of where the documents were coming from. (See A. Neubauer's article, 'Egyptian Fragments', *Jewish Quarterly Review*, pp. 541–561, Vol. VIII, 1895–6; and A. Cowley's article in the same issue, 'Some Remarks on Samaritan Literature and Religion', pp. 562–575. See also Mark R. Cohen's *Jewish Self-Government in Medieval Egypt*, p. 11, Princeton, 1980).

88. **He took with him letters...the Cattaoui family** E. N. Adler, 'An Eleventh Century Introduction to the Hebrew Bible' (*Jewish Quarterly Review*, p. 673, Vol. IX, pp. 669–716, Macmillan, London, 1896–7).

88. **Between them, they granted:** Ibid., p. 673.

89. **'Dear Mrs Lewis,':** A copy of the note is reprinted in Norman Bentwich's *Solomon Schechter,* opp. p. 111.

89. **'All students of the Bible':** *The Academy,* p. 405, No. 1254, 16 May 1896.

90. **'If it could be proved':** S. Schechter, 'A fragment of the Original Text of Ecclesiasticus', p. 1 (*Expositor,* Fifth Series, Vol. IV, London, 1896).

91. **So little did he think:** A. Lutfi al-Sayyid, *Egypt and Cromer: A Study in Anglo-Egyptian Relations,* p. 64 (John Murray, London, 1968).

91. **'We need not...inquire too closely':** Quoted in A. Lutfi al-Sayyid, *Egypt and Cromer,* p. 62.

91. **Schechter was fortunate...that Cromer:** See, for example, N. Bentwich's Introduction to *Solomon Schechter: Selected Writings,* (ed. N. Bentwich, East and West Library, Oxford, 1946). Bentwich writes: 'Lord Cromer, then the British Agent in Egypt, was interested in Schechter's exploration, and helped him to secure the removal of the treasure to Cambridge.' (p. 15).

91. **They decided to make...a present:** See S. D. Goitein, *A Mediterranean Society,* Vol. I, p. 5; and Paul Kahle, *The Cairo Geniza,* p. 7.

92. **It has sometimes been suggested:** Bentwich, for example, writes: 'It was fortunate that the Egyptian Jewish community regarded their archives at that time as little more than a rubbish heap, and were prepared to let him carry away the greater part of their collection to Cambridge...' (Introduction to *Solomon Schechter: Selected Writings*).

92. **In fact...lucrative trade:** Schechter himself was to comment later that the beadles of the Synagogue had 'some experience' in dealing with the documents. (S. Schechter, 'The Cairo Geniza', p. 102, in *Solomon Schechter: Selected Writings*).

92. **'I flirted with him':** Bentwich quotes these letters in his biography, *Solomon Schechter,* p. 129.

93. **'For weeks and weeks':** Ibid., p. 128.

93. **'The whole population':** *Solomon Schechter: Selected Writings,* pp. 102–3.

94. **'with the spoils':** E. N. Adler, 'An Eleventh Century Introduction', p. 673.

98. **So it happened:** My first explorations of Masr owed a great deal to the enthusiasm of Sudhir Vyas. I would like to thank him, and his colleague at the Indian Embassy Shri A. Gopinathan, for their hospitality. I would

also like to thank Shri K. P. S. Menon and Sm. Lalitha Menon for their interest in, and support of my work during their stay in Egypt. Later Laurent Ham's knowledge of the city was to prove invaluable to me: I am deeply grateful to him for his help and for innumerable kindnesses.

99. **Goitein...published in India:** Cf. S. D. Goitein, 'Letters and Documents on the India Trade in Medieval Times', (*Islamic Culture*, Vol. 37, pp. 188–205, 1963).

99. **The complete bibliography:** Robert Attal, *A Bibliography of the Writings of Professor Shelomo Dov Goitein*, Hebrew University, Jerusalem, 1975 (Supplement 1987).

99. **His interest in the Geniza:** See Mark R. Cohen's obituary 'Shelomo Dov Goitein (3 April 1900–6 February 1985)' in the American Philosophy Society *Year Book*, 1987.

100. **His monumental study:** The five volumes of S. D. Goitein's *A Mediterranean Society* were published in the following years, by the University of California Press: Vol. I, 1967; Vol. II, 1971; Vol. III, 1978; Vol. IV, 1983; Vol. V, 1988. The fifth volume appeared posthumously.

100. **Scanning Goitein's...oeuvre:** Goitein did however occasionally write biographical sketches. His posthumously published article 'Portrait of a Medieval India Trader: Three Letters from the Cairo Geniza' (*Bulletin of the School of Oriental and African Studies*, Vol. 50, part 3, pp. 449–64, 1987), for example, deals with the life of the trader 'Allân b. Ḥassûn.

100. *The India Book*: The catalogue numbers of the India Book documents were published in Shaul Shaked's *A Tentative Bibliography of Geniza Documents* (Mouton, Paris, 1964), which was published under the joint direction of D. H. Baneth and S. D. Goitein.

101. **Judæo-Arabic evolved:** This brief account is based largely upon the 'Introduction' in Joshua Blau's *Judæo-Arabic*, (Clarendon Press, Oxford, 1965), the standard work on the subject. Those who wish to learn more about this extraordinary and wonderful language are strongly recommended to consult Blau's excellent study.

104. **Mark Cohen's encouragement:** In case my debt to Mark Cohen is not apparent already, I would like to add a line of acknowledgement here. It was Mark Cohen who convinced me that I could indeed learn Judaeo-Arabic, and he has been very generous with constructive criticism as well as advice and encouragement ever since. My debt to him is incalculable.

105. **Over the next couple of years:** My Geniza research would not have

been possible without the support of a great many people. To begin with, I would like to thank Dr A. Udovitch of the Department of Near Eastern Studies, Princeton and Dr Stefan C. Reif of the Taylor-Schechter Geniza Research Unit of the Cambridge University Library. To Dr Geoffrey Khan, also of the Taylor-Schechter Geniza Research Unit, Cambridge, I owe a very special debt—for guiding my first faltering steps in the field of Geniza studies, for giving me the benefit of his understanding of the material, and for his patience in answering my innumerable queries. Dr Menahem Ben Sasson also helped me a great deal in the early stages of my research and I would like to thank him for his advice, for many valuable suggestions and for checking several of my transcriptions. I need hardly add that neither he nor anyone else is in any way responsible for any of the views expressed here. Finally a tribute is due to the staff of the Manuscripts Reading Room of the Cambridge University Library for their efficiency and unfailing helpfulness.

Nashâwy

153. Since his friends...referred to him as al-Mahdawî: Khalaf Ibn Ishaq for instance, addresses Ben Yiju as al-Mahdawî in his 1148 letter (National and University Library Jerusalem Geniza MS H.6, in Strauss, 'Documents').

153. Mahdia...a major centre of Jewish culture: See H. Z. Hirschberg's *A History of the Jews in North Africa*, Vol. I, pp. 339–41 (E. J. Brill, Leiden, 1974).

153. 'altogether Mahdia offered': Al-Sharîf al-Idrîsî, *Kitâb tazha al-mushtâq fi ihtirâq al-afâq*, p. 257 (Geographie d'Edrisi, ed. and trans. P. A. Jaubert, Vol. I, Paris, 1836).

153. Of Ben Yiju's immediate family: S. D. Goitein believed that Ben Yiju may have had another sister, Yumn (cf. *Letters*, pp. 204 fn).

154. He was called Perahyâ: The Jewish naming system in the medieval Arabic-speaking world was enormously complex being compounded out of two languages, Arabic and Hebrew. Most people had several names, each context-specific—tekonyms, nicknames, (both individual and collective), titles that were the equivalent of surnames, and so on. To simplify matters I have tried to refer to each individual by a single name throughout this narrative. As a rule (if a principle founded on indeterminacy can be called a rule) I have tried to use the name that is most commonly used for them in the documents themselves. I have also generally tried to transcribe the names as they occur in the documents, in the expectation that those spellings provide the nearest available approximation to the manner in which the names were actually pronounced, at the time, by the people who used them. But in such instances when those spellings produce results that are meaningless or absurd I have substituted the etymologically appropriate Hebrew equivalents. Thus I have generally used the Arabic 'Farhîa' instead of the Hebrew 'Peraḥyâ', taking at face value the following statement by Goitein: 'No such Heb. name (Peraḥyâ) exists in the Bible. This is one of the pseudo-biblical names invented during the Geniza period and I suspect that the verb contained in it was understood as Ar. faraḥ ("Joy in God") rather than Heb. peraḥ ("flower") which makes no sense.' (*Letters*, pp. 327). The relationship between the name and the Arabic root was evidently apparent to those who used it, since Farhia is usually twinned with the diminutive Surûr, which has a similar semantic value in Arabic. I have however used 'Berâkhâ' rather than 'Barkha' for example, (which is how the name is spelt by Ben Yiju, in his letter), since it has no Arabic equivalent or referent. I can only beg the indulgence of those who consider this method haphazard, or otherwise objectionable, while pointing out that when a naming system is intended to create multiple levels of identity, any procedure for privileging one name (or even one spelling) is bound to be arbitrary.

154. **and he was a Rabbi:** Khalaf ibn Ishaq once addressed Ben Yiju as the son of the 'R(abbi) Peraḥyâ, son of Yijû' (S. D. Goitein, *Letters*, pp. 192).

155. **Madmun ibn Bundar:** See S. D. Goitein, *Letters*, pp. 177; 181–82; and 'From Aden to India: Specimens of the Correspondence of India Traders of the Twelfth Century', p. 45, (in *Journal of the Economic and Social History of the Orient*, Vol. XXXIII, pts I and II, 1980). For the institution of the nagîd, see Goitein's articles, 'The Title and Office of the Nagid; a Re-examination' (*Jewish Quarterly Review*, pp. 93–119, LIII, 1962–3), and 'Mediterranean Trade in the Eleventh Century: Some Facts and Problems', p. 61 (in *Studies in the Economic History of the Middle East* ed. M. A. Cook, Oxford University Press, London, 1970). The Nagîdate and the interesting historiographical controversies surrounding it are also extensively discussed in Mark Cohen's *Jewish Self-Government in Medieval Egypt*.

156. **Madmun's earliest extant letters:** T–S 20.130. My assumption that this is the first item in Madmun's correspondence with Ben Yiju is based on a comment in the text (recto, lines 4–5) which seems to suggest that Ben Yiju had only recently made the journey to India.

156. **From the tone and content of those...letters:** Their business relations were patterned on a model of informal co-operation, widespread amongst Middle Eastern merchants, in which traders in different countries rendered each other mutual service. For more on the subject of co-operation amongst merchants see S. D. Goitein's article 'Mediterranean Trade in the Eleventh Century: Some Facts and Problems', p. 59; and Abraham L. Udovitch's 'Commercial Techniques in Early Medieval Islamic Trade', (in *Islam and the Trade of Asia*, ed. D. S. Richards).

156. **The letters are full of detailed instructions:** for example, one passage in a letter from Madmun to Ben Yiju in India reads: '...collect yourself all the letters for the people of Mangalore...and be careful with them because they contain things that I need urgently...deliver each one to the person to whom it is addressed, by hand, personally, for God's sake.' (T–S N.S. J 1, verso, lines 6–10). In a departure from the epistolary conventions of the time, Madmun used the second person pronoun, inta, a relatively familiar form, to address Ben Yiju: I have translated it as 'yourself' in this passage. It is a clear indication that there was a certain asymmetry in their relationship.

156. **The other was Khalaf ibn Ishaq:** Khalaf was a fine calligrapher and a prolific correspondent; many of his letters to various different correspondents have been preserved in the Geniza. See S. D. Goitein, 'Portrait of a Medieval India Trader', p. 453–54.

157. **Judah ha-Levi...composed poems in his honour:** See S. D. Goitein's article, 'The Biography of Rabbi Judah Ha-Levi in the Light of the Cairo Geniza Documents' (in *Essays in Medieval Jewish and Islamic Philosophy*, ed. Arthur Hyman, Ktav Publishing House, Inc., New York, 1977).

157. **Abû Sa'id Ḥalfon:** In a letter to Ben Yiju in Mangalore, Madmun refers to a certain 'Nâkhudha Abû Sa'îd' who might be Abu Sa'id Halfon (T–S MS Or 1081, J3, recto, line 3). Although to the best of my knowledge, no letters addressed directly from Ben Yiju to Abu Sa'id Halfon (or vice versa) have been preserved, several letters between others in the circle have survived (e.g. T–S MS Or. 1080 J 211 and T–S Box J 1 fol. 53 [Khalaf to Halfon]. Cf. Shaul Shaked, *Tentative Bibliography*, pp. 47, 150).

157. **The second of the great travellers:** Abû-Zikrî Sijilmâsî and Abu Sa'id Halfon were in fact partners in the Indian Trade, and several documents relating to their joint business dealings have been preserved in the Geniza (e.g. T–S 13 J 22, fol. 33, 'Memorandum to Ḥalfon b. Nethaneel, while on his way to India, from his partner Abû Zikrî' and T–S N.S. J 22, 'Deed of acquittance by Abû Zikrî to Ḥalfon b. Nathaneel in connection with their India business' (Shaul Shaked, *Tentative Bibliography*, pp. 132, 160).

158. **Chief Representative of Merchants:** See S. D. Goitein, *Letters*. p. 62; 'The Beginnings of the Kârim Merchants', pp. 176–7 (*Journal of the Economic and Social History of the Orient*, Vol. I, part 2, E. J. Brill, Leiden, 1958); and 'Bankers Accounts from the Eleventh Century AD', pp. 62–3 (*Journal of the Economic and Social History of the Orient*, IX, pt. I–II, 1966).

158. **References...a shipowner called Maḥrûz:** See T–S 8 J 7, fol. 23, recto, line 3; T–S N.S. J 10, verso 1st Account, line 9; and 2nd Account, line 1.

158. **So close were the...three:** See S. D. Goitein, *Letters*, pp. 62–5.

159. **At the time...gifted Hebrew poets:** Cf. Yosef Tobi, 'Poetry and Society in the works of Abraham ben Ḥalfon (Yemen, twelfth century)' (in *Biblical and Other Studies in Memory of S. D. Goetein*, ed. Reuben Ahroni, *Hebrew Annual Review*, Vol. IX, Dept. of Judaic and Near Eastern Languages and Literatures, Ohio State University, 1985).

159. **instances of Geniza traders living abroad:** See, for example, S. D. Goitein, 'Abraham Maimonides and his Pietist Circle', p. 157 (in *Jewish Medieval and Renaissance Studies*, ed. A. Altmann).

159. **The second reason...lies in a cryptic letter:** T–S MS Or. 1080 J 2 63, verso.

160. **Fortunately the scrap:** Ben Yiju was clearly the recipient of his letter, because the back of the letter is scribbled on in a handwriting which is unmistakably his. Professor Goitein included the catalogue number of this letter in Shaked's catalogue of Geniza documents, and he must have known of its contents for he described it there as the 'first part of a letter sent by Maḍmûn...of Aden to Ben Yijû in India,' (Shaul Shaked, *Tentative Bibliography*, p. 47). But he did not quote it in any of his published references to Ben Yiju and probably did not fully appreciate the implications it has for the story of Ben Yiju's life.

160. **'Concerning what he':** T–S MS Or. 1080 J 263, recto, lines 16–22.

Notes

The meaning of the second part of the last sentence is doubtful, and my reading of it must be taken as provisional at best. The reference to the 'court' may be to the council of foreign merchants (cf. M. N. Pearson, *Merchants and Rulers in Gujarat*, p. 17, University of California Press, Berkeley, 1976).

160. **'His servant spoke to [the king]':** It is not quite clear who the reference is to. Aden in this period was controlled by the Zuray'ids, a dynasty of the Isma'íli sect, nominally linked to the Fatimids of Egypt. The dates and lines of succession within the dynasty are rather obscure, but it would appear that none of the Zuray'id rulers of this period bore the name Sa'id (cf. g. R. Smith, *The Ayyûbids and Early Rasûlids in the Yemen*, Vol. II, pp. 63–7, Luzac & Co. Ltd, London, 1978). However, the name could have been the popularly current name of the Zuray'î ruler of that time.

161. **The word is dhimma:** In Islamic law, members of tolerated religious groups are known as the dhimmi.

174. **In the twelfth century…Qus:** Cf. J-C. Garcin, 'Un centre musulman de la Haute-Égypte médiévale: Qûs' (Cairo, IFAO, 1976) and W. J. Fischel's 'The Spice Trade in Mamluk Egypt', pp. 162–4. The twelfth-century Arab geographer, Al-Idrisi wrote of Qus that it was a big mercantile city with many resources, but its air was unhealthy and few strangers escaped the insalubriousness of the climate (*Kitâb*, p. 127).

174. **'a station for the traveller':** The quotation is from R. J. C. Broadhurst's translation of the *Raḥla* of Abû al-Ḥasan ibn Jubaîr (published as *The Travels of Ibn Jubaîr*, Jonathan Cape, London, 1952).

175. **Over the next seventeen days:** The crossing took Ibn Jubair only seventeen days, but Al-Idrisi asserts that it generally took at least twenty days (*Kitâb*, p. 132).

175. **Ibn Jubair remarked…'whoso deems it lawful':** R. J. C. Broadhurst, *Travels*, p. 60.

176. **The area…inhabited by a tribe:** This was one of the Beja tribes of Sudan and southern Egypt who are referred to frequently by medieval Arab geographers and travellers (e.g. Al-Idrisi, *Kitâb*, p. 133). See also Paul Wheatley's article, 'Analecta Sino–Africana Recensa', p. 82 (in *East Africa and the Orient*, ed. H. Neville Chittick and R. I. Rotberg, Africana Publishing Co., New York and London, 1975).

176. **'Their men and':** R. J. C. Broadhurst, *Travels*, p. 66.

176. **'A sojourn in':** Ibid., p. 67.

371

176. 'It is one': Ibid., p. 63. for the maritime routes of the Red Sea, see G. R. Tibbetts, 'Arab Navigation in the Red Sea', pp. 322–4 (*Geographical Journal*, 127, 1961).

176. For about five hundred years Aidhab functioned: See, for example, H. A. R. Gibb's article on 'Aydhâb (in the *Encyclopaedia of Islam*), and G. W. Murray's article 'Aidhab' (in *The Geographical Journal*, 68, pp. 235–40, 1926).

176. In any case, all that remains: Cf. J-C. Garcin, 'Jean-Léon l'Africain et 'Aydab', p. 190 (*Annales Islamologiques*, XI, 1972).

177. 'The carrier of this letter': T-S N.S. J 1, recto, lines 13–16.

178. But the writing...is clear: Cf. Shaul Shaked, *Tentative Bibliography*, p. 134.

178. 'Shaikh Abraham Ibn Yijû bespoke': T-S 13 J 24, fol. 2, recto, lines 9–22 and margins.

178. 'For the affair of Shaikh Makhluf': T-S MS Ov. 1081 J 3, recto, margin.

227. The first...a legally attested deed: Cf. S. D. Goitein, *Letters*, p. 202.

227. The second...is a rough draft: T-S 12.458 verso, lines 5–13. I would like to thank Dr Geoffrey Khan for translating the Aramaic words in this document for me.

228. 'concubinage is permitted': Al-Idrisi, *Kitâb*, p. 179.

228. 'Let us thank God,': Cf. G. Ferrand, *Voyage du Marchand Arabe Sulayman en Inde et en Chine*, p. 124 (Paris, 1922).

228. 'Public women are everywhere': 'The Travels of Nicolo Conti in the East in the Early Part of the Fifteenth Century', p. 23 (translated from the original of Poggio Bracciolini by J. Winter Jones, in *India in the Fifteenth Century; Being a Collection of Narratives of Voyages to India*, ed. R. H. Major, Hakluyt Society, London, 1857).

228. 'Immediately after midday': 'Narrative of the Voyage of Abd-er-Razzak, Ambassador from Shah Rukh, A.H. 845, A.D. 1442', p. 29 (translated by R. H. Major from the French translation of the Persian by M. Quatremère, in *India in the Fifteenth Century*, ed. R. H. Major).

229. 'I have also sent': T–S N.S. J 1 recto, line 11.

229. The connection seems so obvious: S. D. Goitein, *Letters*, p. 202.

229. In a set of accounts...the name Naîr: T-S 20.137, verso, line 19 (account no.2). The word of Ben Yiju used was sahrî, 'brother-in-law' or male affine. It is worth noting that in Ben Yiju's circle this term was generally used in a specific sense, and not as a portmanteau kinship term

(for a case to point see p. 178 of S. D. Goitein's article 'The Beginnings of the Kârim Merchants').

229. The lucky accident...links her...to the Nairs: This squares well with what is known of the social composition of Mangalore at the time, for it is recorded in contemporary inscriptions that a community of Nairs was indeed resident in the area around that time. Accounts left by later travellers suggest that the Nairs of that region had developed particularly close links with foreign traders. See P. Gururaja Bhatt's *Studies in Tuḷuva History and Culture*, pp. 234–5 (Manipal, Karnataka, 1970).

230. 'And throughout the [land]': Benjamin of Tudela, *The Itinerary*, pp. 120–1 (ed. Michael A. Signer, 1983).

Mangalore

242. When Ben Yiju arrived: See Neville Chittick, 'East Africa and the Orient: Ports and Trade before the arrival of the Portuguese' (in *Historical Relations Across the Indian Ocean*, UNESCO, Paris, 1980).

242. 'living in a suburb': See Ibn Battúta *Travels in Asia and Africa, 1325–1354*, p. 233 (trans. and selected by H. A. R. Gibb, Routledge & Sons, London, 1939).

243. 'China, Sumatra, Ceylon,': Ibid, p. 234.

243. 'Arabs, Persians, Guzarates': Duarte Barbosa, *A Description of the Coasts of East Africa and Malabar in the beginning of the sixteenth century*, p. 202 (trans. H. E. J. Stanley, The Hakluyt Society, London, 1856).

243. '[They] possess...wives': Ibid., p. 202.

243. 'They dress themselves': 'Narrative of the Voyage of Abd-er-Razzak', p. 17 (in *India in the Fifteenth Century*, ed. R. H. Major).

244. ...the Arabic name 'Malabâr': The name is spelt variously as Malâbâr and Malîbâr in the Geniza documents. It also sometimes occurs in plural forms, such as Malîbârât.

244. The language of Mangalore: See K. V. Ramesh, *A History of South Kanara*, xxiv–xxvi (Karnatak University Research Publications, Series 12, Dharwar, 1970); 'Geographical Factors in Tuluva History', p. 7 (*Academy Silver Jubilee Lecture*, Academy of General Education, Manipal, Karnataka, 1981); U. P. Upadhyaya & S. P. Upadhyaya (ed.), *Bhuta Worship: Aspects of a Ritualistic Theatre*, p. 1 (Regional Resources Centre for Folk Performing Arts, M.G.M.College, Udupi, Karnataka, 1984); P. Claus, 'Mayndaḷa: A Legend and Possession Cult of Tuḷunâḍ', p. 96 (*Asian Folklore Studies*, Vol. 38:2, 1979); and G. R. Krishna, *Caste and Tribes of Fishermen*, pp. 103–11 (Discovery Publishing House, New Delhi, 1990).

244. **It is this language:** Tuḷu is spoken by 47 per cent of the population of South Kanara District—the area that was once known as Tuḷanâḍ (*Karnataka State Gazetteer [South Kanara District]*, p. 94, Govt. of Karnataka, Bangalore, 1973).

245. **Writing in Alexandria…Ptolemy:** The name of this dynasty is also spelt, in various inscriptions, as Aḷva, Aḷuka, Aḷupa and Aḷapa (Cf. K. V. Ramesh, *A History of South Kanara*, p. 30; and P. Gururaja Bhatt, *Studies*, p. 18).

245. **For several hundreds of years:** For detailed accounts of the history of the Aḷupas see K. V. Ramesh's *History of South Kanara;* P.Gururaja Bhatt's *Studies,* pp. 18–41; and B. A. Saletore's *Ancient Karnataka*, (*History of Tuluva*, Vol. I, Oriental Book Agency, Poona, 1936).

245. **it was in the reign of…:** Cf. K. V. Ramesh, *History of South Kanara,* p. 115. P.Gururaja Bhatt dates Kavi Aḷupendra's reign from 1115 to 1155 (*Studies* p. 23).

246. **I had been told:** I am indebted to a great many people for offering help, advice and criticism while I was working in Karnataka. I would particularly like to thank Dr C. Veeranna, Dr G. S. Sivarudrappa, Dr M. N. Srinivas, Sm. Tara N. Chandravarkar and Dr Vivek Dhareshwar of Bangalore; Dr Vijaya Dabbe of Mysore; and Dr K. S. Haridas Bhatt, Shri S. A. Krishnaiah, Dr Alphonsus D'Souza and Sm. L. Lobo-Prabhu of Mangalore. The late Shri K. S. Niranjana and Sm. Anupama Nivanjana were also very generous with their time and advice while I was in Bangalore; I would like to record my gratitude to them here.

247. **In the translated version of the letter:** S. D. Goitein, *Letters*, p. 191.

247. **Indeed…an accepted way of spelling the word:** The tenth-century Arab traveller and geographer Masûdî, for example, uses the word brâhma and various cognates frequently in his encyclopaedic compendium, *Murûj al-Dhahab (Les Prairies d'or)*, Vol. I, pp. 149, 154, & 157–8 (Arabic text and French Translation, C. Barbier de Meynard & Pavet de Courteille, Société Asiatique, Paris, 1861). The geographer Al-Idrisi, who happened to be a contemporary of Ben Yiju's, was perfectly familiar with the word although he never went anywhere near the Indian

Ocean. Al-Idrisi uses the word frequently but he sometimes uses it to mean Brahmin (as indeed does Mas'udi often).

248. **The slave-trade in Ben Yiju's time:** A Persian chronicler of the ninth century describes travelling merchants who took 'eunuchs, female slaves (and) boys' from 'the country of the Franks', in Europe, and traded them, in India and China, for 'musk, aloes, camphor and cinnamon', (Ibn Khurdâdhbih, quoted in Reinaud's introduction to Abû al-Fidâ's *Kitâb taqwîm al-buldân* (Géographie d'Aboulfélda), p. 58, Arabic text, ed. M. Reinaud & Baron MacGuckin de Slane, Paris, 1860). A century later, a geographer, Ibn Ḥauqâl, noted that Byzantine, Slavonic and Berber slaves were regularly traded in the cities of the east. (Cf. H. Z. Hirschberg, *Jews in North Africa*, p. 252). Edward H. Schafer deals briefly with the import of foreign slaves into China in *The Golden Peaches of Samarkand*, pp. 43–7 (University of California Press, Berkeley, 1963).

248. **Indeed, an obscure reference:** In one of his letters, Madmun, writing to Ben Yiju, remarks: 'This year the "traders" (jallâb) have not come here yet from Zabîd' (T-S 20.130, recto, lines 45–46). The word jallâb has the connotation of 'slave-traders'. The implication of the passage is that Ben Yiju had been expecting the arrival of a party of slave-traders in Mangalore. Al-Idrisi observes that Zabid was a major destination for Abyssinian slave-traders (*Kitâb*, Vol. I, p. 49).

248. **The slaves...traded in...Egypt:** See S. D. Goitein, 'Slaves and Slavegirls in the Cairo Geniza Records', (*Arabica*, Vol.9, 1–20, 1962); and *A Mediterranean Society*, Vol. I, pp. 130–147.

249. **But the slave's name:** Dr Geoffrey Khan has found the name Bâmah in a third-century AH Arabic papyrus, and he interprets it as a rendering of the Coptic name Pamei/Pame (personal communication). It is extremely unlikely however that the B-M-H of MS H.6 is intended to represent the same name, since it is spelt differently, not just once, but consistently through the whole range of Ben Yiju's correspondence.

249. **I discovered...Mâsaleya Bamma:** R. S. Panchamukhi (ed.), *Karnataka Inscriptions*, Vol. II., pp. 71–2 (Kannada Research Institute, Dharwar, 1951).

249. **Another...Seṭṭi Bamma:** Ibid., pp. 72–73.

250. **Over...but still preserved:** For example, one of the principal matrilineal clans of Tulunad bears the name 'Bommiya-baḷi'. There is also a Bommi-ṣeṭṭiya-baḷi among the many matrilineal baḷis mentioned in medieval inscriptions. See P. Gururaja Bhatt, *Studies*, pp. 243 & 250–1.

251. But divided...the Tuluva: Cf. P. Claus, 'Spirit Possession and Spirit Mediumship from the Perspective of Tulu Oral Traditions', (in *Culture, Medicine & Psychiatry*, 3:94–129, 1979). The distinctively Tuluva matrilineal system of law is known as Aḷiya-santâna law. By the rules of this system, men transmit their immoveable property, not to their own children, but matrilineally, to their sister's children. But it is important to note that among the Tuluva, as with most groups that are characterized as 'matrilineal', these rules apply only to certain categories of property. P. Claus in his article 'Terminological Aspects of Tuḷu Kinship: Kin Terms, Kin Sets, and Kin Groups of the Matrilineal Castes' (in *American Studies in the Anthropology of India*, 1981) has very rightly questioned the usefulness of labels such as 'matrilineal' and 'patrilineal' in these circumstances (p. 213). In his view some Tuluva institutions are suggestive of double unilineal descent (p. 234). Where I have used the term 'matrilineal' without qualification it is purely for convenience; these qualifications must be taken for granted.

251. Equally, they shared in the worship of...Bhûtas: See, for instance, the following articles: Heidrun Brückner, 'Bhûta-Worship in Coastal Karnâṭaka: An Oral Tuḷu myth and festival ritual of Jumâdi', p. 18 (*Studien zur Indologie und Iranistik*, 13/14, Reinbek, 1987); P. Claus, 'Possession, Protection and Punishment as Attributes of the Deities in a South Indian Village', p. 235 (*Man in India*, 53:231–242, 1973); and Mark Nichter, 'The Joga and Maya of Tuluva Buta', p. 140, (*Eastern Anthropologist*, 30:2).

251. By tradition, each of the Tuluva castes: Mark Nichter, 'The Joga and Maya of Tuluva Buta', p. 143.

252. The cult was tied to the land: Mark Nichter, 'Joga and Maya of Tuluva Buta', p. 139. It is also worth noting that Tuluva Brahmins follow patrilineal rules of succession. (See P. Claus, 'Terminological Aspects of Tulu Kinship: Kin Terms, Kin Sets, and Kin Groups of the Matrilineal Castes', p. 214).

252. There was no contradiction: See Mark Nichter's 'Joga and Maya' for a detailed account of the workings of this process.

253. Koti and Chennaya: Cf. G. R. Krishna, *Caste and Tribes*, p. 109.

254. Later, he explained...Berme: I am deeply grateful to Prof. B. A. Viveka Rai for this and many other comments and suggestions, for his unstinting generosity with his time and erudition, and for a great many other kindnesses. On the subject of Berme see H. Brückner, 'Bhûta-

Worship in Coastal Karnâtaka', p. 29; and P. Claus, 'Spirit Possession and Spirit Mediumship from the Perspective of Tulu Oral Traditions', p. 40. Bermeru, or the Tulu Brahma is always depicted as a figure seated on a horse with a sword in hand. Cf. plates 437–8 in P. Gururaja Bhatt, *Studies*; and U. P. Upadhyaya & S. P. Upadhyaya (ed.), *Bhuta Worship: Aspects of a Ritualistic Theatre*, plate 4.

255. The letter in question: T-S 20.137 recto. Ben Yiju used the reverse side of this fragment for jotting down certain invaluable notes and accounts.

255. It is worth adding...this sum of money: These figures are computed on the basis of E. Ashtor's statistics, pp. 200–201, (*A Social and Economic History of the Near East in the Middle Ages*, University of California Press, Berkeley, 1976.). The figures for mutton and olive oil are based on prices prevalent at the beginning of the eleventh century. There were however considerable differences in value between the Malikî dinars of Aden and Fatimid dinars, at various points in time. The reader is cautioned therefore, that these figures are, at best, very rough approximations.

256. Alternatively,...three adult Spaniards: Cf. S. D. Goitein, 'Changes in the Middle East (950–1150)'. The ransom for an adult person in Spain at that time was $33^1/3$ dinars (p. 21).

256. ...the wage of any artisan: E. Ashtor, *Social and Economic History*, p. 200. Standard earnings were remarkably stable throughout the eleventh and twelfth centuries (cf. S. D. Goitein, 'Urban Housing in Fatimid Times', p. 9).

256. Madmun's accounts show: T-S 20.137, recto, line 36–7; T-S N.S. J 1, recto, line 5–6.

256. enough to buy a...mansion in Fustat: See E. Ashtor, *Histoire des prix et des salaires dans l'Orient médiéval*, p. 184, Paris, 1969.

256. The expedition: S. D. Goitein, 'Two Eye-Witness reports on an Expedition of the King of Kish (Qais) against Aden', (*Bulletin of the School of African and Oriental Studies*, XVI/2, pp. 247–57, London, 1956).

257. The Amîrs of Kish...their depredations: Cf. Al-Idrisi, *Kitâb*, pp. 59, 153 & 171.

257. But...the pirates tried not to invite: For the attempts of the Sung government to control piracy in Chinese waters see Jung-Pang Lo's article, 'Maritime Commerce and its relation to the Sung Navy', pp. 57–101 (*Journal of the Economic and Social History of the Orient*, XI, pt. III, 1968). Lo points out: 'the problem of piracy suppression was not just a simple matter of police action. Beside the unscrupulous merchants who were in league with the outlaws, there were respectable merchants who started out their career as pirates', (p.74).

257. ...ever tried to gain control of the seas: The historian K. N. Chaudhuri, for instance remarks: 'Before the arrival of the Portuguese in the Indian Ocean in 1498 there had been no organised attempt by any political power to control the sea-lanes and the long distance trade of Asia...The Indian Ocean as a whole and its different seas were not dominated by any particular nations or empires.' (*Trade and Civilisation in the Indian Ocean*, p. 14, Cambridge University Press, Cambridge, 1985).

258. Sirâf: Sirâf was one of the most important ports of the Persian Gulf in the Middle Ages. See K. N. Chaudhuri's *Trade and Civilisation*, p. 48; and Rita Rose Di Meglio's article, 'Arab Trade with Indonesia and the Malay Peninsula from the eighth to the sixteenth century', p. 106 (in *Islam and the Trade of Asia*, ed. D. S. Richards).

258. Ramisht of Siraf: See S. M. Stern, 'Râmisht of Sîrâf, a Merchant Millionaire of the Twelfth Century', p. 10, (*Journal of the Royal Asiatic Society*, pp. 10–14, 1967).

258. Ramisht's trading empire: Cf. S. D. Goitein, *Letters*, p. 193.

258. 'Thus God did not': S. D. Goitein, 'Two Eye-Witness Reports...', p. 256.

259. 'And after that': T-S 20.137, recto, lines 1–5.

259. entirely different from...'slavery': M. I. Finley, *Ancient Slavery and Modern Ideology*, pp. 58–62, (Chatto and Windus, London, 1990).

260. Slavery...a kind of career opening: S. D. Goitein began the section on slavery in *A Mediterranean Society* (Vol. I) with the observation: 'In order to be able to understand the economic role and the social position of slaves in the society reflected in the Geniza records, we must free ourselves entirely of the notions familiar to us from our readings about life on American plantations or in ancient Rome.' (p. 130). In the extensive anthropological literature on the subject it has of course, long been recognized that it is almost impossible to distinguish formally between slavery and certain other social estates.' (Cf. Claude Meillasoux, *L'esclavage en Afrique précoloniale*, Paris, 1975; and Jack Goody, 'Slavery in Time and Space', in James L. Watson ed. *Asian and African Systems of Slavery*, University of California Press, Berkeley, 1980).

260. In the medieval world, slavery: In various languages words that are now translated as 'slave' actually had the sense of dependant. For a discussion of the meaning and etymology of Chinese slave-terms, see E. G. Pulleybank, 'The Origins and Nature of Chattel Slavery in China', pp. 193–204, *Journal of the Economic and Social History of the Orient*, Vol. I, pt. 2, (E. J. Brill, Leiden, 1958).

261. **In their poetry:** M. Chidanandamurthy, in his account of slavery in medieval Karnataka, in *Pâgaraṇa mattu itara samprabandhagaḷu* ('Pagarana and other research papers', Pustaka Chilume, Mysore, 1984) for instance, draws much of his material from the work of Basavaṇṇa and other Vachanakara saint-poets (I am grateful to Prof. B. A. Viveka Rai for translating portions of the relevant article for my benefit).

261. **Judaism…felt the influence of Sufism:** Cf. Paul Fenton's translation of 'Obadyâh Maimonides', (1228–1265), *Treatise of the Pool*, pp. 2–3 (Octagon Press, London, 1981). Fenton's introduction provides an outline of Sufi influences on Jewish mysticism.

261. **Egypt, in particular:** See for example S. D. Goitein's 'A Jewish Addict to Sufism in the time of the Nagid David II Maimonides', (*Jewish Quarterly Review*, Vol. 44, pp. 37–49 1953–54).

262. **'worthier disciples':** S. D. Goitein, 'Abraham Maimonides and the Pietist Circle', p. 146, (in *Jewish Medieval and Renaissance Studies*, ed. Alexander Altmann).

262. **Their own conceptions:** See Annemarie Schimmel, *Mystical Dimensions of Islam*, p. 141–3 (University of North Carolina Press, Chapel Hill, 1975).

262. **For the Sufis…the notion of being held by bonds:** Forms of the Arabic root which expresses the idea 'to bind, tie up', r-b-ṭ, are threaded through Sufi discourse: they range from the brotherhoods called rabîta to the murâbiṭ (marabouts) of Morocco and rabita kurmak, the Turkish phrase which expresses the tie between the Sufi Shaikh and his disciples. (See Annemarie Schimmel, *Mystical Dimensions*, pp. 231 & 237).

262. **'the slave of his slave':** Ibid., p. 292; see also Franz Rosenthal's *The Muslim Concept of Freedom Prior to the Nineteenth Century*, p. 93, (Leiden, E. J. Brill, 1960).

263. **Amongst the members of:** A large number of documents relating to such esoteric and magical cults, as well as protective talismans etc. have survived in the Geniza. See Norman Golb, 'Aspects of the Historical Background of Jewish Life in Medieval Egypt', pp. 12–16. The custom of visiting saint's graves was followed widely within the congregation of the

Synagogue of Ben Ezra in Fustat (see, for example, S. D. Goitein's article, 'The Sexual Mores of the Common People', p. 58). For the use of talismans in North African Jewish communities in modern times see Yedida Stillman, 'The Evil Eye in Morocco', (in *Folklore Research Centre Studies*, Vol. I, ed. Dov Noy, Issachar Ben-Ami, Hebrew University of Jerusalem, Jerusalem, 1970).

264. it was...dismissed: P. Gururaja Bhatt, for example, writes: 'devil-worship has been, for centuries, the core of the Tuḷuva cult among the non-Brahmins.' (*Studies*, p. 356).

265. The spot was tended by a Pujari: For the role of the Pujari in Bhûtaradhana see G. R. Krishna's *Caste and Tribes*, pp. 175–8.

266. Over the years...Bomma's role: See for example, S. D. Goitein, *Letters*, p. 191; E. Strauss, 'Documents', p. 149 (line 23 'to brother Bomma especially from me, plentiful greetings'); and T-S 18 J 4, fol. 18, recto, line 47, 'and special greetings to Shaikh Bomma'.

267. Among the items he brought back: T-S 20.137, recto, lines 46–48, & T-S N.S. J 1, recto, lines 8–11. Coral was an important product of the medieval Muslim west. It was obtained from the coasts of Spain and North Africa (Cf. Norman Stillman, 'The Merchant House of Ibn 'Awkal', p. 63). Soap was another luxury item exported by the Muslim west. Stillman writes: 'It was the Arabs who first discovered that soap could be made from olive oil instead of foul-smelling animal fats. The Arabs often perfumed their soap, and in Europe soap from the Arab countries was considered an article of luxury.' (p. 66, ibid.). Ben Yiju frequently imported soap from Aden to Mangalore.

267. 'They wear only bandages': R. H. Major, *India in the Fifteenth Century*, p. 17. 'Abd al-Razzaq notes that this apparel was common to 'the king and to the beggar'. See Goitein's discussion of attitudes towards clothing as they are represented in the Geniza documents (*A Mediterranean Society*, Vol. IV, pp. 153–159, 1983).

267. Several...mention imported Egyptian robes: These garments were referred to as fûṭa and maqṭaʿ. See, for example, T-S 1080 J 95, recto, lines 8–9; T-S 10 J 9, fol. 24, lines 14–15; T-S 20.137, recto, line 48; and T-S 10 J 12, fol. 5, verso, line 9, & T-S 10 J 9, fol. 24, recto, lines 14–15 (maqṭaʿ iskandarânî). For cloths that he may have used as turbans, see T-S 8 J 7, fol. 23, recto margin.

268. 'I have also...sent for you': T-S 18 J 2, fol. 7, recto, lines 15–18.

268. In the Middle East...paper: For treatments of the medieval paper industry in the Middle East, see S. D. Goitein, 'The Main Industries of the Mediterranean Area as Reflected in the Records of the Cairo Geniza', pp. 189–193 (*Journal of the Economic and Social History of the Orient*, Vol. IV, 1961); and E. Ashtor, 'Levantine Sugar Industry in the Later Middle Ages—An Example of Technological Decline', pp. 266–73, (*Israel Oriental Studies*, VII, Tel Aviv University, 1977). For the role of paper in medieval Muslim culture, see Qazi Ahmadmian Akhtar, 'The Art of Waraqat', (*Islamic Culture*, pp. 131–45, Jan. 1935); and 'Bibliophilism in Medieval Islam', (*Islamic Culture*, pp. 155–169, April 1938). There is of course an extensive literature on the manufacture of books in the Islamic world in the Middle Ages. See for example, T.W. Arnold & A. Grohmann, *The Islamic Book*, (Paris, Pegasus Press, 1929).

268. 'the best available': T-S K 25. 252, verso, lines 14–15.

268. 'no one has its like': T-S 18 J 2, fol. 7, recto, lines 19–20. For some other references to paper (waraq) in Ben Yiju's correspondence see T-S 8 J 7, fol. 23, verso, line 1 (waraq maṣrî); T-S 18 J 4, fol. 18, recto, line 42; T-S Misc. Box 25, fragm. 103, recto, line 48; & T-S N.S. J 1, recto, line 9.

269. Much of his kitchenware: For mention of 'iron frying-pans' (maqlâ ḥadîd) see T-S 20.137, recto, line 47; for glasses (zajjâj), 20.137, recto, line 45; T-S MS Or. 1081 J 3, recto, lines 7; and for soap (ṣâbûn), T-S 10 J 9, fol. 24, recto, line 16; T-S 8 J 7, fol. 23, recto margin, and T-S 20.137, recto, line 48.

269. For his mats: For references to mats from Berbera (ḥuṣar barbarî) see T-S 18 J 2, fol. 7, recto, line 12; T-S 20.137, recto, line 46; and T-S K 25.252, recto, line 21. For mention of a 'Barûjî ṭanfasa' see T-S K 25.252, recto, line 23.

269. His friends…sent him raisins': For references to sugar (sukkar in Ben Yiju's correspondence) see, T-S 10 J 12, fol. 5, recto, line 22; T-S 10 J 9, fol. 24, recto, line 16; T-S K 25.252, verso, line 13; T-S 18 J 2, fol. 7, recto, line 22; T-S Misc. Box 25. 103, recto, line 43; T-S N.S. J 1, recto, line 9; and (National and University Library, Jerusalem) Geniza MS H.6, line 18 (E. Strauss, 'Documents…'). For raisins (zabîb) see T-S 18 J 5, fol. 1, recto, line 23; T-S N.S. J 1, recto, line 9; T-S K 25.252, verso, line 13; T-S 10 J 9, fol. 24, recto, line 16; T-S 18 J 2, fol. 7, recto, line 22; T-S Misc. Box 25, fragm. 103, recto, line 43; T-S 8 J 7, fol. 23, recto margin; and (National and University Library, Jerusalem) Geniza MS H.6, line 19 (E. Strauss, 'Documents…').

269. The various kinds of palm-sugar: Failing to find sugar in Aden once,

Khalaf ibn Ishaq commented 'Your servant looked for sugar, but there is none to be had this year,' as though in apology for the deprivation he was inflicting on his friend (T-S 18 J 5, fol. 1, recto, margin).

269. **If it seems curious:** Ben Yiju's imports of sugar offer a sidelight on the history of that commodity in India. Sugar cane is, of course, native to India and is even mentioned in the Vedas. In his article, 'Sugar-Making in Ancient India' (*Journal of the Economic and Social History of the Orient*, VII, pt. 1, 1964, pp. 57–72) Lallanji Gopal points out that processes for the manufacturing of refined sugar are mentioned in the Jatakas and were evidently well-known in India since antiquity. Yet, the travellers who visited the Malabar in the later Middle Ages (such as Marco Polo), generally refer to sugar made from palm products, not cane-sugar (p. 68, fn.). This must mean either that cane-sugar was not manufactured in India on a commercial scale or that the process was not widely in use on the Malabar coast. At any rate, the fact that Ben Yiju imported sugar from the Middle East indicates clearly that refined sugar was not generally available in the Malabar coast, and was probably not commercially produced in India at the time. By the sixteenth century, however, sugar had become a major export in Bengal (cf. Archibald Lewis, 'Maritime Skills in the Indian Ocean', *Journal of the Economic and Social History of the Orient*, XVI, pts. II–III, 1973). This means that processes of sugar manufacturing had been widely adopted in India in the intervening centuries—possibly from the Middle East. This may be the reason why the names of certain sugar products in India still invoke Middle Eastern origins.

269. **In the Middle Ages, it was Egypt:** The reader is referred to E. Ashtor's excellent article 'The Levantine Sugar Industry in the Later Middle Ages—An Example of Technological Decline', (*Israel Oriental Studies*, VII, Tel Aviv Univ., 1977). See also Norman Stillman's 'The Merchant House of Ibn 'Awkal', p. 47.

270. **As fishermen...free of restrictions:** However, it is worth noting that the origins and nature of the prohibition on sea travel for Hindus ('crossing the black water') of which so much was made in the nineteenth century, are extremely obscure. The indications are that the privileging of restrictions on sea-travel amongst Hindus was a relatively late, possibly post-colonial development. For a useful discussion of this question the reader is referred to M. N. Pearson's excellent article 'Indian Seafarers in the Sixteenth Century', p. 132, (in M. N. Pearson, *Coastal Western India*,

Notes

Studies from the Portuguese Records, Concept Publishing Co., New Delhi, 1981).

271. **Soon after I reached Mangalore...Bobbariya-bhuta**: See U. P. Upadhyaya & S. P. Upadhyaya, *Bhuta Worship*, p. 60; B. A. Saletore, *Ancient Karnataka*, p. 461, (Oriental Book Agency, Poona, 1936); and K.Sanjiva Prabhu, *Special Study Report on Bhuta Cult in South Kanara District*, pp. 143–4, (*Census of India*, Series 14, Mysore, 1971). The legends and rituals associated with the Bobbariya-Bhuta are discussed at some length in G. R. Krishna's *Caste and Tribes*, (pp. 180–5), which is a detailed study of the Magavira caste.

271. **No Magavira settlement...without its Bobbariya shrine**: U. P. Upadhyaya & S. P. Upadhyaya, *Bhuta Worship*, p. 60.

275. **'With a whole temple'**: Allama Prabhu, trans. A. K. Ramanujan, *Speaking of Siva*, p. 153 (Penguin Books, London, 1987).

275. **'The kâ[r]dâr'**: T-S 20.137, verso, 2–4. In this account Ben Yiju misspells the word 'kârdâr' as kâdâr.

276. **'You my master'**: S. D. Goitein, *Letters*, p. 193. I have substituted the words 'disgrace' and 'censure' for the words 'excommunicate' and 'excommunication'. The words used in the manuscript (T-S 12.320 recto) are two forms of the Arabic root 'sh-m-t'. I am informed by Dr Geoffrey Khan that this is not the root that is normally used to designate excommunication in the Geniza documents; it should be read instead as 'the metathesized form of sh-t-m (to insult, defame), which is used in Maghrebî Arabic...' The letter would, therefore, be referring to some form of public defamation, or 'rogues gallery' (personal communication). Prof. Goitein probably used the term 'excommunicate' on the assumption that the 'kârdâl' was Jewish. The evidence, as we shall see, suggests otherwise.

276. **kârdâl**: The word must have been unfamiliar to Yûsuf ibn Abraham for he misspelled it as 'kârdâl'.

276. **'As for the delay'**: T-S 18 J 4, fol. 18, recto, lines 25–28. It is worth noting that among Khalaf and his friends 'reminding a person of a debt was almost an insult', (S. D. Goitein, 'Portrait of a Medieval India Trader', p. 452).

276. **He and Yusuf continued**: For a somewhat fuller version of the affair of the kârdâr's cardamom see my article, 'The Slave of MS H.6', (in *Subaltern Studies*, Vol. VII, Oxford University Press, New Delhi, 1992). I would like to take this opportunity to thank the faculty of the Centre for

Studies in Social Sciences, Calcutta (where this book was mainly written) for their comments and criticisms of an earlier version of that article. I also wish to thank Professor Asok Sen, Ranabir Samaddar, Tapati Guha Thakurta, Anjan Ghosh, Pradip Bose and Tapti Roy for the many discussions and arguments with which they have enriched my thinking. Partha Chatterjee has been a constant (if laconic) source of support and encouragement for many years and his comments and suggestions on this manuscript have been invaluable to me. To thank him would be an impertinence.

276. The clue lies...in a throwaway scrap: The sentence goes thus: 'Remaining (with me) for Nâîr, the brother of the kârdâr, 3 fîlî dirham-s.' T-S N.S. J 10, verso, margin.

278. Long active...Gujarati merchants: Cf. M. N. Pearson, *Merchants and Rulers in Gujarat*, pp. 7–12 (University of California Press, Berkeley, 1976). The Vanias were usually referred to as a single group in Ben Yiju's papers—Baniyân—but they were actually composed of many different sub-castes (see Pearson's *Merchants and Rulers*, p. 26). For the transoceanic dispersal of Gujarati traders in the Middle Ages, see Paul Wheatley's *The Golden Khersonese*, p. 312 (University of Malaya Press, Kuala Lumpur, 1961). Wheatley quotes an observation by Tomé Pires, the sixteenth-century Portuguese chronicler, that of the 4,000 foreign merchants resident in Malacca in 1509, 1,000 were Gujaratis. See also R. B. Serjeant, *The Portuguese off the South Arabian Coast*, p. 10 (Clarendon Press, Oxford, 1963); M. N. Pearson's article, 'Indian Seafarers in the Sixteenth Century', p. 132; and Archibald Lewis's article, 'Maritime Skills in the Indian Ocean', pp. 243–4.

278. Madmun, for one: In one of his letters Madmun asked Ben Yiju to inform his Gujarati contacts about the probable behaviour of the prices of pepper and iron in the Middle East in the coming year (T-S 18 J 2, fol. 7, verso, lines 3–6). See also S. D. Goitein's article, 'From Aden to India', p.53.

278. Ben Yiju...served as a courier: Cf. T-S N.S. J 1, verso, line 4–10.

278. Madmun...proposed a joint venture: T-S 18 J 2, fol. 7, verso, lines 1–2. Curiously Ishaq is referred to as 'the Bâniyân'. The names of the others are spelt: Kanâbtî and Sûs Sîtî respectively. I am grateful to Prof. B. A. Viveka Rai for the suggestion that the latter could be 'Sesu Shetty'. Cf. also Goitein, ibid.

278. Equally, the ships: S. D. Goitein thought it possible that the name of the powerful Kârimî merchants association was derived from the Tamil word kâryam, 'which, among other things, means "business, affairs"' ('The Beginnings of the Kârim Merchants', p. 183).

278. Among the...nâkhudas: For 'Pattani-svâmi' see Goitein, *Letters*, p. 188, fn. One NMBRNI is mentioned as a shipowner by Madmun (T-S K 25.252 recto, line 13). For a discussion of the meaning of the term nâkhuda (which is spelt in various different ways in Ben Yiju's documents), see M. N. Pearson's 'Indian Seafarers in the 16th. century', p. 118.

279. 'between him and me': Goitein, *Letters*, p. 64. The letter was addressed to Abu Zikri Sijilmasi, who was in Gujarat.

279. In addition, Ben Yiju...connected with...metalworkers: Bronze objects and utensils that Ben Yiju shipped to his friends are referred to repeatedly in the documents. See, for example, T-S K 25.252, verso, line 11; T-S Misc. Box 24, fragm. 103, recto, line 34; ; T-S 18 J 5, fol. 1, line 13; T-S 18 J 4, fol. 18, recto, line 35; & T-S 8 J 7, fol. 23 recto, line 4. Locks are referred to it the following documents, T-S K 25.252, verso, line 11 & T-S 18 J 2, fol. 7, recto, line 7. See also S. D. Goitein, *Letters*, p. 192–5.

279. The names of these craftsmen: The workmen's names, spelt 'Iyârî and LNGY appear to be variants of the Tamil Brahmin name Ayyar and the name-element Linga. Imports of copper, lead and bronze for the workshop are frequently alluded to in his papers. See for example, T-S K 25.252, recto, lines 6 & 28; & T-S 8 J 7, fol. 23, verso, line 6. See also S. D. Goitein, *Letters*, pp. 192–194.

279. Membership...involved binding understandings: The economy of Fatimid Egypt was, to use Goitein's words, largely a 'paper economy'— that is payments were generally made not in cash, but by debt transfers, letters of credit and orders of payment. Cf. S. D. Goitein, 'Changes in the Middle East (950–1150)', p. 19; 'Bankers Accounts from the Eleventh Century AD', pp. 28–68; and *A Mediterranean Society*, Vol. I, pp. 241–62. See also W. J. Fischel, 'The Spice Trade in Mamluk Egypt', p. 170; and A. L. Udovitch, 'Commercial Techniques', p.53–61. Ben Yiju's papers and accounts suggest that this paper economy was not localized in Egypt or the Middle East. There are several references in Ben Yiu's papers to credit arrangements between himself, his friends in Aden and Indian merchants.

280. Common sense suggests...the language: The cultural and linguistic diversity of the regions surrounding the Indian Ocean were represented in microcosm in all its major ports. A Portuguese observer, Tomé Pires, who spent two and a half years in Malacca at the beginning of the sixteenth century, reported that eighty-four languages could be heard in the streets of that city—Babel realized! (Cf. Paul Wheatley, *The Golden Khersonese*, p. 312). Taken at face value, that figure would suggest that communication had effectively ceased in Malacca—or that it was possible only within tiny speech communities.

281. **Given what we know:** See Kees Versteegh, *Pidginization and Creolization: The Case of Arabic*, p. 114 (*Current Issues in Linguistic Theory: 33*, Amsterdam, 1984); and Keith Whinnom, 'Lingue France: Historical Problems', p. 296 (in A.Valdman (ed.) *Pidgin and Creole Linguistics*, Indiana University Press, Bloomington, 1977).

281. **The Arab geographer Mas'udi:** S. Muhammad Husayn Nainar, *The Knowledge of India Possessed by Arab Geographers down to the 14th. century AD with special reference to Southern India*, p. 95 (Madras University Islamic Series, University of Madras, 1942).

282. **Ben Yiju's usage:** See for example, Mas'udi, *Murûj*, Vol. I, p. 163, and Al-Idrisi, *Kitâb*, Vol. I, pp. 162–183. The names 'Ṣîn' and 'China' may of course derive from Sanskrit and Prakrit words (see the article 'The Name China' by Berthold Laufer in *T'oung Pao*, II/13, pp. 719–26, 1912, and Paul Pelliot's article 'L'Origine du nom de <Chine>', in the same issue (pp. 727–742).

282. **India,...as the Arab geographers well knew:** G. Ferrand, V*oyage du Marchand Arabe Sulayman*, p. 48; and Mas'udi, *Murûj*, p. 162.

282. **For several centuries...a king called the Ballahrâ:** Several medieval Arab geographers and travel writers asserted that the 'Ballahrâ' was India's 'king of kings', the pre-eminent ruler in the land. Thus, Ibn Khurdadhbih, writing in the ninth century remarked 'the greatest king of India is the Ballahrâ or king of kings,' while one of his contemporaries noted: "The Ballahrâ is the most noble of the princes of India; the Indians recognise his superiority.' (Gabriel Ferrand, *Relations de Voyages et Textes Géographiques, Arabes, Persanes et Turks, Relatifs à l'Extrème-Orient du VIIIe au XVIIIe Siècles*, Vol. I, pp. 22 & 42, Ernest Leroux, Paris, 1913). Mas'udi, writing in the tenth century, observed: 'The most powerful of the kings of India is the Ballahra, the lord of the city of Mankir. Most Indian chiefs turn towards him when they say their prayers.' (*Murûj*, Vol. I, p. 177). Al-Idrisi was to add his considerable authority to these statements a couple of

BONNEVILLE TRAVEL   CLIENT: NUNO/DOMINGO
3901 WESTERLY PLACE STE 101
NEWPORT BEACH   CA   714 476-8383   INVOICE: 84732   PAGE:01

09 MAY   NORTHWST AIR   FLIGHT: 356   CLASS: V   SEAT: 37G
FR   SAN FRANCISCO   DEPART: 305P
          MPLS/ST PAUL   ARRIVE: 833P

09 MAY   NORTHWST AIR   FLIGHT: 1504   CLASS: V   SEAT: 13E
FR   MPLS/ST PAUL   DEPART: 925P
          CLEVELAND   ARRIVE: 1202A 10MAY

11 MAY   NORTHWST AIR   FLIGHT: 625   CLASS: V
SU   CLEVELAND   DEPART: 615P
          MPLS/ST PAUL   ARRIVE: 719P

TICKET: 012 1294159405   USD277.00

THE WORLD LABOUR MARKET

A HISTORY OF MIGRATION

LYDIA POTTS

ISBN 0-86232-833

ZED BOOKS 1990

el siete

centuries later (see *Kitâb*, p. 47, and G. Ferrand, *Relations*, p. 196). See also André Miquel, *La Géographie humaine du Monde Musulman jusqu'au milieu du 11e siècle*, Vol. II, p. 84 (Mouton, Paris, 1975).

282. An eminent scholar: S. M. H. Nainar, *The Knowledge of India*, pp. 138–140.

283. …small kingdoms and principalities: As Ibn Battuta put it: 'In (the Malabar) there are twelve infidel sultans, some of them strong with armies numbering fifty thousand men, and others weak with armies of three thousand. Yet there is no discord whatever between them, and the strong does not desire to seize the possessions of the weak.' (*Travels*, p. 232).

284. The place…known as 'Jurbattan': S. M. H. Nainar, *The Knowledge of India*, p. 41.

284. After about two days…'Budfattan': S. M. H. Nainar, *The Knowledge of India*, pp. 29–30. The town is also known as Valarapattanam.

285. For much of the distance: Ibn Battuta, *Travels*, p. 232.

285. 'Dahfattan'…lies: S. M. H. Nainar, *The Knowledge of India*, p. 32. The town is also known as Dharmapattanam.

285. A little further…Pantalayini Kollam: S. M. H. Nainar, *The Knowledge of India*, p. 35.

286. Cabral delivered a letter: Cf. K. N. Chaudhuri, *Trade and Civilisation*, p. 68.

286. The Portuguese fleet sailed: Cf. R. S. Whiteway, *The Rise of Portuguese Power in India 1497–1550*, pp. 86–7.

286. A year…later…da Gama returned: Cf. George D. Winius, 'From Discovery to Conquest', p. 224, (in *Foundations of the Portuguese Empire, 1415–1580*, by Bailey W. Diffie and George D. Winius, University of Minnesota Press, Minneapolis, 1977).

287. 'The heathen [of Gujarat]': Quoted by M. N. Pearson, in 'Indian Seafarers in the Sixteenth Century', p. 121.

288. 'between resistance and submission': M. N. Pearson, *Merchants and Rulers*, p. 69. See also C. R. Boxer, *The Portuguese Seaborne Empire, 1415–1825*, p. 46 (A. A. Knopf, New York, 1969).

288. As far as the Portuguese were concerned: In 1595 Philip II of Spain took matters a step farther and 'decreed that no non-Christian resident in Western India could trade, either directly or through an intermediary, to places other than those on the Western India coast.' (M. N. Pearson, *Merchants and Rulers*, p. 53).

288. In 1509AD: See M. N. Pearson, *Merchants and Rulers*, p. 31; George

D. Winius, p. 240–1 (in *Foundations of the Portuguese Empire*) and S. A. I. Tirmizi, 'Portuguese problems under the Muzaffarids' (in *Some Aspects of Medieval Gujarat*, Munshiram Manoharlal, Delhi, 1968).

Going Back

299. The news…from Ifriqiya: H. Wieruszowski, 'The Norman Kingdom of Sicily and the Crusades', p. 22.

299. 'Shaikh Abû Isḥâq': T-S 18 J 4, fol. 18, recto, lines 33–5.

300. 'Concerning the news': T-S Misc. Box 25, fragm. 103, recto, lines 27–9.

300. 'My master [Ben Yiju]': T-S 13 J 7, fol. 27, recto, lines 15–18. Altogether, five of Ben Yiju's letters, three from Khalaf ibn Ishaq and two from Yusuf ibn Abraham, refer to Mubashshir. These letters appear to have been written over a relatively short period of time. The last in the sequence is probably the letter of MS H.6 (from Khalaf ibn Ishaq) which has been dated by Strauss as having been written in 1148AD. Another letter from Khalaf, (T-S Misc. Box 24, fragm. 103) has been dated to 1147 by S. D. Goitein (cf. S. Shaked, *Tentative Bibliography*, pp. 147). Since Mubashshir's stay in Egypt was probably not a very long one, it seems likely that the others were written in the couple of years immediately preceding 1147. The five letters are: T-S 12.235 (from Yusuf ibn Abraham); T-S 13 J 7, fol. 27 (from Yusuf ibn Abraham);T-S 18 J 4, fol. 18, (from Khalaf ibn Ishaq); T-S Misc. Box 25, fragm. 103, (from Khalaf ibn Ishaq); MS H.6, E. Strauss, 'Documents', (from Khalaf ibn Ishaq).

300. 'As for the news': T-S 13 J 7, fol. 27, recto, lines 18–19;

300. Disease and famine had followed: Cf. H. Wieruszowski, 'The Norman Kingdom of Sicily and the Crusades', p. 23.

300. In western Europe: Cf. Virginia G. Berry, 'The Second Crusade', p. 463–512, in K. M. Setton (Gen. ed.) *A History of the Crusades*, Vol. I, University of Wisconsin Press, Madison, 1969.

301. 'Behold the days of reckoning': *The Jews and the Crusaders (The Hebrew Chronicles of the First and Second Crusades)*, p. 123, (translated and edited by Shlomo Eidelberg, University of Wisconsin Press, Madison, 1977).

301. They were relatively lucky: H. Z. Hirschberg, *History of the Jews in*

North Africa, p. 128, and 'The Almohade Persecutions and the India Trade', in *Yitzhak F. Baer Jubilee Volume* (ed. S. W. Baeon et. al., History Society of Israel, Jerusalem, 1960).

301. The letter...by Abu Zikri's son: H. Z. Hirschberg, 'The Almohade Persecutions and the India Trade'. This letter contains an extraordinary usage: the writer uses the Arabic word fataḥ (victory, lit. 'opening'), which has the sense of 'liberated', to describe the Almohad entry into Tlemcen—an event that he clearly regarded as a disaster. It is a striking instance of the ironies that Judæo-Arabic sometimes imposed on its users (line 41, p. 142).

301. Not long before: Cf. S. D. Goitein, *Letters*, pp. 62–65.

301. On that occasion, Ben Yiju: The nakhuda Mahruz frequently acted as a courier for Ben Yiju and his friends and is mentioned several times in their letters (Cf. T-S 8 J 7, fol. 23, recto, line 3; T-S N.S. J 10, verso, 1st. Account, line 9, 2nd. Account, line 1. See also S. D. Goitein, *Letters*, pp. 62–5. Goitein notes there that Mahruz's sister was married to Judah b. Joseph ha-Kohen (Abu Zikri Sijilmasi).

302. 'I asked [some people]': Cf. E. Strauss, 'Documents', p. 149 (lines 10–14, MS H.6).

302. 'Every year you speak': Cf. E. Strauss, 'Documents' p. 149 (lines 23–4, MS H.6).

302. 'I do not know': The catalogue number of this document is T-S 10 J 10, fol. 15. This letter was first transcribed and published by J. Braslawsky in *Zion*, (7, pp. 135–139) in 1942. Goitein also published an English translation of it in 1973 (*Letters*, pp. 201–6). All except one of the following quotations from this document are taken from Goitein's translation.

303. '[Therefore], I ask you': I have made the word 'brother' plural here to preserve the implied sense of the passage.

303. 'I heard of what happened': I have translated this passage directly from Braslawsky's transcription (Cf. *Zion*, 7, p. 138), (T-S 10 J 10, fol. 15, lines 41–44 [verso 5–8]).

304. 'I wished to ask': Bod. Lib. Ox. MS Hebr., d. 66, fol. 139, recto, lines 6–12.

313. Such were the misfortunes: The chronology of this period of Ben Yiju's life is not easy to establish. The document T-S 12.337 appears to have been written some three years or so after T-S 10 J 10, fol. 15, which Goitein has dated as being written on 11 September 1149 (*Letters*, p.

201). This plus the sequence of documents and events that follow upon it, suggest that T-S 12.337 was written in 1152–3 or thereabouts.

313. 'I wrote a letter to you': T-S 12.337, recto, lines 4–6.)

314. 'I did all...in my power': T-S 12.337, recto, lines 6–8.)

314. 'As for Mubashir':T-S 12.337, recto margin.

314. ...the joyful name Surûr: 'Surur' was of course, the diminutive for Farḥia (Peraḥyâ), and both names derive from roots that have the connotation of 'joyfulness' (cf. Goitein, *Letters*, p. 327, fn.). Farhia was also Ben Yiju's father's name which was why both he and his brother Yusuf named their first-born sons Farhia (Surur). Ben Yiju was in fact sometimes addressed by the tekonym 'Abû Surûr' or 'father of Surur'

314. 'two children like sprigs': T-S 12.337, recto, line 13.

314. 'And the elder': T-S 12.337, recto, lines 14–16.,

315. Dhû Jibla: G. R. Smith, *Ayyûbids and Early Rasûlids*, p. 66.

315. 'The news reached your...slave: T-S 10 J 13, fol. 6, lines 13–17. The second part of the quotation (lines 14–17) are in Hebrew, and were kindly translated for me by Dr Geoffrey Khan. See also S. Shaked's *Tentative Bibliography*, p. 102.

315. Ben Yiju...a Hebrew poem: T-S 8 J 16, fol. 23. Cf. S. Shaked's *Tentative Bibliography*, p. 86.

315. Such documentation as there is: Such was his position that one of his correspondents of that time used phrases such as 'the gracious sage', 'the head of the community' and other such honorifics to address him. Cf. T-S 10 J 13, fol. 6, lines 5 and 7 (I am grateful to Dr Geoffrey Khan for translating these honorifics for me). A document containing parts of three legal opinions written by Ben Yiju, suggest that he had some judicial functions within the community. They are written on the reverse side of a letter that Yusuf ibn Abraham had sent to him in Mangalore (T-S 10 J 9, fol. 24), but Goitein was of the opinion that the drafts were written after Ben Yiju's departure from India, 'probably in Yemen' (S. Shaked, *Tentative Bibliography*, p. 100).

315. Yet there must...have been anxieties: The letter in question is Bod. Lib. Ox. MS Hebr. d. 66 (Catalogue n. 2878), fol. 61. Lines 10–15 deal with the safety of the roads and were evidently written in answer to a query from Ben Yiju. The Yemen in this period was riven by struggles between the Mahdids and the Najâḥids (see G. R. Smith, *Ayyûbids and Early Rasûlids*, p. 58).

316. ...such marriages were commonplace: Khalaf's relative Madmun for

example, was married to the sister of Abu Zikri Sijilmasi, who was, of course, originally from the Maghreb (see S. D. Goitein, *Letters*, p. 62).

316. **Instead, he began to dream:** For a brief review of the literature on cousin marriage in the Middle East see J. M. B. Keyser's article, 'The Middle Eastern Case: Is There a Marriage Rule?', (*Ethnology*, 13, pp. 293–309).

316. **'Shaikh Khalaf [ibn Ishaq]':** T-S 12.337, recto, lines 20–25.

317. **'and we will rejoice':** T-S 12.337, recto, line 19.

317. **'Address your letters to me':** T-S 12.337, recto, lines 30–32.

317. **'Suliman and Abraham':** T-S 12.337, recto, line 34 & margin.

325. **But it had other compensations:** At this time, and until well afterwards, the Jews of Sicily looked to North Africa in matters of liturgy and religion (see David S. H. Abulafia, 'The End of Muslim Sicily', in *Muslims Under Latin Rule*, ed. James M. Boswell, Princeton University Press, Princeton, 1990).

325. **The young Surur:** My description of Surur's voyage to Messina is based on S. D. Goitein's translation of the letter he wrote home after reaching that city (Letters, pp. 327–330).

326 **Sulîmân ibn Ṣaṭrûn:** Mentioned in Ben Yiju's second letter to Yusuf (T-S 12.337, recto, lines 25–6)

326. **In this instance,…in a letter:** In his letter home Surur evidently spelt this name as 'Ben Siṭlûn'. Goitein points out in his translation of this letter, that the name is identical with 'Ibn Ṣaṭrûn' and it seems almost certain the individual in question was the same person that Ben Yiju referred to in his letter to his brother Yusuf (T-S 12.337, lines 25–26.)

326. **The letter…was a short one:** The letter contains a reference to one 'Abû'l Fakhr al-Amshâṭî' who was a family friend, and Surur's contact in Fustat.

326. **But Surur had…another reason:** T-S 8 J 36, fol. 3, recto, lines 4–6.

327. **Their parents, already prostrate:** Surur's letter home has not survived, but the letter his brother Shamwal wrote back in reply has. Its catalogue number is Bod. Lib. Ox. MS Hebr., b. 11 (Cat. no. 2874), fol. 15 (S. Shaked, *Tentative Bibliography*, p. 207).

327. **'We were seized with grief':** Bod. Lib. Ox. MS Hebr., b. 11 (Cat. no. 2874), fol. 15, recto, lines 8–9. I would like to thank Dr Geofrrey Khan for translating the Hebrew phrase in this passage (in italics).

327. **'well and in good cheer':** T-S 13 J 20, fol. 7, recto, lines 22–23.

327. **Food was short:** Bod. Lib. Ox. MS Hebr., b. 11 (Cat. no. 2874), fol.

15, recto, lines 34–35 & 36–37.

327. 'If you saw [our] father': Bod. Lib. Ox. MS Hebr., b. 11 (Cat. no. 2874), fol. 15, lines (recto) 45—(verso) 4 & (verso) 8–13.

328. 'Come quickly home': T-S 16.288, recto, lines 10–11.

328. The marriage did indeed take place: S. D. Goitein, *Letters*, pp. 202.

328. Both Surur and Moshe: Ibid., pp. 186 & 328.

342. I discovered that the name Abu-Hasira: The most important scholarly work on the cult of saints amongst North African Jews is that of the eminent Israeli folklorist, Issachar Ben-Ami. See, for example, his article 'Folk Veneration of Saints among Moroccan Jews', (in *Studies in Judaism and Islam*, ed. Shelomo Morag et al., Hebrew University, Jerusalem, 1981). In the course of their fieldwork amongst Moroccan Jews Ben Ami and his associates compiled a list of 571 saints, twenty-one of whom were women. The French scholar, L. Voinot, estimated in 1948 that forty-five Jewish saints in Morocco were revered by Muslims and Jews alike while thirty-one were claimed by both Jews and Muslims as their own (quoted by Ben-Ami in 'Folk Veneration of Saints', p. 283).

342. 'The tomb of Rabbi': See Alex Weingrod's article, 'Saints and Shrines, politics and culture: a Morocco-Israel comparison', pp. 228 (in *Muslim Travellers*, ed. Dale F. Eickelman and James Piscatori, University of California Press, Berkeley, 1990); Gudrun Krämer, *The Jews in Modern Egypt*, 1914–1952, pp. 114. University of Washington Press, Seattle, 1989; Issachar Ben-Ami, 'Folk Veneration of Saints', pp. 324–328; and Baba Sali, His Life, Piety, Teachings and Miracles (Rav Yisrael Abuchatzeirah), by Rav Eliyahu Alfasi & Rav Yechiel Torgeman, written and edited by C. T. Bari, trans. Leah Doniger (Judaica Press Inc., New York, 1986).

Epilogue

349. The document is one of Ben Yiju's sets of accounts: Dropsie 472. The following are the other Geniza documents I have used in reconstructing Bomma and Ben Yiju's lives. This list includes only those documents with which I have worked principally or in part from my own transcriptions, made directly from the manuscripts (in such instances where I have worked with published transcriptions or translations, the references are provided in the endnotes). I would like to thank the Syndics of the University Library, Cambridge, for giving me permission to use and quote from these documents. I would also like to thank the Bodleian Library, Oxford, and the Annenberg Research Centre, Philadelphia, for allowing me to consult their Geniza collections.

1. T-S 12.235
2. T-S 12.337
3. T-S 16.288
4. T-S 20.130
5. T-S 20.137
6. T-S N.S. J 1
7. T-S N.S. J 5
8. T-S N.S. J 10
9. T-S K 25.252
10. T-S MS Or. 1080 J 95
11. T-S MS Or. 1080 J 263
12. T-S MS Or. 1081 J 3
13. T-S Misc. Box. 25, fragm. 103
14. T-S 6 J 4, fol. 14
15. T-S 8 J 7, fol. 23
16. T-S 8 J 36, fol. 3
17. T-S 10 J 9, fol. 24
18. T-S 10 J 10, fol. 15
19. T-S 10 J 12, fol. 5
20. T-S 10 J 13, fol. 6
21. T-S 13 J 7, fol. 13
22. T-S 13 J 7, fol. 27
23. T-S 13 J 20, fol. 7
24. T-S 13 J 24, fol. 2
25. T-S 18 J 2, fol. 7
26. T-S 18 J 4, fol. 18
27. T-S 18 J 5, fol. 1
28. Bod. Lib. Ox. MS Hebr., b. 11, fol. 15
29. Bod. Lib. Ox. MS Hebr., d. 66, fol. 61
30. Bod. Lib. Ox. MS Hebr., d. 66, fol. 139

A NOTE ON THE TYPE

This book was set in a type face called Garamond. Jean Jannon has been identified as the designer of this face, which is based on Garamond's original models but is much lighter and more open. The italic is taken from a font of Granjon, which appeared in the repertory of the Imprimerie Royale and was probably cut in the middle of the sixteenth century.

Composed in Great Britain

Printed and bound by The Haddon Craftsmen, Scranton, Pennsylvania